The Essential Guide to Web3

Develop, deploy, and manage distributed applications
on the Ethereum network

Vijay Krishnan

BIRMINGHAM—MUMBAI

The Essential Guide to Web3

Group Product Manager: Ali Abidi
Publishing Product Manager: Heramb Bhavsar
Content Development Editor: Priyanka Soam
Technical Editor: Sweety Pagaria and Kavyashree K S
Copy Editor: Safis Editing
Project Coordinator: Shambhavi Mishra
Proofreader: Safis Editing
Indexer: Pratik Shirodkar
Production Designer: Aparna Bhagat
Marketing Coordinator: Nivedita Singh

First published: November 2023

Production reference: 1221123

Published by Packt Publishing Ltd.
Grosvenor House
11 St Paul's Square
Birmingham
B3 1RB, UK.

ISBN 978-1-80181-347-1

www.packtpub.com

In loving memory of my dad

– Vijay Krishnan

Contributors

About the author

Vijay Krishnan, an experienced expert in blockchain and Web3, holds the position of head of SysOps for Linea, a Layer 2 blockchain at Consensys. With a rich background in blockchain, he's guided Fortune 100 companies from ideation to product build. With over 50 projects and 300+ use cases to his credit, Vijay has left an indelible mark on the industry.

Prior to Consensys, he pioneered the AWS Partner Blockchain ecosystem and led IBM North America's Blockchain Practice. With two decades on Wall Street, he possesses deep financial and tech insights.

Vijay, a leader and subject matter expert, empowers clients in DeFi, NFTs, gaming, and the metaverse. Beyond work, he's a mentor, speaker, author, and organic farmer. His knowledge and innovation continue to shape the blockchain and Web3 landscape.

Acknowledgments

I extend my heartfelt gratitude and acknowledgement to S.Sidarth for his invaluable contribution to this book. His extensive expertise in blockchain has enriched the content with a deep understanding of the subject matter. Sidarth's hands-on example with the Hardhat Pet Store serves as a valuable educational resource for readers, bringing real-world insights to the forefront. His active engagement within the blockchain community and commitment to knowledge sharing exemplify his dedication to advancing the field. Thank you, Sidarth, for your outstanding contribution to this book.

I would like to express my sincere appreciation and acknowledgement to Kavya Vijay for her exceptional contributions to this book. As a talented student at the **National Institute of Design** (**NID**) specializing in Exhibition Design, Kavya's graphic designs have added a unique and visually captivating dimension to the content. Her creative prowess and dedication to crafting exceptional experiences through design are truly commendable. Kavya's artistic talents have significantly enhanced the book's visual appeal and overall quality. I am grateful for her valuable contributions and the positive impact they have had on this book. Thank you, Kavya, for your outstanding work and artistic flair.

About the reviewers

Pradeep Raj is an Open Group Master Certified Architect, having 20 years of experience in various domains and technologies in the industry. He has a strong background in leading market-edge technologies such as the cloud, mobile, data platforms and AI/ML, blockchain, and supply chain analytics. He has handled many successful client projects as a lead architect. He has in-depth knowledge of financial markets, industrial products, and supply chain and trade promotion domains.

I appreciate Mr. Vijay Krishnan for putting tremendous effort into creating an easy path to learn about Ethereum and its concepts.

I enjoyed reviewing this book. Also, I gained new insights from this book. Thank you!

Mayukh Mukhopadhyay started his career as a BI developer. After the 2008-09 financial crisis, he was at Tata Consultancy Services for one of their Fortune 500 clients in the telecom sector. Holding a master's in software engineering from Jadavpur University, he is presently working as a data insight developer, where he focuses on applying data science and machine learning to raw telecom equipment logs to generate business insights. He has a varied list of academic interests, ranging from audio signal processing, structural bioinformatics, and bio-inspired algorithms to consciousness engineering. Apart from being an Oracle Certified Specialist, he is a Certified Bitcoin Professional, recognized by **C4 (Crypto Currency Certification Consortium)**. He applies blockchain as a technology to different business domains.

Table of Contents

3

Your First Ethereum Transaction   59

Part 2 – All about Smart Contracts

4

Introduction to Smart Contracts   79

5

Creating and Deploying Your First Smart Contract   113

6

Smart Contract Security and Access Controls   131

Part 3 – Writing Your DApps for Web3

7

Developer Tools and Libraries for Web3 Development   151

8

Writing and Testing Your First dApp on Web3   171

Part 4 – Fungible Tokens

9

10

Part 5 – Non-Fungible Tokens

11

12

Creating Your First Non-Fungible Token   253

Part 6 – Web3 Advanced Topics

13

Understanding Oracles   277

14

Zero-Knowledge Proofs and Zero-Knowledge EVMs   295

Preface

The Ethereum blockchain and Web3 technology have gained immense traction in recent years, transforming the way we perceive and interact with the digital world. As the demand for blockchain professionals surges, both newcomers and seasoned individuals from diverse backgrounds are eager to harness the potential of this revolutionary field. However, diving into Ethereum and Web3 can be intimidating, especially for those without prior experience or a technical background.

This book is tailored to bridge that knowledge gap, providing a comprehensive guide that demystifies Ethereum and Web3 for all readers. While crafting this book, I endeavored to weave together complex concepts in a coherent manner, ensuring that you can grasp these transformative ideas with ease.

By the time you reach the last chapter, you will have gained the confidence to navigate the Ethereum blockchain and harness the capabilities of Web3. From fundamental concepts to advanced topics in smart contracts and tokens, this book will equip you with the skills needed to explore this exciting realm. Moreover, if you are gearing up for a career in blockchain or Web3, the seamless integration of theoretical knowledge and practical code examples will prepare you for success. Embark on this journey with me as we unlock the full potential of Ethereum and Web3, making these groundbreaking technologies accessible to all. Welcome to the future of the decentralized digital landscape!

Who this book is for

This book is crafted for individuals seeking to bridge their knowledge gaps in Ethereum blockchain and Web3 technology. It will be equally valuable to seasoned blockchain enthusiasts, offering an engaging and informative read. The book is thoughtfully designed with the assumption of minimal prior technical knowledge, making it accessible and comprehensive.

Whether a beginner or an experienced professional, you can navigate this book effortlessly, building a solid foundation in Ethereum and Web3 concepts step by step. Its approach is intentionally thorough and detailed, ensuring that even novices can utilize it as a self-contained resource to progressively enhance their understanding.

Whether you are new to blockchain or an intermediate expert, this book provides a holistic and enjoyable journey into the world of Ethereum and Web3. It welcomes readers of all backgrounds to explore and grasp these transformative technologies effectively, chapter by chapter, from the ground up. Welcome to a comprehensive exploration of Ethereum and Web3 that is accessible to all!

What this book covers

Chapter 1, Fundamentals of Blockchain and Web3, introduces the basic concepts in blockchain and Web3.

Chapter 2, Getting Started with Ethereum, offers an extensive overview of Ethereum, concepts, managing keys, wallets, and the state of Ethereum.

Chapter 3, Your First Ethereum Transaction, introduces Hardhat, preparing wallets, initiating a transfer, and verifying the results of transactions.

Chapter 4, Introduction to Smart Contracts, provides a detailed deep dive into Solidity smart contracts, writing a "Hello World" contract, and getting started with Hardhat.

Chapter 5, Creating and Deploying Your First Smart Contract, is a hands-on walk-through on writing a smart contract, compiling, creating ABIs, deploying, verifying, and debugging.

Chapter 6, Smart Contract Security and Access Controls, explores some of the smart contract security issues, access controls, and using tools to audit smart contracts.

Chapter 7, Developer Tools and Libraries for Web3 Development, examines Web3 developer stacks, Ethereum clients, Infura, and IPFS.

Chapter 8, Writing and Testing Your First dApp on Web3, offers a hands-on walk-through to create and deploy your first Dapp in Web3.

Chapter 9, Introduction to Tokenization, introduces the concept of tokenizing real-world objects as tokens, looking at some of the common token standard uses and tokenization use cases.

Chapter 10, Creating Your First Token, provides a hands-on example of creating your first ERC-20 token, minting tokens and testing it.

Chapter 11, Non-Fungible Token Standards, explores the most common standards for an NFT, including ERC-721 and ERC-1155.

Chapter 12, Creating Your First Non-Fungible Token, offers a hands-on example of creating your first NFT, minting it, and adding it to a wallet.

Chapter 13, Understanding Oracles, introduces the concept of oracles, the oracle problem in Web3, an example of Chainlink as an oracle service, and running a Chainlink oracle node.

Chapter 14, Zero-Knowledge Proofs and Zero-Knowledge EVMs, covers the basics of zero-knowledge proofs and zero-knowledge Ethereum virtual machines.

Chapter 15, L2 Networks and Rollups, discusses L2 networks, how Polygon works, and rollups.

Chapter 16, Decentralized Autonomous Organizations – Overview, introduces several important concepts and provides an overview of DAOs.

To get the most out of this book

Software/hardware covered in the book	Operating system requirements
Browser (Chrome, Safari, Firefox)	Windows, macOS, or Linux
Node.js 16 or greater	
Hardhat 2.19.0 or later	
The latest Visual Studio Code version	
The latest MetaMask version	
Infura – an account and API key	
Pinata – an account and API key	

Download the example code files

You can download the example code files for this book from GitHub at `https://github.com/PacktPublishing/The-Essential-Guide-to-Web3`.

If there's an update to the code, it will be updated in the GitHub repository.

We also have other code bundles from our rich catalog of books and videos available at `https://github.com/PacktPublishing/`. Check them out!

Conventions used

There are a number of text conventions used throughout this book.

`Code in text`: Indicates code words in text, database table names, folder names, filenames, file extensions, pathnames, dummy URLs, user input, and Twitter handles.

A block of code is set as follows:

```
pragma solidity ^0.8.0; contract MyContract {  uint256 public value =
10;  bool public isGreater = value > 5; }
```

When we wish to draw your attention to a particular part of a code block, the relevant lines or items are set in bold:

```
contract BadAccessControl {
    address public owner;

    constructor() {
        owner = tx.origin;
```

```
    }

    function sensitiveFunction() public {
        require(tx.origin == owner, "BadAccessControl: Not
authorized");// Sensitive code
    }
}
```

Any command-line input or output is written as follows:

```
contract MultiSigWallet {
    uint minApprovers;
    address payable dealProposer;
    address payable beneficiary;
    mapping (address => bool) approvedBy;
    mapping (address => bool) isApprover;
    uint approvalsNum;
```

Bold: Indicates a new term, an important word, or words that you see on screen. For instance, words in menus or dialog boxes appear in **bold**. Here is an example: "Once you've signed up for an Infura account, you can create a new project by clicking on the **Create New Project** button on the dashboard."

> **Tips or important notes**
> Appear like this.

Get in touch

Feedback from our readers is always welcome.

General feedback: If you have questions about any aspect of this book, email us at customercare@ packtpub.com and mention the book title in the subject of your message.

Errata: Although we have taken every care to ensure the accuracy of our content, mistakes do happen. If you have found a mistake in this book, we would be grateful if you would report this to us. Please visit www.packtpub.com/support/errata and fill in the form.

Piracy: If you come across any illegal copies of our works in any form on the internet, we would be grateful if you would provide us with the location address or website name. Please contact us at copyright@packt.com with a link to the material.

If you are interested in becoming an author: If there is a topic that you have expertise in and you are interested in either writing or contributing to a book, please visit authors.packtpub.com.

Share Your Thoughts

Once you've read *The Essential Guide to Web3*, we'd love to hear your thoughts! Scan the QR code below to go straight to the Amazon review page for this book and share your feedback.

https://packt.link/r/1-801-81347-7

Your review is important to us and the tech community and will help us make sure we're delivering excellent quality content.

Download a free PDF copy of this book

Thanks for purchasing this book!

Do you like to read on the go but are unable to carry your print books everywhere? Is your eBook purchase not compatible with the device of your choice?

Don't worry, now with every Packt book you get a DRM-free PDF version of that book at no cost.

Read anywhere, any place, on any device. Search, copy, and paste code from your favorite technical books directly into your application.

The perks don't stop there, you can get exclusive access to discounts, newsletters, and great free content in your inbox daily

Follow these simple steps to get the benefits:

1. Scan the QR code or visit the link below

https://packt.link/free-ebook/9781801813471

2. Submit your proof of purchase

3. That's it! We'll send your free PDF and other benefits to your email directly

Part 1 – Introduction to Web3

Introduction to Web3 is your gateway to understanding the fundamentals of blockchain technology and diving into the exciting world of Ethereum. This part takes you on a journey, starting with the foundational concepts of blockchain and Web3 technology. It provides a clear and beginner-friendly introduction, making complex ideas accessible. As you progress, you'll explore the Ethereum ecosystem and embark on your first Ethereum transaction, gaining hands-on experience in a step-by-step manner. Whether you're a newcomer curious about blockchain or an enthusiast eager to enter the Web3 realm, this part offers a solid foundation and practical guidance to get you started on your blockchain journey.

This section has the following chapters:

- *Chapter 1, Fundamentals of Blockchain and Web3*
- *Chapter 2, Getting Started with Ethereum*
- *Chapter 3, Your First Ethereum Transaction*

1

Fundamentals of Blockchain and Web3

This chapter will lay the foundation for the rest of this course. We will walk through some of the basic blockchain fundamentals required to understand the rest of the concepts and other chapters in this book. You will be introduced to blockchain and the basic anatomy of a blockchain, including nodes, blocks, consensus, and the elements of a blockchain transaction. You'll be introduced to private, public, and hybrid blockchains and learn when to use private and public blockchains. By learning all of the required basics, you'll be fully prepared to learn Web3.

In this chapter, we're going to cover the following main topics:

- Getting started with blockchain

- Understanding the role of cryptography in blockchain

- The basic components of a blockchain

- Types of blockchain

- The anatomy of a blockchain transaction

- Getting started with Web3

- The fundamentals of Web3

Getting started with blockchain

Let's start with some fundamentals about blockchain and topics related to blockchain. If you are already a blockchain expert, this will be a good refresher on the basic concepts.

A blockchain is a type of database that is used to store transactions across a network of computers. It is called a **blockchain** because it consists of a series of blocks that are chained together. Each block contains a list of transactions that have occurred since the last block was added to the chain.

The key feature of a blockchain is that it is decentralized, meaning it is not controlled by a single entity, such as a bank or government. Instead, it is maintained by a network of computers that work together to validate and record transactions. This makes it difficult for anyone to alter the data on the blockchain, as they would need to convince a majority of the computers on the network to accept their changes.

Blockchains are often used to store and track financial transactions, but they can be used to store any type of data that needs to be securely recorded and shared. For example, they are used in supply chain management to track the movement of goods, and in voting systems to ensure that votes are counted accurately.

The following figure is a simple illustration of Ethereum blocks and how they are chained to form the blockchain.

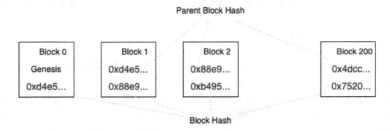

Figure 1.1 – The blocks in a blockchain

Overall, blockchains provide a secure and transparent way for people to exchange information and value without the need for a central authority.

> **Blockchain definition**
> A blockchain is a trusted distributed data and ledger that can be shared and accessed by multiple parties simultaneously, acting as a single source of truth.

Understanding the role of cryptography in blockchain

It is essential to understand the role of cryptography and how it helps blockchain technology with the privacy, trust, and security of transactions. Currently, there are more than 350 cryptographic libraries available globally, but only a few of them are used in blockchain technology.

In a blockchain, each transaction is secured with the use of a unique digital signature, which is generated using a private key. This signature is used to verify the authenticity of the transaction and ensure that it has not been tampered with.

Cryptography is a key element of the security of blockchain technology. It is used to secure the transactions on the blockchain and ensure that the information on it is kept private and cannot be altered.

Cryptography is also used to secure the blocks on a blockchain. To maintain the chain's integrity and prevent any tampering, each block in a blockchain carries a cryptographic hash of the one before it.

Additionally, cryptography was used in the consensus process to help ensure the security of the blockchain. Consensus mechanisms use cryptographic hashes to solve complex mathematical problems, create new blocks, and add them to the chain.

One of the major implementations of blockchains is public and private key cryptography. These keys define how the accounts operate and sign transactions and how the transactions are understood between a buyer and seller, for example. Key generation and management will be covered in depth in *Chapter 2*.

The following diagram shows a simple way to create a private and public key, using custom input and cryptography. This technique is used in many public blockchains.

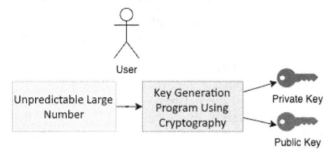

Figure 1.2 – Key creation using cryptography

Overall, cryptography plays a vital role in ensuring the security and integrity of blockchain technology. It helps to ensure the privacy of transactions, prevent tampering with the blockchain, and secure the mining process.

Next, we'll take a look at components that are essential in a blockchain.

The basic components in a blockchain

Understanding the anatomy of a blockchain is key and a basic requirement to access Web3. Here, we will go over the components and architecture of a blockchain.

We are aware that a blockchain is a distributed database made up of a number of blocks, connected by cryptography and safeguarded with it. Each block has a list of several transactions, and once data has been recorded on a block, it cannot be altered. Let us look at the most common components of a blockchain, which includes but is not limited to the following:

- **Blocks**: A block is a collection of transaction data that is added to a blockchain. Each block contains a unique code called a "hash" that distinguishes it from other blocks in the chain.

- **Nodes**: A node is a computer that participates in the operation of a blockchain network. Nodes can validate transactions and add them to a blockchain.

- **Miners**: Miners are nodes that perform the work of verifying transactions and adding them to a blockchain. In return for this work, they are typically rewarded with a small amount of the cryptocurrency used on the network.

- **Cryptography**: Cryptography is the use of mathematical algorithms to secure communication. In the context of a blockchain, cryptography is used to secure data within blocks and ensure that blocks are linked together in a way that is tamper-resistant.

- **Consensus protocol**: A consensus protocol is a set of rules that determines how nodes on a blockchain network reach agreement about the state of a network. There are several different consensus protocols that are used in different blockchain systems, including proof of work, proof of stake, proof of verification, proof of importance, proof of capacity, and proof of authority.

- **Smart contracts**: A self-executing software program known as a "smart contract" contains the details of an agreement between numerous parties, written directly into its source code. The blockchain serves as a repository for both the agreements and the underlying code.

Depending on the blockchain product or framework that we use, the components may vary. For example, Ethereum, one of the most popular blockchains, recently moved away from mining and adopted **staking** for its consensus mechanism. However, most blockchains have components with common features, which perform similar functions and operations. Some of these components are summarized in this section.

> **What is staking?**
>
> Staking is a way to keep money in a cryptocurrency wallet that helps to run the blockchain network. By staking your coins, you essentially hold them as collateral to verify network transactions. Users receive a portion of the transaction fees and block rewards for their contribution to the network, in exchange for staking their coins. A portion of the total number of coins staked is typically the reward for staking. A **proof-of-stake** (**PoS**) blockchain network allows users to take part in the consensus process through staking. The number of staked coins determines how likely it is that a new block will be validated in a PoS system. This implies that the more coins you stake, the more likely it is that you will be chosen to validate a new block and receive the corresponding reward. Staking is a replacement for networks such as Bitcoin's **proof-of-work** (**PoW**) consensus mechanism. To validate transactions and produce new blocks in a PoW system, miners compete to find solutions to challenging mathematical puzzles. This procedure uses a significant amount of computational resources and energy.

Types of blockchain

There are several types of blockchains, including public, private, consortium, and hybrid. Let us look at some of the popular types and some examples. In this book, we will deep-dive into Ethereum, the first blockchain to support smart contracts, also called programmable money.

Public blockchains

Public blockchains are open to anyone and are decentralized, meaning they are not controlled by a single entity. Let us look at the most popular blockchains and how they operate.

The following table shows a basic comparison of three popular blockchains, with high-level information. We will take a deep dive into Ethereum in the next chapter, and it will be our focus in the Web3 topics throughout this book.

Public Blockchains			
Name	Bitcoin	Ethereum	Solana
Logo			
Popularity	#1	#2	Top 10
Symbol	BTC	ETH	SOL
Year Launched	2009	2012	2020
Supports Smart Contract	No	Yes	Yes

Figure 1.3 – A public blockchain comparison

Bitcoin (`https://bitcoin.org/en/`), the first cryptocurrency and the first public blockchain, continues to be the most popular and market leader.

Bitcoin is a digital currency that is not regulated by any government or financial organization, and it employs encryption for security. It was developed in 2009 by a person or group of people going under the alias *Satoshi Nakamoto*. Users can access their bitcoins using a wallet that houses private keys, which are required to access their Bitcoin address. Transactions are recorded on a public ledger known as the Bitcoin blockchain.

Bitcoins can be used to purchase goods and services online and also exchanged for other currencies. The value of a bitcoin is determined by supply and demand on exchanges, and it has fluctuated significantly since it was first introduced. Bitcoin is the first decentralized cryptocurrency, and it has gained a reputation as a safe and secure way to store and transfer value.

Ethereum (`https://ethereum.org/en/`) is a decentralized platform for building **decentralized applications (dApps)**. It was launched in 2015 and is powered by a cryptocurrency called **ether (ETH)**. Ethereum is designed to be a flexible and adaptable platform, allowing developers to build decentralized applications that run on a blockchain. These applications can be used for a variety of purposes, including finance, gaming, identity verification, and supply chain management. Smart contracts are one of the key features of Ethereum and are self-executing contracts, with business logic embedded in them directly, written in high-level programming languages. They are used to automate complex financial transactions, enable peer-to-peer payments, and create **decentralized autonomous organizations (DAOs)**. Ethereum also has a highly active developer community and is home to many **decentralized finance (DeFi)** applications, which have grown significantly in popularity in recent years.

The Ethereum platform is powered by ether, a cryptocurrency that can be used to pay for transaction fees and services on the Ethereum network. The value of ether has fluctuated significantly since it was first introduced, but it has consistently remained one of the top cryptocurrencies by market capitalization.

Ethereum blockchain introduced the concept of smart contracts. You can develop your own smart contracts, which are programs running on various blockchain nodes. This introduces a new way for developing business logics using smart contracts. Ethereum is also popularly known as the first **programable blockchain**.

Solana (`https://solana.com/`) is a public blockchain platform that is designed to support high scalability and low transaction fees. It uses a novel consensus algorithm called **proof of history (PoH)** to achieve fast transaction speeds and low fees, making it suitable for dApps that require high performance. Solana also has features such as smart contracts, which allow developers to build complex dApps, and a **decentralized exchange (DEX)** for trading cryptocurrencies. The Solana network is maintained by a decentralized network of validator nodes, which are responsible for verifying transactions and adding them to the blockchain.

When it comes to solutions involving public blockchain, there are a number of factors to take into consideration. It is not a very simple task to settle on a particular blockchain for all your needs. Every blockchain has its own pros and cons, and the choice of blockchain depends on the specific needs and use cases. Next, we will take a look at the private blockchains.

Private blockchains

Private or permissioned networks are only accessible to a certain group of individuals. They are often used by organizations that want to keep their data private and secure. The following table gives you an overview of the three popular private or permissioned blockchains.

Private or Permission Blockchains			
Name	Hyperledger Fabric	R3 Corda	Quorum
Logo			
Enterprise Friendly	Yes	Yes	Yes
Supports Tokens	Yes	Yes	Yes
Year Launched	2016	2015	2016
Supports Smart Contract	Yes	Yes	Yes

Figure 1.4 – Private blockchain comparisons

- We will take three of the popular private blockchains and go over them quickly. This will be only an introduction to private or permissioned blockchains, as we will focus on Ethereum, which is a public blockchain. **Hyperledger Fabric** (https://www.hyperledger.org/use/fabric) is an open source platform for building enterprise-grade blockchain applications. It is one of the initiatives under the Hyperledger umbrella, an open source collaborative initiative to improve blockchain technologies across industries.

  Hyperledger Fabric is designed to support modularity and flexibility, allowing developers to easily build and deploy blockchain applications that meet their specific needs. It is suitable for use in a variety of industries, including finance, supply chain, and healthcare.

  One key feature of Hyperledger Fabric is its support for private and permissioned networks, which allows organizations to control access to their data and ensure that only authorized parties can participate in the network. It also uses a modular architecture, which allows developers to plug in different components and customize the behavior of their applications.

  Overall, Hyperledger Fabric is a powerful platform for building enterprise-grade blockchain applications that can be used in a variety of industries and contexts.

- **R3 Corda** (https://www.r3.com/products/corda/) is an open source blockchain platform that is specifically designed for use in the financial industry. It was developed by R3, a technology company that focuses on building blockchain-based solutions for financial institutions.

Corda is built on the principle of "shared ledger" technology, which allows participants to share a ledger of transactions without the need for a central authority. This allows financial institutions to streamline their operations and reduce the need for intermediaries.

Corda is unique in that it is not a fully decentralized platform like other blockchains. Instead, it is a distributed ledger platform that is designed to be private and secure, while still allowing participants to share data and transact with one another. It also uses smart contract technology to automate business logic, especially multi-party agreements between buyers and sellers, with programs written in a high-level language.

Overall, R3 Corda is a highly secure and efficient platform for building financial applications that can be used by banks, insurance companies, and other financial institutions.

- **GoQuorum** (`https://consensys.net/docs/goquorum/en/latest/`) is an open source platform for building enterprise-grade blockchain applications, using the Ethereum code base. It is a fork of Ethereum that has been modified to support private and permissioned networks, making it suitable for use in enterprise contexts where data privacy is a concern.

  GoQuorum is built on top of the **Ethereum Virtual Machine** (**EVM**), which is a runtime environment for executing smart contracts. It supports the Solidity programming language, which is the most popular language for writing smart contracts on the Ethereum platform.

One key feature of GoQuorum is its support for private transactions, which allows participants to transact with one another without revealing the details of the transaction to the entire network. It also has a feature called private smart contracts, which allows organizations to deploy smart contracts that are only accessible to a specific group of individuals.

Overall, GoQuorum is a powerful platform for building enterprise-grade blockchain applications that can be used in a variety of industries and contexts.

Let's now move on to consortium blockchains.

Consortium blockchains

Consortium blockchains are partially decentralized, as they are controlled by a group of organizations rather than a single entity. They are often used in industries where multiple parties need to work together, such as the financial industry.

For example, the following diagram shows a consortium of banks to solve specific banking industry problems.

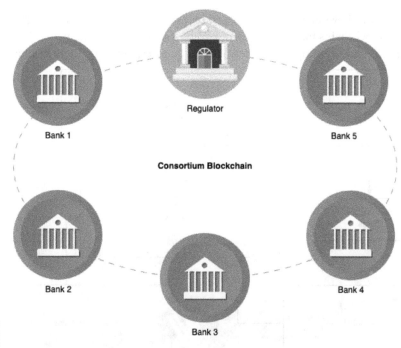

Figure 1.5 – A banking industry blockchain consortium

Banks and regulators can come forward to form a consortium-based blockchain network and take specific banking or regulatory-related industry problems to solve them. Some of the popular financial use cases include letters of credit in trade finance, custody and clearing and settlements in capital markets, new fund launches from asset and wealth management, and cross-border payments from payments and remittances.

Consortium-based blockchain networks can be public or private chains, but they are usually private due to confidentiality and privacy requirements. The consortium blockchains were popular from 2017 to 2020, and there have been many consortium-based blockchain networks formed by large enterprises.

Even though they all were very appealing and performed successfully during and after the launch, these consortiums had operational constraints. Governing consortiums added another level of complexity, and companies spent a lot of time planning, operating, and executing plans. The investments to become part of a consortium and keep it running took a lot of investment from these consortium members. Eventually, most of the consortium-based blockchains failed.

Hybrid blockchains

Hybrid blockchains are blockchains that combine aspects of both public and private blockchains. They can be open to the public but also have certain elements that are restricted to certain individuals or groups.

The following diagram shows an example of hybrid blockchains and network convergence, which is the near future of blockchains for enterprises and Web3 use cases, where L2 networks, cross-chain bridges, and roll-ups play very important roles. We will do a deep dive into these in later chapters.

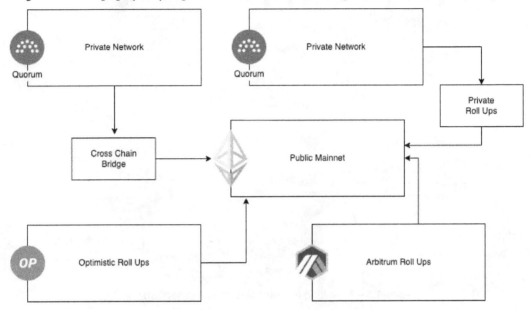

Figure 1.6 – Ethereum-based hybrid blockchains

We have covered different blockchain types and some pros and cons here; next, we'll move on to the anatomy of a blockchain. Here, we'll understand the various elements of a blockchain transaction and why they are important, and we'll take a closer look into these elements later when we do a deep dive into Ethereum.

The anatomy of a blockchain transaction

Transaction is the core of everything that happens in a blockchain. It is important to understand what a blockchain transaction consists of and how the various elements hold valuable information about the transaction. This is also a good primer to understand how blockchain transactions are different from transactions of a traditional system.

A blockchain transaction typically consists of the following elements:

- **Input**: The input refers to the previous transaction output that is used as the input for the current transaction.

- **Output**: The output is the result of the transaction, which can be either the payment to a recipient or the creation of new units of a cryptocurrency.

- **Transaction fee**: A transaction fee is a small amount of cryptocurrency that is included in the transaction and paid to the miner, who processes the transaction and adds it to the blockchain.

- **Signature**: A signature is a piece of data that is used to verify the authenticity of a transaction. It is created using a private key and can be verified using the corresponding public key.

- **Timestamp**: A timestamp is a record of the time at which the transaction was added to the blockchain.

- **Block hash**: A block hash is a unique identifier for each block in the blockchain. It is created using the data in the block and used to verify the integrity of the block.

As we discussed earlier, depending on the blockchain product or framework that we use, the elements/fields of a blockchain transaction vary. We will deep-dive in the next chapter into Ethereum transactions, where we will study these elements in detail.

In the following figure, a sample Ethereum transaction is shown from **Etherscan** (`https://etherscan.io/`), a popular blockchain explorer, which provides a user interface for developers and other users to browse the blockchain, abstracting the complexity of running various commands to get the transaction details.

A total of 244 transactions found

First < Page 1 of 5 > Last

	Txn Hash	Method	Block	Age	From		To	Value	Txn Fee
⊕	0x1a9fb8c23c9be9bbd...	Set Approval ...	17019532	17 secs ago	⟨⟩ seneca.eth	→	Opepen Edition: OPEPE...	0 ETH	0.00131662
⊕	0xc235f669f55f8dd27...	Transfer	17019532	17 secs ago	0x538765...D258E38a	→	0x04DBD6...55d67491	0.01062855 ETH	0.00054285
⊕	0x80837eb5658a3243...	Append Sequ...	17019532	17 secs ago	Optimism: Sequencer	→	Optimism: Canonical Tr...	0 ETH	0.0077222
⊕	0xe38c0d5480368a1e...	Add Sequenc...	17019532	17 secs ago	Arbitrum: Batch Submit...	→	Arbitrum: Sequencer In...	0 ETH	0.04765099
⊕	0x240422978d4f0f4e0...	Transfer	17019532	17 secs ago	0x27899f...9EE60FD6	→	0x975924...9482AcF6	0.017957907 ETH	0.00054295
⊕	⏱ 0x79a77e2633603ae7...	Mint	17019532	17 secs ago	⟨⟩ 0xhsien.eth	→	0x73dde6...CC9b013a	0 ETH	0.00073858
⊕	0x1da047cb2c2c8aaf3...	Request L2Tr...	17019532	17 secs ago	0x14D2C4...daCEefa0	→	zkSync Era: Diamond P...	0.313805749 ETH	0.00307231
⊕	0xfc10df60f939ab819...	Fulfill Availabl...	17019532	17 secs ago	⟨⟩ graphilix.eth	→	Seaport 1.4	0.059 ETH	0.013785b7
⊕	0x84ffc928a68a6d638...	Unstake	17019532	17 secs ago	0x8fdb48...886757aa	→	Illuvium: Migrate	0 ETH	0.00343713
⊕	⏱ 0xb845d46a3654fa7c6...	Mint	17019532	17 secs ago	0xd9b205...E671aE6f	→	0x73dde6...CC9b013a	0 ETH	0.00073875
⊕	0x2bfe44cd78b3552ee...	0x00000000	17019532	17 secs ago	⟨⟩ naravv.eth	→	Seaport 1.4	0.0949 ETH	0.00325573
⊕	0xe0b7b3047b01a5a4...	Transfer	17019532	17 secs ago	0x11271C...02FAab71	→	Tether: USDT Stablecoin	0 ETH	0.00119284
⊕	0x178b380145eb5336...	Transfer	17019532	17 secs ago	0x52B4CD...02a5894c	→	0x3486E0...1448961C	0.3 ETH	0.00054341
⊕	0x8192f9e15f2ee86ef...	Transfer	17019532	17 secs ago	⟨⟩ sincerepallas.eth	→	0x263E96...67647078	0.189696377 ETH	0.00054341
⊕	0x78ee9ed724f682f79...	Claim Self MA...	17019532	17 secs ago	0x987627...0048c101	→	Apecoin: Staking	0 ETH	0.00207231

Figure 1.7 – The Etherscan blockchain explorer

Getting started with Web3

We need to understand Web1 and Web2 to understand Web3. Let us understand what Web1 stands for first.

Web1, or the first generation of the **World Wide Web** (**W3**), refers to the earliest stage of the web, which was primarily used to access and share information. It was characterized by static HTML pages that could be linked using hyperlinks. Web1 focused on the dissemination of information, rather than on interactive and dynamic content. It was also limited in terms of the types of media that could be shared, as it was primarily text-based. It is important to know that Web1 is the foundation for many modern technologies and frameworks that we have in the world today.

So, Web2 is simply the next generation of technologies that evolved from Web1. Web2, or the second generation of the W3, refers to the stage of the web that focuses on the development of interactive and dynamic content, and on improving the user experience. Some key features of Web2 include the following:

- **Social media**: Web2 saw the rise of social media platforms, which enabled users to connect with one another and share content

- **Collaboration**: Web2 technologies such as wikis and blogs made it easier for users to collaborate and work together online

- **Personalization**: Web2 technologies enabled personalized experiences for users, such as recommendations based on their browsing history

- **Mobile access**: Web2 technologies made it easier for users to access the web from their mobile devices

Overall, Web2 was characterized by the shift from a web of static pages to a web of dynamic and interactive content, and by the increasing centralization of the web as large companies emerged as key players in the industry.

While serving content and data in a centralized web has many advantages, the birth of cryptocurrencies and blockchain technology proved how decentralization can improve data availability and content served on the internet, which we call **Web3**.

Web3, also known as the decentralized web or the decentralized internet, refers to the use of blockchain technology to create a more secure and decentralized internet. It is a set of protocols and technologies that aims to give users more control over their online data and interactions, making the internet more resistant to censorship and interference.

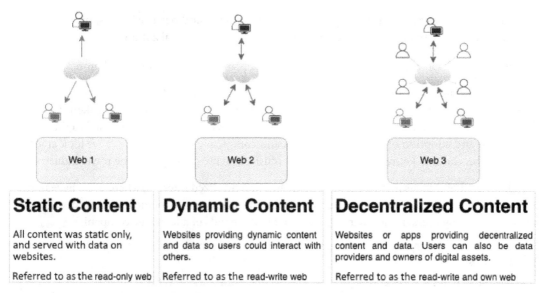

Static Content	**Dynamic Content**	**Decentralized Content**
All content was static only, and served with data on websites.	Websites providing dynamic content and data so users could interact with others.	Websites or apps providing decentralized content and data. Users can also be data providers and owners of digital assets.
Referred to as the read-only web	Referred to as the read-write web	Referred to as the read-write and own web

Figure 1.8 – Understanding Web1, Web3, and Web3

Web3 technologies, such as Ethereum and other smart contract platforms, enable the creation of dApps, which can operate on a blockchain and are not controlled by any single entity. These dApps can be used to create a wide range of applications, from social networks and marketplaces to voting systems and supply chain management tools.

Web3 also includes protocols for secure peer-to-peer communication, such as **Inter-Planetary File System (IPFS)**, which can be used to store and share data without the need for a central server.

Newer business ideas that originated based on the decentralization and tokenization of real and virtual assets are now commonly called **digital assets**. With new financial digital assets and blockchain, the world was introduced to a completely new set of financial services called **Decentralized Finance (DeFi)**.

DeFi refers to financial applications and services that are built on decentralized networks, such as blockchain. DeFi aims to provide the same financial services as traditional finance but in a decentralized and trustless manner.

Some of the key features of DeFi include the following:

- **Decentralization**: DeFi applications are decentralized, meaning that they are not controlled by any single entity
- **Trustless**: DeFi applications are designed to be trustless, meaning that users do not need to trust a third party to handle their transactions
- **Interoperability**: DeFi applications are often built on open protocols, which enables them to work together and exchange information seamlessly

- **Permissionless access**: DeFi applications are often open and permissionless, meaning that anyone can use them without the need for approval from a central authority

DeFi applications include DEXs, lending and borrowing platforms, Stablecoins, and more.

With regard to non-financial services, creating digital assets based on real-world objects created a new economic model for humans. This kind of tokenization is called **Non-Fungible Tokens** (**NFTs**). Creators and artists gained a new monetization model with NFTs. This new model led to the rapid development and adoption of Web3 technologies and completely changed the way we look at arts, collectibles, fan clubs, ticketing systems, royalties, music, movies, gaming, and the travel industry.

Overall, the goal of web3 is to create a more open and decentralized internet, where users have more control over their data and interactions, and where the power and control of the internet is distributed more evenly among users, rather than concentrated in the hands of a few large companies.

Stablecoins

Stablecoins are digital assets that are designed to maintain a stable value relative to a specific asset or basket of assets. One of the primary goals of stablecoins is to provide a more stable store of value compared to cryptocurrencies such as Bitcoin, which can be highly volatile.

The fundamentals of Web3

Web3 refers to the third generation of the World Wide Web, which emphasizes the use of decentralized technologies such as blockchain and peer-to-peer networking. Some of the key features of Web3 include the following:

- **Decentralization**: In contrast to the centralized nature of Web2, Web3 technologies are decentralized and distributed, meaning that they are not controlled by any single entity.

- **Blockchain**: A key technology underlying Web3 is the blockchain, which is a decentralized, distributed ledger that records transactions in a secure and transparent manner.

- **Smart contracts**: Smart contracts are typically used in dApps that run on blockchain networks, such as Ethereum. They are used to automate the execution of complex financial transactions, enforce rules and regulations, and ensure that all parties involved in the contract are held accountable.

- **Interoperability**: Web3 technologies are designed to be interoperable, meaning that they can work together and exchange information seamlessly.

- **Security**: Web3 technologies are designed to be secure and resistant to tampering, making them well suited for a variety of applications, including financial transactions and data storage.

- **DApps**: Web3 technologies enable the creation of dApps, which are applications that run on a decentralized network rather than a single server.

It is difficult to predict the exact future of Web3, as it is a rapidly evolving field. However, it is likely that Web3 technologies will continue to play a significant role in shaping the future of the internet and industries such as finance and supply chain management. Some potential future developments for Web3 include the following:

- **Increased adoption**: It is likely that Web3 technologies will see increased adoption in a variety of industries, as more organizations become aware of the benefits they offer.

- **Improved scalability**: One of the challenges facing Web3 technologies is scalability, or the ability to handle a large volume of transactions. It is likely that efforts will continue to be made to improve the scalability of Web3 technologies in the future.

- **Integration with Web2**: It is possible that Web3 technologies will become more integrated with the existing Web2 infrastructure, allowing for a seamless transition between the two.

- **Development of new applications**: As Web3 technologies mature, it is likely that new applications and use cases will be developed, enabling a wider range of industries to benefit from the features they offer.

Overall, the future of Web3 is likely to be marked by continued innovation and growth, as more organizations and individuals become aware of the benefits it offers.

Summary

Let's summarize what we learned in this chapter. We started by understanding blockchain as a technology and framework. Then, we saw how cryptography plays a very important and integral part in the blockchain technology stack. We also covered some of the basic components of a blockchain. We looked at the anatomy of a blockchain transaction and how it plays an important role, followed by a few common types of blockchain and how they are used. This chapter also laid out the foundation to get started with Web3 and the core fundamentals required for Web3.

In the next chapter, we'll start looking at the Ethereum blockchain to understand its core fundamentals and basics. We'll look into concepts such as **Ethereum Improvement Proposals (EIP)** and **Ethereum Request For Comment (ERCs)** and the importance of key management. We'll also learn how to use a wallet and deep-dive into the history of Ethereum.

Getting Started With Ethereum

The chapter gives an extensive overview of the Ethereum ecosystem. The chapter summarizes its origin to its current state, explaining the complete anatomy of Ethereum, accounts, nodes, smart contracts, consensus mechanisms, and much more. You will learn about the basics of Ethereum as a cryptocurrency and the blockchain that powers it. You will also gain exposure to different consensus mechanisms such as proof-of-work and proof-of-stake, which are very essential to understanding the rest of the chapters and how blockchain works.

This chapter will introduce you to the types of Ethereum keys, the significance of private keys, and how they are used to sign a transaction. You will also get an introduction to wallets and learn about the different types of wallets. You will also learn about how to create your first wallet using MetaMask. The chapter also covers some of the important things to consider when storing secret phrases and how to use them to recover a wallet and address.

In this chapter, we're going to cover the following main topics:

- Getting started with Ethereum
- Ethereum ecosystems and essentials
- Understanding ERC and EIP
- Creating and managing your keys
- A self-custodial wallet, MetaMask
- The state of Ethereum

Getting started with Ethereum

Let's start with Ethereum. The book focuses on Ethereum as the preferred blockchain for Web3, and all examples and code samples will be using the Ethereum blockchain.

Ethereum is a unique open source and decentralized blockchain platform that enables users and developers to create smart contracts and **decentralized applications** (**dApps**). It features its own cryptocurrency, called **Ether** (**ETH**), which is the mode of payment for transactions and computational work on the network.

Ethereum was first proposed in 2013 by Vitalik Buterin, a Canadian–Russian programmer, and was officially launched on July 30, 2015. Buterin had previously worked on **Bitcoin** (**BTC**) but became convinced that the blockchain technology could be used for more than just a digital currency.

Buterin published the Ethereum white paper (`https://ethereum.org/en/whitepaper/`), which outlined his vision for a decentralized platform that would allow developers and users to create dApps and smart contracts. The Ethereum network went live in July, 2015 with the launch of the Frontier version of the Ethereum software.

Since then, Ethereum has upgraded its network numerous times, such as with the Metropolis and Serenity upgrades. Ethereum 2.0 is the current version and is still under development. It aims to address scalability and security issues, and will also make significant changes to the Ethereum network.

Ethereum has grown to become one of the most popular and widely used blockchain platforms, and its native cryptocurrency, ETH, is the second-largest digital currency by market capitalization after BTC.

The following figure describes the history and the major releases and milestones of the Ethereum ecosystem. These releases became the foundation for the ecosystem and everything that we build on Ethereum today.

The first five years of Ethereum provided the foundation required for developers and Ethereum to set up a platform to build the future.

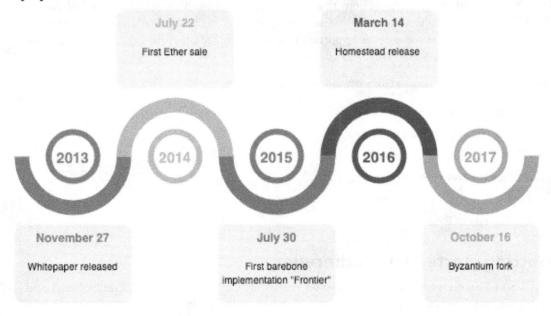

Figure 2.1 – Ethereum from 2013 to 2017

In 2019, Ethereum started gaining more traction from both cryptocurrency and blockchain perspectives. Some of the updates that core foundation capabilities have gone through are considered the most signification innovations and milestones in the technology space over the last two years. The following figure shows some of the important milestones.

Figure 2.2 – Ethereum from 2019 to 2023

We will start learning about the basics of Ethereum and the Ethereum virtual machine in the next section.

Ethereum ecosystems and essentials

Let us look at some of the essentials that we need to know about Ethereum. These fundamentals will help you align with the rest of the book and are required to understand the code and other advanced topics covered later in this book.

The Ethereum virtual machine

The **Ethereum virtual machine** (**EVM**) is an execution and runtime environment that executes smart contracts on the blockchain network. It is a virtual machine that can execute arbitrary computations, similar to the way a traditional computer's CPU executes instructions. The EVM is referred to as a Turing-complete virtual machine very often, meaning it can run any program that can be expressed in code.

The EVM is responsible for executing the bytecode that makes up a smart contract, which is generated from the contract's high-level programming language code. It processes the smart contract's code and performs the required operations, such as updating the contract's state and interacting with the Ethereum blockchain.

The EVM is designed to be a global, decentralized, and public resource. It is implemented in the client software of every node in the Ethereum network, and it runs independently of the underlying hardware or operating system. This ensures that the EVM is a consistent and reliable environment for executing smart contracts across the entire Ethereum network.

This allows for the creation of dApps and the implementation of various use cases, such as digital assets, digital identity, and **decentralized finance (DeFi)**.

ETH

ETH is the native cryptocurrency of the Ethereum network, also known as Ether. It is used to pay for transactions and computational services on the Ethereum network, similar to how BTC is used as a means of payment on the BTC network.

ETH is used to pay for the cost of executing smart contracts and transactions on the Ethereum network, which is known as a gas fee. The gas fee is calculated in Ether and is required to be paid by the user or contract creator to execute a transaction or smart contract on the Ethereum network.

In addition to its use as a means of payment, ETH is also used as a store of value and can be traded on various cryptocurrency exchanges. It is also used as collateral for various DeFi applications and platforms.

It is important to note that ETH is not just a digital currency but also a digital asset that has value and can be traded like any other asset. The value of ETH fluctuates based on supply and demand in the market, and it can be affected by several factors such as regulations, adoption, and the overall performance of the Ethereum network.

Ethereum accounts

In Ethereum, an account is a fundamental concept that represents an identity on the Ethereum network. Ethereum has two types of accounts: **externally owned accounts (EOAs)** and **contract accounts**.

EOAs are controlled by private keys and are used to send transactions and execute smart contracts. They are controlled by a single private key and can be used to send Ether or other tokens, as well as interact with smart contracts. EOAs are similar to BTC addresses; they are used to receive and send transactions.

Contract accounts, also called smart contract accounts, are like digital agreements that automatically follow the rules written in their code. These agreements work by themselves without the need for someone to enforce them. It's like a computer program that takes care of things according to the instructions it's given. Just imagine a robot that knows what to do based on the code you've given it.

These contracts have their own address on the Ethereum blockchain and can hold Ether or other tokens. They can also perform actions such as sending Ether or other tokens and interacting with other smart contracts.

Both EOAs and contract accounts have a public key (address) and a balance, which represents the amount of Ether or other tokens they hold. Accounts also have a **nonce**, which is a number that tracks the number of transactions that have been sent from a particular Ethereum account.

In summary, Ethereum accounts are digital identities that can hold Ether and other tokens, send transactions, and execute smart contracts on the Ethereum network. EOAs are controlled by private keys, while contract accounts are self-executing smart contracts.

Gas and fee structure

The Ethereum fee structure is based on the concept of gas, which is a unit of computational work to execute a transaction or run a smart contract on the Ethereum blockchain network. Gas is also used as a technique to prevent spamming and denial-of-service attacks on the network.

The cost of executing a transaction or running a smart contract on the Ethereum network is measured in gas and the cost is paid in ETH. The price of gas is measured in gwei, which is one billionth of an Ether. Gwei is named after the Chinese word *gwei*, which means "giga" (billion). A gwei is equivalent to one billionth (10^{-9}) of an ETH.

The way fees work on Ethereum is like this: when you want to do something on the network, such as send money or run a smart contract, you need to pay a fee. This fee is based on two things: the price you're willing to pay for each unit of gas (like fuel) and the maximum amount of gas you're allowed to use.

Think of it like a car. The gas price is how much you're ready to pay for each gallon, and the gas limit is how much gas your car's tank can hold. Transactions offering a higher gas price get to go first, just like a higher offer gets you a spot in line. This way, people can bid more to get their stuff done quicker.

The exact fee for a transaction depends on the complexity of the operation and the current state of the network. Transactions that involve more computational work, such as deploying a contract or running a complex smart contract, require more gas and therefore have higher fees.

Ethereum has also implemented a new fee market mechanism called EIP-1559, which introduces a base fee that is adjusted dynamically based on network usage and burns a portion of the fees, which helps to reduce the supply of Ether over time, making it a scarce resource.

For example, if a user wants to execute a smart contract that requires 300,000 units of gas and the current gas price is 20 gwei, the total cost of the transaction would be:

300,000 x 20 = 6,000,000 gwei = 6 Ether

Smart contracts

A smart contract is a set of business logic or computational instructions, written in code, that can be executed automatically when required. These conditions can be based on the value of variables, such as the value of a digital asset, or on the outcome of a predefined event, such as the expiration of a time limit. Smart contracts can be executed either when the conditions are met or by triggering an event that executes the contract automatically without the need for intermediaries or manual intervention.

Smart contracts are used to automate a broad range of business processes, such as supply chain management, digital identity, and DeFi applications. They can also be used to create dApps that run on the Ethereum blockchain.

Smart contracts are stored and replicated on the Ethereum blockchain, and they each have their own unique address. They can hold Ether or other tokens, and they can also perform actions such as sending Ether or other tokens and interacting with other smart contracts.

Smart contracts are transparent, auditable, and tamper-proof. Once they are deployed on the Ethereum network, their code and their execution can be audited by anyone. This ensures that the contract will be executed as intended and that the terms of the contract are enforced.

Let us look at an example of a sample smart contract here and the simplest smart contract. The following code blocks show the Solidity code to see the balance of an Ethereum account:

```solidity
// Solidity program to get a balance of an Ethereum account
pragma solidity ^0.8.13;
// Creating a contract to get the balance of an account
contract Balance
{
// Private state variable address private owner;
// Defining a constructor
constructor() public{
owner=msg.sender;
}
// Function to return current balance of owner
function getBalance(
) public view returns(uint256){
return owner.balance;
}
}
```

We will get into the details of such code in the next few sections, but for now, this code shows that a smart contract is nothing but a collection of functions and/or instructions for a computer to execute when it is called or triggered. The programming language used here is Solidity, which is a JavaScript-like language.

A smart contract in Ethereum can be written in several programming languages, including the following:

- **Solidity**: This is the most popular language for writing Ethereum smart contracts and is supported natively by the Ethereum platform
- **Vyper**: This is a Python-based language for writing smart contracts that is more secure and simple than Solidity
- **Bamboo**: This is a JavaScript-based language for writing smart contracts that is still in development
- **Lisp Like Language** (**LLL**): This is a low-level language for writing smart contracts that is used for optimization and performance
- **Assembly**: This is the lowest-level language for writing smart contracts, and it is used for writing complex, low-level functions and interacting with the Ethereum virtual machine

We will use only Solidity as our smart contact language in this book.

Ethereum transactions

An Ethereum transaction can be of two types. The first transfers Ether that is sent from one address (or account) to another on the Ethereum blockchain, and the second is a smart contract call. The latter contains several key components, including the following:

- **Nonce**: A nonce is a unique number that is used to identify the transaction and prevent replay attacks. It is incremented for each transaction sent from a particular address.
- **Gas price**: The gas price is the amount of ETH that the sender needs to pay per unit of gas consumed by the transaction. The gas price is measured in gwei (1 gwei = 10^{-9} ETH).
- **Gas limit**: The gas has limits. It is the maximum ETH in the amount of gas that the user agrees to pay for the transaction. The gas limit is based on the complexity of the operation and the current state of the network, and it is measured in units of gas.
- **To address**: The To address is the Ethereum address of the recipient of the transaction. This can be an externally owned account address or a smart contract address.
- **Value**: The value is the amount of Ether that is being transferred in the transaction. It is measured in Wei (1 Wei = 10^{-18} ETH).
- **Data**: The data field is an optional field that can be used to include additional information in the transaction, such as the bytecode of a smart contract or the parameters of a function call.
- **Signature**: The signature is a digital signature that is used to authenticate the transaction and prove that the sender is the owner of the address that is sending the transaction.

Once a transaction is sent to the Ethereum network, it is included in a block by a miner and becomes part of the blockchain. Once the transaction is wrapped in a block, it is confirmed. The time that it takes for a transaction to be confirmed depends on the gas price, the current network conditions, the miner's preference, and a few other parameters.

Consensus mechanism

The consensus mechanism in the Ethereum blockchain was **proof-of-work (PoW)**. This mechanism required nodes in the network to perform a mathematical calculation, called **mining**, to validate transactions and add them to the blockchain. The first node to solve the calculation adds the block to the blockchain and receives a reward for doing so. The other nodes in the network then validate the solution and add the block to their own copies of the blockchain.

PoW has several advantages, such as increased security and resistance to malicious actors, but also has significant disadvantages, such as energy consumption and the centralization of mining power. Therefore, Ethereum moved to **proof-of-stake (PoS)**, a new consensus mechanism that allows validators to earn rewards based on the amount of Ether they hold and their stake in the network. This mechanism is expected to be more efficient, secure, and scalable than PoW.

We'll dive deeper into PoS in an upcoming section about the Merge.

Ethereum testnets and mainnet

Testnets in Ethereum are alternative blockchain networks that are used for testing and development purposes. They are separate from the main Ethereum network, which allows developers to test their applications and smart contracts in a safe and secure environment without the risk of affecting the main network.

Ethereum has two testnets: **Sepolia** and **Goerli**. Both these testnets provide a sandbox platform for developers and testers to prepare smart contracts and test them under different conditions so that they can deploy them into the mainnet when they are ready to go live.

The Sepolia testnet emerged in October 2021 as a proof-of-authority testnet developed and maintained by Ethereum core developers. Sepolia, along with the Goerli testnet, transitioned to a PoS consensus mechanism to closely resemble the Ethereum mainnet.

Testnets serve as blockchain environments that mirror the functionalities of the mainnet but operate on separate ledgers. They provide developers with a secure platform to test their applications and smart contracts before deploying them on Ethereum's mainnet, minimizing risks and ensuring smooth deployments.

Sepolia was specifically designed to replicate challenging network conditions, incorporating shorter block times. This feature allows faster transaction confirmations and offers valuable feedback to developers during the testing phase.

The Goerli testnet is a widely used Ethereum test network that provides developers and users with a sandbox environment to test their applications and smart contracts before deploying them on the Ethereum mainnet. It was launched in 2019 and has gained popularity due to its reliability and community support.

Goerli operates on the **proof-of-authority** (**PoA**) consensus algorithm, which allows for quick block generation times and efficient testing. This consensus mechanism relies on a set of trusted validators who are responsible for creating new blocks and maintaining the network's integrity. Unlike the Ethereum mainnet, Goerli does not require expensive mining equipment or extensive computational power, making it accessible for developers of all levels.

Goerli has become an integral part of the Ethereum ecosystem, serving as a vital testing ground for developers, auditors, and projects to ensure their applications are secure and efficient. Its collaborative nature and robust infrastructure make it a valuable tool for the Ethereum community to advance the development and adoption of dApps.

Mainnet refers to the production blockchain network of Ethereum or any other cryptocurrency. It is the actual, live blockchain network where real transactions occur, and the transfer of cryptocurrency or tokens has real-world value. The mainnet operates on the consensus mechanism agreed upon by the network participants and is secured by the full power of the network's computing resources. Transactions recorded on the mainnet are permanent and can be audited by anyone. It contrasts with testnets, which are used for testing and development purposes, may use dummy tokens, and may have different consensus mechanisms and reduced security.

Like operating on a testnet, you can open the URL `https://etherscan.io/` (*Etherscan Mainnet*) in a browser and see that there are transactions submitted to this network and blocks created with these transactions.

Ethereum clients

An Ethereum client is a software implementation of Ethereum that enables interactions with the Ethereum blockchain. It allows users to connect to the Ethereum network, mine blocks, transfer Ether and other tokens, deploy smart contracts, and interact with the EVM.

A client is a full node implementation that stores the entire Ethereum blockchain and validates and relays transactions and blocks. A full node is responsible for maintaining a copy of the Ethereum blockchain and enforcing the rules of the Ethereum protocol. It also allows for the creation of new blocks and the execution of smart contracts.

Ethereum clients can be divided into two main categories: full nodes and light nodes. A full node stores the entire Ethereum blockchain and is responsible for validating transactions and blocks. This means that they must download and store the entire blockchain, which can take up a significant amount of storage space. Light nodes rely on full nodes to validate transactions and blocks, they are typically used for mobile and light clients, and they do not store the entire blockchain data locally.

There are several Ethereum clients available for use on the Ethereum network, including Geth, Parity, Nethermind, Besu, and OpenEthereum. They can be written in different programming languages and have unique features that make them suitable for different use cases.

There are several Ethereum clients, or implementations, available for use on the Ethereum network. Some of the most popular Ethereum clients include the following:

- **Geth** (`https://geth.ethereum.org/`) is the most widely used Ethereum client. It is written in Go and maintained by the Ethereum Foundation. Geth is a full node implementation of the Ethereum protocol, which means that it can be used to mine, transfer, and deploy smart contracts on the Ethereum network.

- **Parity** (`https://github.com/openethereum/parity-ethereum`) is another popular Ethereum client. It is written in Rust and maintained by Parity Technologies. Parity is a full-node implementation of the Ethereum protocol, and it offers a unique feature called **warp sync**, which allows faster synchronization of the node with the blockchain.

- **Nethermind** (`https://docs.nethermind.io/nethermind/`) is another Ethereum client. It is written in C# and is maintained by Nethermind. It is also a full-node implementation of the Ethereum protocol, and it offers high performance, low latency, and other features, such as fast sync and light client support.

- **Besu** (`https://besu.hyperledger.org/en/stable/`) is an open source Ethereum client. It is written in Java and is maintained by PegaSys. It supports both private and public networks and it has a built-in privacy feature called privacy groups, which allows the creation of private transactions.

- **OpenEthereum** (`https://openethereum.github.io/`) is an open source Ethereum client. It is written in Rust and is community-driven. It is a full-node implementation of the Ethereum protocol, and it is compatible with Geth and Parity.

These are some of the most popular Ethereum clients, but there are many other Ethereum clients available, including Trinity and Teku. The choice of client depends on the specific use case, requirements, and personal preferences.

Ethereum Request for Comments (**ERC**) is a standard that defines guidelines for token and contract implementation, while **Ethereum Improvement Proposals** (**EIP**) are proposals for improving the Ethereum network and its functionality and features. Both ERCs and EIPs play essential roles in shaping the evolution of the Ethereum ecosystem. Now, let us look at both EIPs and ERCs in depth.

Ethereum Improvement Proposals

EIPs are suggestions for changes and improvements to the Ethereum protocol and ecosystem. They are used to propose new features, updates, and modifications to the Ethereum network. EIPs are used to gather feedback and consensus from the Ethereum community and developers before any changes are made to the protocol.

EIPs are created by members of the Ethereum community, including developers, researchers, and users. They are submitted to the Ethereum community for review and discussion, and if they are deemed to be beneficial for the network, they may be included in a future Ethereum network upgrade.

EIPs cover a wide range of topics, including the following:

- Modifications to the EVM
- Changes to the consensus mechanism
- New opcodes and instructions for smart contracts
- Updates to the network's security
- Changes to the network's scalability and performance
- Improvements to the privacy and anonymity of the network
- The interoperability between Ethereum and other blockchain networks

Each EIP is assigned a unique number, and they are tracked and discussed on the EIP GitHub repository.

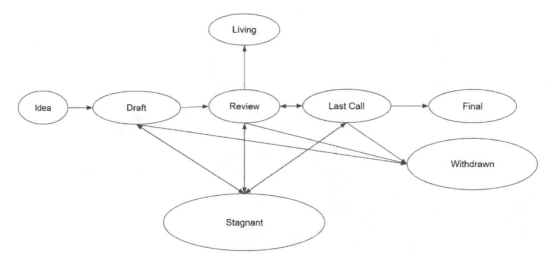

Figure 2.3 – EIP process

> **Note**
> Source: `https://eips.ethereum.org/EIPS/eip-1`

Please note that not all EIPs are accepted and included in a network upgrade; they must go through a review process and require the community's consensus to be implemented.

Why EIPs are important

EIPs are important because they provide a framework for the development and standardization of the Ethereum protocol. They allow the community to propose and discuss changes to the protocol and to come to a consensus on the best course of action.

EIPs allow for the evolution of the Ethereum protocol in a decentralized and community-driven way. They provide a way for developers and users to propose new features, improvements, and modifications to the protocol and for the community to review and discuss these proposals. This ensures that protocols are constantly being improved and updated to meet the needs of users.

EIPs also help to ensure that the Ethereum protocol is secure, efficient, and interoperable. By providing a framework for the development and standardization of the protocol, EIPs help to ensure that changes to the protocol are made in a thoughtful and deliberate way rather than in a haphazard or ad hoc manner.

EIPs also provide a way for the community to come to a consensus on the best course of action for the protocol. By allowing for open and transparent discussion of proposed changes, EIPs ensure that the community is informed and engaged in the process of developing the protocol.

EIP workflow

The EIP workflow is a process that is used to propose, review, and implement changes to the Ethereum protocol. The workflow typically involves the following steps:

Figure 2.4 – EIP workflow

The following is each step in detail:

1. **Proposal**: An individual or a team of developers will write and submit an EIP, which outlines the proposed change to the Ethereum protocol. The EIP should include a detailed explanation of the problem that the proposal is intended to solve, as well as a detailed description of the proposed solution.

2. **Discussion**: After an EIP is submitted, it will be discussed by the Ethereum community, typically on the Ethereum research forum or the EIPs repository on GitHub. Community members will provide feedback and suggestions on the proposal, and the proposal's authors may make revisions based on this feedback.

3. **Review**: After a period of discussion, the EIP will be reviewed by the EIP editors and the Ethereum core developers. The review process will evaluate the technical feasibility of the proposal, as well as its alignment with the Ethereum roadmap and overall goals.

4. **Approval**: If the EIP passes the review, it will be marked as "final" and scheduled for implementation. The decision to implement an EIP is usually made by the Ethereum core developers and the Ethereum community.

5. **Implementation**: After an EIP is approved, it will be implemented in a future Ethereum software release. The implementation process typically involves writing new code, testing the code, and deploying the code to the Ethereum mainnet.

6. **Monitoring**: Once an EIP has been implemented, the Ethereum community will monitor its effects on the network and make any necessary adjustments.

The EIP process is a living document, and it is subject to improvements and modifications as the network and the community evolves. Also, the period for each step of the process can vary depending on the proposal, and some EIPs can take months or even years to fully implement.

Contents of a successful EIP

A successful EIP should include certain elements that clearly and effectively communicate the proposed change and its potential impact on the Ethereum protocol. Here are some key elements that a successful EIP should include:

- **Clear problem statement**: A successful EIP should clearly define the problem that the proposal is intended to solve and explain why the problem is important. This should include a detailed description of the current limitations of the Ethereum protocol that the proposal aims to address.

- **Well-defined solution**: The EIP should provide a clear and detailed description of the proposed solution, including any new features, optimizations, or changes to the existing protocol. The proposal should explain how the solution addresses the problem identified in the problem statement, and it should be technically sound and feasible to implement.

- **Evaluation of the impact**: The EIP should provide an evaluation of the potential impact of the proposal on the Ethereum protocol and its users. This should include an analysis of the benefits and drawbacks of the proposal, as well as any potential risks or trade-offs.

- **Implementation details**: A successful EIP should provide a clear and detailed description of how the proposal will be implemented, including any changes to the existing code base, testing procedures, and deployment plans.

- **Backward compatibility**: The EIP should consider the potential impact on existing contracts and dApps, and it should also explain how the proposal will have backward compatibility and how it will impact the existing ecosystem.

- **Security considerations**: The EIP should include a comprehensive evaluation of the potential security risks of the proposal and it should describe how they will be mitigated.

- **References**: The EIP should include any relevant references to other EIPs, research papers, or external resources that were used as inspiration or to support the proposal.

- **Authorship**: The EIP should mention the authors, their affiliations, and their contact information.

By including these elements, an EIP can effectively communicate the proposed change, its potential impact, and the reasoning behind it, making it more likely to be accepted and implemented by the Ethereum community.

Popular EIPs

Many EIPs have been proposed and implemented on the Ethereum network, but some of the most popular and widely adopted EIPs include the following:

- **EIP-20 (ERC-20)**: This EIP defines a common standard for fungible tokens on the Ethereum blockchain. It was first proposed in 2015 and has since become the most widely adopted token standard on the Ethereum network. ERC-20 tokens are used for a wide range of applications, including **initial coin offerings (ICOs)** and DeFi platforms.

- **EIP-721 (ERC-721)**: This EIP defines a standard for **non-fungible tokens (NFTs)** on the Ethereum blockchain. It was first proposed in 2017 and has since become the standard for creating and trading unique digital assets on the Ethereum network, such as collectible items, digital art, and game items.

- **EIP-1559**: This is a plan to make Ethereum work better. It suggests changing how fees are paid on the network. Instead of guessing fees, there would be a fair price that changes based on how busy the network is. Also, a portion of each fee would disappear over time, making less Ethereum available, kind of like rare coins. This was intended to make Ethereum faster and more valuable.

- **EIP-1108**: This EIP reduces the cost of executing precompiled contracts on the EVM and makes it more affordable for developers to use them.

- **EIP-1344**: This EIP proposes a new standard for creating and managing decentralized identities on the Ethereum network. It aims to provide a secure and privacy-preserving way to interact with dApps on the Ethereum network.

- **EIP-1702**: This EIP suggests changing and improving smart contracts on Ethereum to make them simpler. It posits a new way of building things so that you can easily make them better in the future. This helps developers make updates without starting from scratch every time. It's like adding new features to your favorite game instead of making a whole new game.

There are several EIPs with Ethereum. The ones mentioned are some of the most commonly used and referenced. For detailed information on these EIPs, visit `https://ethereum.org`.

Ethereum Request for Comments

Ethereum Request for Comments (ERC) is a formalized process for the development and standardization of smart contracts on the Ethereum blockchain. It is a community-driven process for the creation and improvement of smart contract standards, such as the **Internet Engineering Task Force** (IETF) process for the development of internet protocols.

ERC is used to propose and discuss new standards for smart contracts on the Ethereum network, covering a wide range of topics including token standards, decentralized identity, and NFTs. The ERC process involves ideas proposed by members of the Ethereum community, including developers, researchers, and users, and they are submitted to the Ethereum community for review and discussion.

The ERC process is intended to help standardize smart contracts, making it easier for developers to create and deploy them and for users to understand and interact with them. The ERC process also ensures that smart contract standards are secure, efficient, and interoperable.

The most well-known ERC standards are ERC-20 and ERC-721, which are token standards that define how a token should work on the Ethereum blockchain. ERC-20 defines a common standard for fungible tokens, while ERC-721 defines a standard for non-fungible tokens. These standards have been widely adopted by the community and have become the de facto standard for creating and trading tokens on the Ethereum blockchain.

Popular ERCs

ERC is a formalized process for the development and standardization of smart contracts on the Ethereum blockchain. Some of the most popular and widely adopted ERCs include:

- **ERC-20**: This is the most widely adopted and popular ERC. It defines a common standard for fungible tokens on the Ethereum blockchain, which makes it easier for developers to create, issue, and manage tokens on the Ethereum network. This standard is widely used for ICOs, DeFi platforms, and other applications.

- **ERC-721**: This ERC defines a standard for NFTs on the Ethereum blockchain, making it easier for developers to create and manage unique digital assets such as collectible items, digital art, game items, and more.

- **ERC-1155**: This ERC defines a standard for multi-token contracts, which allows for the creation and management of both fungible and non-fungible tokens in a single contract. It aims to increase the efficiency and flexibility of the token creation process.

- **ERC-827**: This ERC defines a standard for token transfer and token approval extensibility, which allows for the transfer of tokens between smart contracts and for the approval of smart contracts to execute transactions on behalf of a token holder.

- **ERC-1400**: This ERC defines a standard for security tokens. It aims to provide a framework for creating, managing, and trading security tokens on the Ethereum blockchain. It covers topics such as compliance, ownership, and more.

- **ERC-777**: This ERC defines a standard for token operations and token hooks, which allows for more flexibility in the way tokens are transferred. It also allows for the creation of new token operations and hooks.

These are some of the most popular and widely adopted ERCs, but there are many other ERCs that have been proposed and implemented on the Ethereum network.

Creating and managing your keys

In Ethereum, a public key is a string of letters and numbers that represents a user's address on the Ethereum blockchain. Public keys are derived from private keys, which are also a string of letters and numbers, but they are meant to be kept secret.

A public key is used for the following:

- **Receiving Ether or other tokens on the Ethereum network**: Other users can send Ether or tokens to a user's public key address
- **Verifying the identity of a user when they sign a transaction**: By using the corresponding private key, a user can sign a message to prove that they own the associated public key
- **Deriving public keys from private keys using a one-way cryptographic function called a hash function**: This ensures that it is computationally infeasible to determine a private key from a public key, making it safe to share a public key with others

It is important to note that Ethereum public keys are different from the public keys used in other blockchains such as BTC. It is also important to keep the private key safe and not share it with anyone.

In Ethereum, a private key is a string of letters and numbers that generates a user's public key, also known as an address. A private key is a secret/secured code that should only be known to the owner of the public key.

A private key is used for the following:

- **Sign transactions**: When a user wants to send Ether or other tokens, they must use their private key to sign the transaction and prove that they are the owner of the associated public key
- **Generate a public key**: A private key can be used to derive the corresponding public key via a one-way cryptographic function called a hash function

It is important to keep the private key safe and not share it with anyone because whoever has the private key has full access to the Ethereum address and its funds. Private keys can be stored in various forms, such as a plain text file, a QR code, or a hardware wallet.

It is also important to back up the private key. If you lose it, the funds will be lost as well, and there is no way to recover them.

Managing Ethereum public and private keys involves creating, storing, and protecting them. Here are some best practices for managing your Ethereum public and private keys:

- **Create a new address**: Use a secure wallet or software to generate a new address and private key. Each address should only be used once for added security.

- **Store your private key**: Keep your private key in a safe and secure place, such as a hardware wallet or a password-protected file. Avoid storing it on your computer or in the cloud.

- **Back up your private key**: Create multiple copies of your private key and store them in separate locations. This will ensure that you can access your funds even if you lose one copy of your private key.

- **Use a strong password**: Protect your private key with a strong and unique password. Avoid using easy ones that are commonly used and remember on daily basis.

- **Use a hardware wallet**: A hardware wallet is a physical hardware device. It can be used to store your private key offline. Use a hardware wallet only when required to make a transaction. By using a hardware wallet, the likelihood of being hacked is lower.

- **Beware of phishing**: Be aware of phishing attempts that may trick you into giving away your private key. Only enter your private key on legitimate websites or applications.

- **Keep your software up to date**: Keep your wallet software and operating system up to date to protect against security vulnerabilities.

By following these best practices, you can ensure the safety and security of your Ethereum public and private keys and protect your funds from unauthorized access.

Creating public keys

Creating a public key in Ethereum involves the following steps:

1. Choose a wallet. The first step is to choose a wallet that supports Ethereum. This could be a software wallet, such as MetaMask or MyEtherWallet, or a hardware wallet, such as Trezor or Ledger.

2. Create a new address. Once you have chosen a wallet, create a new address. The process for creating a new address will vary depending on the wallet you have chosen. Some wallets will generate a new address automatically, while others will require you to manually create a new address.

3. Store your private key. Your wallet will also generate a private key, which should be stored in a safe and secure place. Some wallets will allow you to write down or print the private key, while others will store it on the device.

4. Back up your private key. Create multiple copies of your private key and store them in separate locations. This will ensure that you can access your funds even if you lose one copy of your private key.

5. Use the public key. Once you have created your new address, you can use the public key as your Ethereum address. You can share this address with others so they can send you Ether or other tokens.

The public key, on the other hand, can be shared with others and can be used to receive funds.

Creating private keys

Creating a private key in Ethereum is typically done as part of creating a new address. The private key is generated by the wallet software, and the process for creating a new private key will vary depending on the wallet you are using. Here are the general steps for creating a private key for Ethereum:

- **Choose a wallet**: First, choose a wallet that supports Ethereum. This could be a software wallet, such as MetaMask or MyEtherWallet, or a hardware wallet, such as Trezor or Ledger.

- **Create a new address**: Once you have chosen a wallet, create a new address. The process for creating a new address will vary depending on the wallet you have chosen. Some wallets will generate a new address automatically, while others will require you to manually create a new address.

- **Store your private key**: Your wallet will also generate a private key, which should be stored in a safe and secure place. Some wallets will allow you to write down or print the private key, while others will store it on the device.

- **Backup your private key**: Create multiple copies of your private key and store them in separate locations. This will ensure that you can access your funds even if you lose one copy of your private key.

It is important to keep the private key in a secret and safe location and not share it with anyone. Whoever has the private key has full access to the Ethereum address and its funds.

> **Important note**
> Some wallets allow you to create a private key using a seed phrase. This is a list of words that can be used to recover the private key.

MetaMask: a self-custody wallet

A self-custody wallet, or a non-custodial wallet, is a type of cryptocurrency wallet where you as a user are in full control of your private keys. This means that you are responsible for the safekeeping of your own keys and have full access to your funds without the need for a third party or an intermediary.

With self-custody wallets, users can generate and store their own private keys and sign transactions on the blockchain themselves without the need to rely on a centralized intermediary. This provides users with more control over their funds and greater security.

Examples of self-custody wallets include the following:

- Hardware wallets such as Trezor or Ledger

- Software wallets such as MyEtherWallet or MetaMask

- Paper wallets, where private keys are written down on a piece of paper

It is important to note that self-custody wallets come with the added responsibility of keeping the private key safe. If the private key is lost, the funds will be lost as well and there is no way to recover them.

In contrast, custodial wallets are controlled by a third party who holds the private keys on behalf of the user. This can be more convenient, but it also means that users must trust the custodian to keep their funds safe and to follow their instructions for transactions.

MetaMask is a browser extension-based Ethereum wallet through which users can securely store, manage, and interact with Ethereum and other tokens. It is available for Google Chrome, Firefox, Brave, Edge, and Opera. There are mobile based apps/wallets available for MetaMask both on Android and iOS platforms.

MetaMask allows users to easily create and manage multiple Ethereum addresses, each with its own private key. It also makes it easy to interact with dApps on the Ethereum network for sending and receiving tokens and participating in DeFi activities.

Figure 2.5 – A MetaMask wallet

One of the key features of MetaMask is its built-in browser extension, which allows users to interact with dApps directly in their browser without the need to run a full Ethereum node. This makes it easy for users to access and use dApps without having to download and run additional software.

MetaMask also supports multiple networks, including the main Ethereum network and testnets such as Goerli, Sepolia, and Polygon, allowing users to easily switch between networks for testing and development purposes.

> **Important note**
> MetaMask is a self-custody wallet, which means that users are in control of their own private keys and are responsible for the safekeeping of them.

Let us quickly create a MetaMask wallet now!

Creating a wallet using MetaMask is a straightforward process. Here are the general steps:

1. Install the MetaMask browser extension. Go to the MetaMask website (`https://metamask.io/download/`) and download the browser extension for your preferred browser (Chrome, Firefox, Brave, Edge, or Opera). Once the extension is installed, click on the MetaMask icon in the browser to open it:

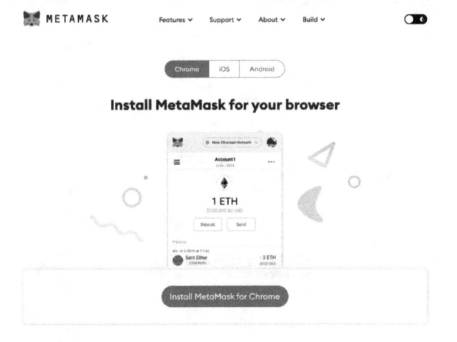

Figure 2.6 – The MetaMask wallet download page

The following screenshot shows a sample of the next page that will let you install the Chrome extension. If you are using a different browser, the page may look a little different from what is shown:

Figure 2.7 – MetaMask Chrome extension

2. Create a new account. Click the **Create a wallet** button and do what it tells you. You'll need to make a strong password and write down a set of words called a seed phrase. This seed phrase is like a secret code that can help you get your account back if you forget your password.

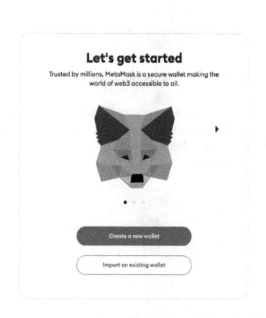

Figure 2.8 – Creating a new wallet in MetaMask

You will see two buttons on the screen. We will use the **Create a new wallet** button to create a new wallet. If you already have a MetaMask wallet, you can skip these steps and go to the next section.

Figure 2.9 – MetaMask terms and conditions

3.   Accept the terms and conditions and make sure to read the privacy policy at least once. It is important to understand what you are signing up for and what personal data you are sharing by installing the MetaMask wallet. The next step is to create a password. You will see a screen like that in the following screenshot:

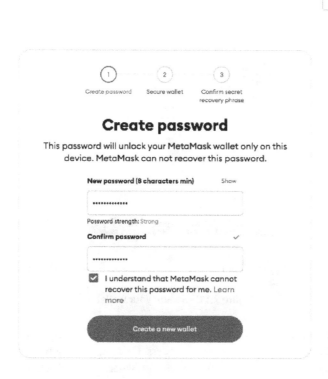

Figure 2.10 – MetaMask Create password

4.   Create a strong password. Follow the best practices for creating a strong password and remember it, as you will be prompted to enter the password every time you use your MetaMask wallet. Once you create a strong password, it is time to secure the wallet. You will see something like the following screenshot:

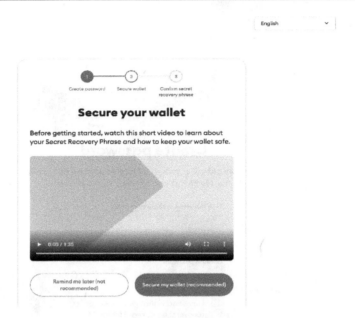

Figure 2.11 – Secure your wallet

5. Please watch the video at least once. The video explains how to perform the next steps. This is the most crucial step in the wallet setup process. Once up are ready, you will be taken to the next screen, as shown in the following screenshot, where you will secure your wallet:

Figure 2.12 – Securing your wallet

6. There are various methods for securing your wallet and protecting your seed phrase. Save the seed phrase somewhere secure so you can use it to restore the wallet or to import it to a new device.

7. Back up your seed phrase. After creating your account, you will be prompted to write down your seed phrase and store it in a safe place. This seed phrase can be used to restore your account if you lose access to it.

8. Secure your account. MetaMask will now display your public address (also called a wallet address), which is a string of letters and numbers that represents your account on the Ethereum network. This address can be used to receive Ethereum and other ERC-20 tokens. You will see the following screen, which confirms the successful setup of your MetaMask wallet:

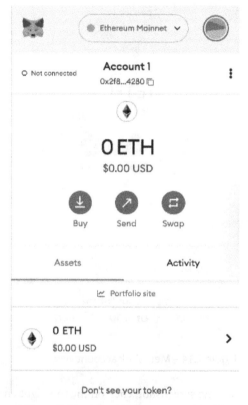

Figure 2.13 – MetaMask account view (1)

Now that we have a wallet, let us add/create new accounts and make the wallet operational so that we can use it in the next chapter to import accounts and make simple transactions.

1. Add tokens. If you want to add other tokens to your wallet, you can do so by clicking on the **Add Token** button and entering the token contract address.

2.   Secure your private key. Your private key is generated and stored by MetaMask and is used to sign transactions. It should be kept private and never be shared with anyone.

3.   Start using your wallet. You can now use your MetaMask wallet to send and receive Ethereum and other ERC-20 tokens and interact with decentralized dApps on the Ethereum network.

You can add multiple EOAs with a few clicks. We will now add an account to the wallet. You will start with the following screen, which is the landing page:

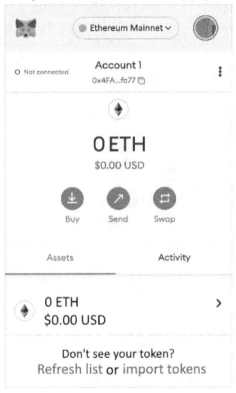

Figure 2.14 – MetaMask account view (2)

4.   As highlighted in the following screenshot, click on the top-right circular icon. This will take you to the account management screen:

Figure 2.15 – Adding accounts

5. On the account management screen, you will see several options. Each option will let you perform a specific activity. We are interested in creating a new account:

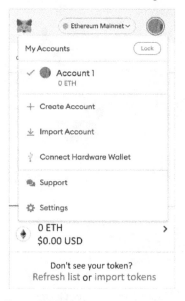

Figure 2.16 – Account management

6. Click on the **Create Account** option, as shown in the following screenshot:

Figure 2.17 – The Create Account button

7. Now, you will be presented with the following screen. All you need to do is to enter an **Account Name**:

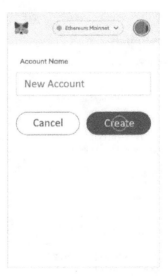

Figure 2.18 – Account Name

8. Once you enter an **Account Name** and click on **Create**, as shown in the screenshot, your new account will be created.

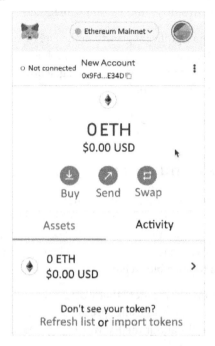

Figure 2.19 – A new account is created

Now you have a new account, and you can choose to use one of the two accounts that is part of MetaMask. This also shows you that you can hold multiple accounts in a single wallet and can transfer tokens and assets between these accounts, similar to how you use your bank accounts.

It is important to remember that MetaMask is a self-custody wallet, which means that users are in control of their own private keys and are responsible for their safekeeping. Your MetaMask wallet is ready to use. In the upcoming chapters, we will use this wallet to do some basic transactions and experience the power of Web3.

The state of Ethereum in 2023

As of 2021, Ethereum is the second-largest blockchain network by **total value locked** (**TVL**) after BTC. The Ethereum network has been growing rapidly in recent years, with an increasing number of dApps and DeFi platforms being built on top of it.

One of the biggest changes made to Ethereum was when it started using PoS. This made the network run faster and use less energy. Before that, Ethereum used PoW like BTC, but it required a lot of energy and couldn't handle too many things at once.

Ethereum 2.0, also known as Serenity, is the name for the upgrade that aims to bring the Ethereum network to a full PoS consensus. It was rolled out in phases. The first phase, called the **Beacon Chain**, has already been launched and is currently running on the mainnet.

The Ethereum network has also seen significant growth in the DeFi space, with an increasing number of platforms and protocols being built on top of it. DeFi protocols and platforms provide a wide range of decentralized financial services, such as insurance, trading, lending, and borrowing, and they are accessible to anyone with an internet connection.

It is important to understand when and how it all started and where we stand. Let us get into the details now.

2013: Milestones, forks, and updates

Vitalk Buterin published a whitepaper (`https://ethereum.org/en/whitepaper/`) containing some of the core architecture and fundamental operating principles for Ethereum on November 27, 2013. The Ethereum whitepaper describes the technical details and the overall design of the Ethereum blockchain platform. It outlines the vision for a decentralized platform that would allow for the creation of smart contracts and dApps on top of a blockchain network.

The whitepaper talks about a "world computer" that works using lots of computers connected all around the world. This computer can do tasks using special code, and it would be fair and safe because no one person controls it. It also talks about the EVM, which is like the special room where smart contracts work on the Ethereum network.

The whitepaper also introduced the concept of gas, which is used to pay for computational services on the Ethereum network, and ETH, the native cryptocurrency of the Ethereum network, which is used to pay for transactions and gas.

It also lays out the design of the consensus mechanism, PoW, that Ethereum uses to secure its network and validate transactions and how it's different from BTC's consensus mechanism.

The Ethereum whitepaper is considered a seminal work in the blockchain and cryptocurrency space, and its ideas and concepts have had a significant influence on the development of other blockchain platforms and projects.

2014

Dr. Gavin Wood, who was one of the co-founders of Ethereum and its former chief technology officer, authored the *Ethereum Yellow Paper* (`https://github.com/ethereum/yellowpaper`), which outlines the core technical definition of Ethereum. The paper was released on April 1st. The *Ethereum Yellow Paper* is a technical document that provides a formal specification of the EVM, which is the runtime environment for smart contracts on the Ethereum network.

The paper is considered a more detailed and formal document than the Ethereum whitepaper. The *Ethereum Yellow Paper* provides a precise and unambiguous definition of the EVM's instruction set, its memory model, and its rules for computation and execution.

It also provides the specifications of Ethereum's consensus algorithm, PoW, and its internals, such as the block header, transactions, and so on.

The paper is intended for a technical audience and is a useful resource for developers, researchers, and other individuals interested in understanding the inner workings of the Ethereum platform at a low level.

It is also considered as the reference implementation of Ethereum and Ethereum-based projects.

The first Ethereum crowdsale, also known as the Ethereum ICO, took place from July 22, 2014 to September 2, 2014. During this crowdsale, participants could purchase ETH using BTC. The crowdsale was organized to fund the development of the Ethereum platform and its associated ecosystem.

In total, 60 million ETH were sold during the crowdsale, raising a total of 31,591 BTC, which was equivalent to approximately $18.4 million at the time. The crowdsale was considered a success, with the Ethereum team raising more than their initial goal of 18,000 BTC.

The ETH sold during the crowdsale was distributed to the buyers over several weeks, with the first batch being released on August 11, 2014.

It is worth mentioning that Ethereum's crowdsale was one of the first and most successful examples of an ICO, and it has since become a popular fundraising method for blockchain and cryptocurrency projects.

2015

The Ethereum **Frontier** release was the first official version of the Ethereum software, which was launched on July 30, 2015. It marked the beginning of the Ethereum network and the first release of the Ethereum blockchain.

The Ethereum Frontier release was a pre-release version of the Ethereum software, which was essentially a testnet that allowed developers to experiment with the Ethereum platform and its features before the network went live. It was intended for developers and early adopters to test and build on the Ethereum network.

The Ethereum Frontier release included basic functionalities such as the ability to create new accounts, the issuance of the first Ether, and the execution of the first smart contracts on the Ethereum network. It also enabled mining on the Ethereum network, allowing users to earn rewards for validating transactions and creating new blocks.

The Ethereum Frontier release was followed by the Ethereum Frontier **thawing fork**, which marked the official launch of the Ethereum network and the transition of the network from a testnet to a live production network.

It was the first step toward the Ethereum network becoming fully functional and was a significant milestone in the development of the Ethereum platform.

The Ethereum Frontier thawing fork was a planned upgrade to the Ethereum network that took place on July 30, 2015. It was the first hard fork of the Ethereum network, and it marked the official launch of the Ethereum network, known as the Frontier release.

The main goal of the fork was to "thaw" the Ethereum network, which had been in a pre-release state since its launch in July, 2015. The thawing fork enabled the network to transition from a testnet to a live production network and to release the first version of the Ethereum software.

The Ethereum Frontier thawing fork also enabled the creation of new accounts, the issuance of the first Ether, and the execution of the first smart contracts on the Ethereum network. It also enabled mining on the Ethereum network, allowing users to earn rewards for validating transactions and creating new blocks.

This fork was the first step toward the Ethereum network becoming fully functional and was a significant milestone in the development of the Ethereum platform.

2016

The Ethereum **Homestead fork** was a planned upgrade to the Ethereum network that took place on March 14, 2016. It was the first major upgrade of the Ethereum network and it marked the transition of Ethereum from its experimental phase to a more stable and secure network.

The main goal of the Homestead fork was to provide stability and security to the Ethereum network by addressing several issues that had been identified. Some of the main improvements included the following:

- The addition of the DELEGATECALL opcode, which allows smart contracts to call other smart contracts without the need to know their addresses
- Improvements to the EVM, which aimed to improve the performance and scalability of the Ethereum network
- The introduction of a new gas pricing mechanism, which aimed to make the network more resistant to spam and denial-of-service attacks
- Changes to the mining difficulty algorithm, which aimed to improve the stability of the network

The Homestead fork was considered to be a major milestone for Ethereum, and it marked the transition of the Ethereum network from a testnet to a production network. It was also the first hard fork of the Ethereum network and was intended to provide a more stable and secure network for users and developers.

The network transition was smooth, with no disruption of services for most users. It is considered a major step toward Ethereum's maturity and stability.

The Ethereum **decentralized autonomous organization (DAO)** fork was a hard fork of the Ethereum network that took place in 2016. It was implemented as a response to the hacking of the DAO, which was built on the Ethereum blockchain. The hack resulted in the theft of 3.6 million ETH, which was equivalent to around $50 million at the time.

For further reading, please follow this link: `https://blog.ethereum.org/2016/07/20/ hard-fork-completed`.

The DAO was a decentralized organization that was built on the Ethereum network and was intended to operate as a decentralized venture capital fund. It allowed investors to vote on proposals for funding Ethereum-based projects, and the funds were stored in a smart contract on the Ethereum blockchain.

On June 17, 2016, an attacker exploited a vulnerability in the DAO smart contract, allowing them to drain the funds stored in the contract. This caused panic among investors and raised questions about the security of the Ethereum network.

In response to the hack, the Ethereum community proposed a hard fork of the Ethereum network, which would effectively undo the effects of the hack and return the stolen funds to the original investors. This proposal was implemented on July 20, 2016, and the hard fork resulted in the creation of two separate Ethereum blockchains: ETH and **Ethereum Classic (ETC)**. For more information on ETC, please visit `https://ethereumclassic.org/`.

The ETH chain is the one that adopted the hard fork, and the stolen funds were returned to the original investors. The ETC chain, on the other hand, is the one that did not adopt the hard fork and continues to follow the original blockchain without any changes.

The Ethereum DAO fork is considered a significant event in the history of Ethereum and blockchain technology, as it highlights the challenges and potential risks of decentralized autonomous organizations. It also sparked a lot of debates on immutability and the censorship resistance of the blockchain.

The Ethereum **Tangerine Whistle fork** was a planned upgrade to the Ethereum network that took place on October 18, 2016. It was the first hard fork of the Ethereum network, and it intended to address a specific issue that had been identified in the Ethereum network.

The main goal of the Tangerine Whistle fork was to address a vulnerability in the Ethereum network, which was named the *gas limit bug* The vulnerability allowed attackers to create a large number of contracts that would exhaust the available gas, causing the network to grind to a halt.

The Tangerine Whistle fork included a change to the Ethereum protocol, which reduced the block gas limit from 8,000,000 gas to 4,700,000 gas. This change effectively limited the number of contracts that could be executed in a block and thus prevented the network from being overloaded.

The Tangerine Whistle fork was a relatively small change and the network transition was smooth, with no disruption of services for most users. The upgrade was done to address the specific vulnerability and was not intended to introduce any new features or significant changes to the Ethereum network.

It is worth mentioning that this was the first hard fork of the Ethereum network, and it was considered a proactive measure to prevent a potential attack on the network.

The Ethereum **Spurious Dragon fork** was a planned upgrade to the Ethereum network that took place on November 22, 2016. It was the second hard fork of the Ethereum network, and it was intended to address several issues that had been identified in the Ethereum network.

The main goal of the Spurious Dragon fork was to improve the security and stability of the Ethereum network, by addressing several issues that had been identified in the Ethereum network. One of the main improvements was the reduction of the block reward for miners from five ETH to three ETH per block, which aimed to reduce the inflation rate of the Ethereum network.

The Spurious Dragon fork also included several changes to the EVM, which aimed to improve the performance and scalability of the Ethereum network. It also included a new opcode, **DELEGATECALL**, which allows smart contracts to call other smart contracts without the need to know their addresses.

The fork also included a change that would allow the Ethereum network to better handle the high number of transactions that were being processed on the network at the time. It also changed the mining difficulty algorithm, which aimed to improve the stability of the network.

The Spurious Dragon fork was considered a relatively minor upgrade and the network transition was smooth, with no disruption of services for most users.

2017

The Ethereum **Byzantium fork** was a planned upgrade to the Ethereum network that took place on October 16, 2017. It was the first of two hard forks, which together make up the Ethereum Metropolis upgrade. The Metropolis upgrade was intended to improve the scalability and privacy of the Ethereum network.

The main goal of the Byzantium fork was to implement a number of protocol-level changes to improve the performance and scalability of the Ethereum network. Some of the main improvements included the following:

- The introduction of a new opcode, called REVERT, which allows smart contracts to return an error message to the user

- The addition of several new opcodes to the EVM, which aimed to improve the performance and scalability of the Ethereum network

- The introduction of a new mining algorithm, **ProgPoW**, which aimed to make the network more resistant to ASIC mining hardware

- Changes to the gas pricing mechanism, which aimed to make the network more resistant to spam and denial-of-service attacks

The Byzantium fork also includes several changes related to privacy, such as the introduction of **zero-knowledge proofs (zk-SNARKs)** and the ability to create private transactions.

The network transition was smooth, with no disruption of services for most users. It is considered a major step toward Ethereum's scalability and privacy. The second part of the Metropolis upgrade, Constantinople, was activated in February 2019.

In 2019, the Ethereum community shifted their focus to making the network much safer, faster, and easier for everyone to use. One of the major accomplishments in this journey was to move away from the consensus mechanism PoW toward PoS, which reduced energy consumption by 99.95%. Next, we'll explore the Merge in more detail.

2019

The Ethereum **Constantinople fork** was a planned upgrade to the Ethereum network that took place on February 28, 2019. It was the second of the two hard forks, which together make up the Ethereum Metropolis upgrade. The Metropolis upgrade was intended to improve the scalability and efficiency of the Ethereum network.

The main goal of the Constantinople fork was to implement a number of protocol-level changes that aimed to improve the performance and scalability of the Ethereum network. Some of the main improvements included the following:

- The reduction of the block rewards for miners from three ETH to two ETH per block, which aimed to reduce the inflation rate of the Ethereum network

- The introduction of EIP 1234, which delayed the "difficulty bomb" (also known as the "Ice Age") and reduced the block rewards by 33% to encourage the adoption of Ethereum 2.0

- The introduction of EIP 145, which added native bitwise shifting instructions to the EVM to improve the performance of smart contracts and dApps

- The introduction of EIP 1014, which allows for the creation of scalable off-chain transaction through the use of "state channels"

- The introduction of EIP 1052, which enables contract addresses to be verified more efficiently, and EIP 1283, which reduces the gas cost of certain SSTORE operations

The Constantinople fork did not result in a separate blockchain and the network transition was smooth, with no disruption of services for most users. The Constantinople fork is considered a major step toward Ethereum's scalability and efficiency.

The Ethereum **Istanbul fork** was a planned upgrade to the Ethereum network that took place on December 7th, 2019. It was a hard fork that aimed to improve the network's security, efficiency, and compatibility with other blockchain networks.

The main goal of the Istanbul fork was to implement a number of protocol-level changes to improve the performance and scalability of the Ethereum network. Some of the main improvements are the following:

- The introduction of EIP-152, which introduced the new opcode, bitwise shifting instructions, to the EVM to improve the performance of smart contracts and dApps

- The introduction of EIP-1108, which reduced the cost of the elliptic curve multiplication operation used in the generation of cryptographic keys

- The introduction of EIP-1344, which introduced a new opcode, ChainID, that allows smart contracts to determine the chain on which they are running

- The introduction of EIP-1884, which increased the gas cost of certain opcodes to prevent denial-of-service attacks

- The introduction of EIP-2028, which reduced the cost of data storage on the Ethereum network, making it more efficient and cost-effective

The Istanbul fork did not result in a separate blockchain and the network transition was smooth, with no disruption of services for most users. The Istanbul fork is considered a major step toward Ethereum's security, efficiency, and compatibility with other blockchain networks.

2020

The Ethereum **Muir Glacier fork** was a planned upgrade to the Ethereum network that was scheduled to take place on January 1, 2020. Its main goal was to delay the "Ice Age," also known as the "difficulty bomb," which is a mechanism built into the Ethereum protocol that increases the difficulty of mining blocks over time. The purpose of the difficulty bomb was to encourage the transition to Ethereum 2.0, which uses the new consensus mechanism, PoS, instead of the current PoW mechanism.

The difficulty bomb was originally intended to gradually increase the mining difficulty, making it more challenging for miners to create new blocks, thus encouraging the transition to Ethereum 2.0. However, as the launch of Ethereum 2.0 has been delayed, the difficulty bomb is set to activate before Ethereum 2.0 is ready.

The Muir Glacier fork was intended to delay the activation of the difficulty bomb for approximately 4,000,000 blocks, or about 611 days. This will provide more time for the Ethereum community to complete the development of Ethereum 2.0 and ensure a smooth transition to the new network.

The fork was a minor and non-contentious upgrade, and it did not result in a new chain or any disruption of services for most users.

The Ethereum **staking deposit contract** is a smart contract that allows users to deposit their ETH into the Ethereum 2.0 network in order to participate in the PoS consensus mechanism. This smart contract was deployed on October 14, 2020.

In Ethereum 2.0, instead of miners solving complex mathematical problems to validate transactions, validators are selected based on the amount of ETH they have staked or locked up in the Ethereum 2.0 network using the deposit contract. The more ETH a validator stakes, the higher their chances of being selected to validate transactions and earn rewards.

The deposit contract acts as a mechanism for users to lock up their ETH in the Ethereum 2.0 network and become validators, and it also serves as a way for the Ethereum 2.0 network to keep track of the total amount of ETH staked.

Users must meet the minimum stake limit of 32 ETH. Then, they can deposit their ETH into the deposit contract by sending it to a specific Ethereum address. Once the deposit is confirmed, the ETH is locked up in the contract and cannot be transferred until the validator decides to withdraw their stake or the contract is closed.

The deposit contract is a crucial component of the Ethereum 2.0 network, as it ensures the security of the network by making it more expensive for an attacker to launch a 51% attack. It also allows the network to function smoothly by providing enough validators to validate transactions.

The Ethereum **Beacon Chain genesis block** is the launch of the Ethereum 2.0 mainnet, which is the next iteration of the Ethereum blockchain. Ethereum 2.0 (or Serenity) is a long-awaited upgrade that aims to improve the scalability, security, and sustainability of the Ethereum network by introducing a new consensus algorithm called PoS.

The Beacon Chain is the central component of Ethereum 2.0; it acts as a hub for all the different shards (smaller chains) that will make up the Ethereum 2.0 network. The Beacon Chain is responsible for maintaining the overall state of the Ethereum 2.0 network and coordinating the activity of all the shards.

The genesis of the Beacon Chain refers to the moment when the Beacon Chain is officially launched and the PoS consensus algorithm is activated on the Ethereum network. It is a critical moment in the development of Ethereum 2.0, as it marks the beginning of the transition from the current Ethereum network (based on PoW) to the new Ethereum 2.0 network (based on PoS).

The Beacon Chain genesis happened on December 1st, 2020, and it attracted a huge amount of stake from the community, reaching the threshold of 524,288 ETH in a short period of time. This was considered a significant milestone in the development of Ethereum 2.0, as it marked the beginning of the transition to a more scalable, secure, and sustainable network.

2021

The Ethereum **Berlin upgrade** was a planned upgrade to the Ethereum network that took place on April 14, 2021. It was the eleventh network upgrade to Ethereum's mainnet, and it made several changes and improvements to the network.

The main focus of the Berlin upgrade was to improve the overall performance and security of the Ethereum network. Some of the key improvements included in the upgrade are as follows:

- The introduction of EIP 2929, which aimed to increase the block gas limit and, in turn, improve the scalability of the Ethereum network by allowing more transactions to be processed in each block

- The introduction of EIP-2718, which aimed to improve the security of the Ethereum network by reducing the cost of certain opcodes, making it more expensive for an attacker to launch a 51% attack.

- The introduction of EIP-2930, which aimed to improve the efficiency of the EVM by reducing the costs of certain opcodes

- The introduction of EIP-2933, which aimed to improve the interoperability of the Ethereum network with other blockchain networks by allowing meta-transactions

The Berlin upgrade was a minor upgrade that did not result in a new chain or any disruption of services for most users. It was an important step toward Ethereum's scalability, security, and interoperability.

The Ethereum **London upgrade** was a planned upgrade to the Ethereum network that took place in July, 2021. It was the twelfth network upgrade to Ethereum's mainnet, and it included several changes and improvements to the network.

The main focus of the London upgrade was to improve the overall performance and scalability of the Ethereum network. Some of the key improvements that are expected to be included in the upgrade include the following:

- The introduction of EIP-3298, which aims to improve the efficiency of the EVM by reducing the cost of certain opcodes

- The introduction of EIP-1559, which aims to improve the gas cost of certain transactions, making it more affordable for users to use the Ethereum network

- The introduction of EIP-2565, which aims to improve the interoperability of the Ethereum network with other blockchain networks by allowing meta-transactions

- The introduction of EIP-2929, which aims to improve the scalability of the Ethereum network by increasing the block gas limit

The London upgrade was a minor upgrade that did not result in a new chain or any disruption of services for most users. It is important to note that the Ethereum network upgrade is a complex process, and the final list of EIPs included in the upgrade may change as the development process continues.

The **Arrow Glacier network upgrade**, like the Muir Glacier update before it, makes modifications to the Ice Age parameters, effectively delaying its impact by several months. This adjustment mirrors the approach taken by previous network upgrades, such as Byzantium, Constantinople, and London. Apart from addressing the Ice Age, no additional changes or modifications were introduced as part of the Arrow Glacier upgrade. The focus remains on extending the time before the Ice Age takes effect, ensuring the smooth functioning of the Ethereum network.

2022: the Paris upgrade (the Merge)

This is the most significant upgrade to Ethereum since its launch in 2015. Crypto approached an inflection point of mainstream adoption, and the concern for sustainability, security, and scalability was at its peak. Ethereum knew that these concerns were caused by the consensus mechanism PoW, which allowed miners to do the majority of the work by rewarding them.

The following image represents how Ethereum moved from PoW to the PoS consensus mechanism:

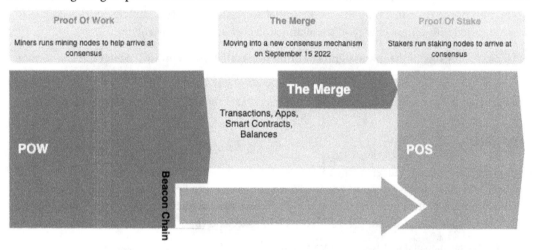

Figure 2.20 – The Merge

After multiple years of research and effort, Ethereum produced a design that makes the Ethereum economical model more durable, its infrastructure more scalable, and the consensus mechanism more sustainable.

The process of moving away from the PoW to PoS is called the Merge. The Merge reduced Ethereum's energy consumption by approximately 99.95%.

PoS is a method that blockchains, such as Ethereum, use to reach agreements. Instead of races using lots of computer power, PoS relies on how much cryptocurrency you own. Having more cryptocurrency gives you more say in making new blocks, similar to having a larger voice in a decision-making group.

In a PoS system, people who join (validators) put some of their cryptocurrency aside as a deposit. Those who have more cryptocurrency have a better chance of being chosen to do tasks such as making new blocks. It's like picking someone to lead a game, and the bigger their share, the more likely they are to be chosen.

Validators are responsible for proposing and validating new blocks. They are incentivized to act honestly because their stakes can be slashed or confiscated if they engage in malicious behavior. This design promotes network security and discourages validators from attempting to manipulate the system.

PoS has several advantages over PoW. It significantly reduces energy consumption since validators do not need to compete in computationally intensive mining processes. It also allows for greater scalability, as PoS networks can process more transactions per second compared to PoW networks.

Furthermore, PoS encourages more widespread participation and decentralization. With PoS, individuals with smaller stakes can participate in block validation, contributing to a more inclusive network.

Ethereum is in the process of transitioning from PoW to PoS with its Ethereum 2.0 upgrade. The introduction of the Beacon Chain marks the initial step toward the full implementation of PoS in Ethereum, providing a more energy-efficient and scalable network infrastructure.

The Merge is only one of the many significant milestones that Ethereum will achieve in the coming years. Ethereum could become the ultimate power of decentralization in the future.

In the next chapter, you will see how to execute your very first Ethereum blockchain transaction. Let's go!

Summary

In summary, Ethereum is currently the second-largest blockchain network by market capitalization. It has been growing rapidly in recent years, with an increasing number of dApps and DeFi platforms being built on top of it. Ethereum moved to a PoS consensus algorithm called Ethereum 2.0. The network has also seen significant growth in the DeFi space and the NFT market.

In this chapter, we delved deeply into the EVM to unravel the inner workings of smart contract execution on the Ethereum network. As you embarked on this journey, you gained a profound understanding of the EVM's architecture and its pivotal role in powering the decentralized world of Ethereum.

We uncovered the complexities of the EVM's components, starting with the execution environment. Here, we discovered how the EVM provides a secure sanctuary for smart contracts, housing crucial elements such as code, data storage, and the execution state. With this foundation, we also saw the EVM's capability to orchestrate the execution of contract logic in a controlled environment.

We also gained a comprehensive understanding of the EVM's architecture, components, and opcodes, grasping the significance of this virtual machine in the realm of Ethereum. You will recognize its role as the bedrock of dApps, ensuring the secure, consistent, and deterministic execution of smart contracts across the Ethereum network.

Finally, we provided a comprehensive summary of the state of Ethereum up to 2023 to understand the long journey that Ethereum has been on so far.

Your First Ethereum Transaction

Now we are ready to learn how to make our first transaction using the **Ethereum blockchain**. Even though executing a transaction with Ethereum is simple enough, it has steps that we need to follow and it is essential to understand these steps to know what we are doing. In this chapter, we will prepare the wallet, initiate a transaction, sign the transaction, and submit it to the public Ethereum blockchain. We'll learn how to look for this transaction using a blockchain explorer. Then, we'll summarize everything so that you can try submitting new transactions and get your hands dirty before we dive deep into programming smart contracts.

In this chapter, we're going to cover the following main topics:

- Setting up Hardhat
- Preparing your wallet
- Initiating a transfer transaction
- Viewing and verifying results

There are many ways to submit an Ethereum transaction. It also depends on what kind of transaction we are doing with the blockchain. The most popular and simple transaction is an account-to-account transfer of some **Ethereum (ETH)**. This can be done using a simple wallet such as **MetaMask**, or we can do this programmatically. We'll do both of these methods in this chapter. First, we need a test or local blockchain to play with. Let us set up a local Ethereum blockchain and make use of it to do our first transaction.

Setting up Hardhat

There are multiple options when it comes to Ethereum blockchain tooling. The simplest and easiest one to get started is Hardhat.

Hardhat is a popular development framework for Ethereum-based blockchain applications. It provides developers with a suite of tools to develop, test, and deploy smart contracts and **decentralized applications (Dapps)** on the Ethereum network.

Hardhat includes a development environment, a testing framework, and a deployment pipeline. It also provides built-in support for various popular Ethereum development standards, such as ERC-20 and ERC-721, as well as integration with popular Ethereum testnets such as **Goerli** (`https://goerli.net/`) and **Sepolia** (`https://sepolia.dev/`), and node providers such as **Infura** (`https://www.infura.io/`).

With Hardhat, developers can write and test their smart contracts in a sandbox environment, simulate blockchain transactions, and deploy their Dapps to the Ethereum network. Hardhat simplifies the process of building Dapps, making it easier for developers to create and deploy blockchain-based solutions.

Hardhat is a development or local blockchain for Ethereum that allows developers to test and deploy smart contracts easily. Hardhat provides a local development environment for Ethereum-based applications, allowing developers to test and debug their code before deploying it to the public Ethereum network. Hardhat creates a local, private blockchain network that can be used to run and test smart contracts, execute transactions, and inspect the blockchain state.

Hardhat offers a **command-line interface (CLI)** and advanced features such as contract debugging, transaction tracing, and gas usage monitoring. It also comes with built-in tools that enable developers to simulate different blockchain scenarios, such as network congestion or contract failures.

Hardhat is an option for Ethereum developers who want to test and debug their smart contracts locally before deploying them to the public Ethereum network. It simplifies the development process and helps developers build and deploy more secure and efficient Dapps. We will use the Hardhat CLI throughout this book to explore code and examples and run tests.

Now, let us set up Hardhat locally on your computer (laptop or desktop).

Installing Hardhat

Navigate to the Hardhat *Getting started* page (`https://hardhat.org/hardhat-runner/docs/getting-started#installation`) and you will find all the steps required. We will go over the steps here to install Hardhat, but it is very straightforward.

Before proceeding, let us make sure you have the following software installed on your desktop/laptop:

- **Node.js** version 20
- **Node Package Manager (npm)** 7 or higher

It is a best practice to have **Node Version Manager (nvm)** installed and pointing to version 20. Once you are ready with these requirements, the installation takes only a minute.

Now, run the following command in your terminal:

```
npm install -save-dev hardhat
```

The following example (*Figure 3.1*) is from a macOS computer:

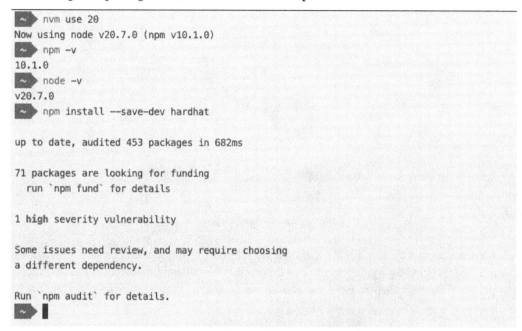

```
~  nvm use 20
Now using node v20.7.0 (npm v10.1.0)
~  npm -v
10.1.0
~  node -v
v20.7.0
~  npm install --save-dev hardhat

up to date, audited 453 packages in 682ms

71 packages are looking for funding
  run `npm fund` for details

1 high severity vulnerability

Some issues need review, and may require choosing
a different dependency.

Run `npm audit` for details.
~  
```

Figure 3.1 – Hardhat setup

Now the installation is complete. You can ignore the warnings saying that there are failures for dependencies and you need to fix them by installing the required npm modules.

That is it! We have installed Hardhat!

Now, let us check whether the installation works correctly. Follow along and execute the commands one by one as described here:

1. First, create a folder:

    ```
    mkdir myhardhat && cd myhardhat
    ```

2. Now, let us create a simple project using the hardhat command. Please note the change in the casing of hardhat:

    ```
    npx hardhat init
    ```

This command will open a new menu, as shown in the following figure:

```
~/myhardhat   npx hardhat init
888        888                         888 888                    888
888        888                         888 888                    888
888        888                         888 888                    888
8888888888  8888b.   888d888 .d88888 88888b.    8888b.   888888
888        888     "88b 888P"  d88" 888 888 "88b    "88b 888
888        888 .d888888 888     888  888 888  888 .d888888 888
888        888 888   888 888     Y88b 888 888  888 888   888 Y88b.
888        888 "Y888888 888      "Y88888 888  888 "Y888888  "Y888

☰ Welcome to Hardhat v2.17.4 ☰

? What do you want to do? …
> Create a JavaScript project
  Create a TypeScript project
  Create an empty hardhat.config.js
  Quit
```

Figure 3.2 – Creating a project using the hardhat Menu

This confirms that the Hardhat installation is working correctly. Select the Create an empty hardhat.config.js option to exit this menu. We will get into the details of the menu options in the next chapter. Now, you should see the output shown in the following figure:

```
x  ~/myhardhat   npx hardhat init
888        888                         888 888                    888
888        888                         888 888                    888
888        888                         888 888                    888
8888888888  8888b.   888d888 .d88888 88888b.    8888b.   888888
888        888     "88b 888P"  d88" 888 888 "88b    "88b 888
888        888 .d888888 888     888  888 888  888 .d888888 888
888        888 888   888 888     Y88b 888 888  888 888   888 Y88b.
888        888 "Y888888 888      "Y88888 888  888 "Y888888  "Y888

☰ Welcome to Hardhat v2.17.4 ☰

? What do you want to do? · Create an empty hardhat.config.js
  Config file created

You need to install hardhat locally to use it. Please run:

npm install --save-dev "hardhat@^2.17.4"

Give Hardhat a star on Github if you're enjoying it!

    https://github.com/NomicFoundation/hardhat
~/myhardhat
```

Figure 3.3 – Create a project using hardhat

3. Next, let us explore the local blockchain functionality Hardhat provides out of the box. Make sure you are still in the myhardhat folder and execute the following command:

```
npm install --save-dev hardhat@^2.17.4
```

4. Then, use the following command:

```
npx hardhat node
```

This command will initiate a locally running Ethereum blockchain with 20 accounts with public and private keys for you to use. *Figure 3.4* shows an example of a locally running blockchain using the command we ran:

Figure 3.4 – Hardhat local blockchain

Hardhat provides an environment with 20 default Ethereum accounts. These are the **Externally Owned Account (EOAs)** that we discussed in the previous chapter.

We have now installed the Hardhat tool for running a local Ethereum blockchain. Next, we will see how to install and interact with this blockchain.

We are ready with the tooling, and the next steps will show us how to prepare the MetaMask wallet to interact with the locally installed Ethereum blockchain environment.

Preparing your MetaMask wallet

Open the MetaMask wallet that we installed and configured in the previous chapter in the *A self-custodial wallet, MetaMask* section. Before we initiate a transfer transaction, we need to do some preparation on the wallet by setting up accounts and connecting the wallet to the blockchain. Follow the next steps to prepare your wallet first:

1. The following figure shows the main login page for MetaMask; enter the password for your wallet here:

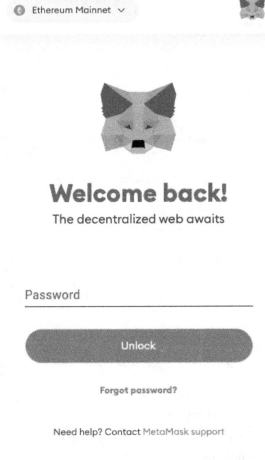

Figure 3.5 – Logging in to MetaMask

2. Now, click on the three dots on the right of **Account 1** and click **Expand view**. *Figure 3.6* shows you a visual representation of the steps:

Figure 3.6 – Opening MetaMask in Expand view

3. You will see something as shown in the following figure where a new page in a browser will open with an expanded view of the MetaMask wallet:

Figure 3.7 – MetaMask expanded view

This view is easy to operate and navigate if you are using MetaMask for the first time.

4. Open MetaMask by going to the browser plugins and clicking on the *MetaMask* icon. Now, let us connect the wallet and the locally running Ethereum blockchain that we created using Hardhat.

5. Switch to the local network by using the drop-down on the left top section on the screen where it shows Ethereum Mainnet as default. The following figure shows the list of networks available. We need to select **Localhost 8545**, which is the network that we create using Hardhat.

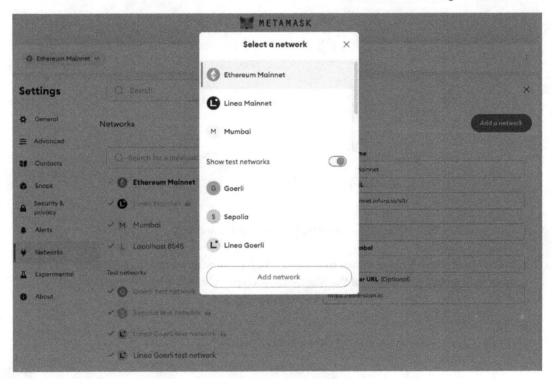

Figure 3.8 – Switching networks in MetaMask

6. If you do not see **Localhost 8545**, you can use the **Add network** button to add the newly created and locally running blockchain using the following options. The following figure shows the value to input when adding a new local network:

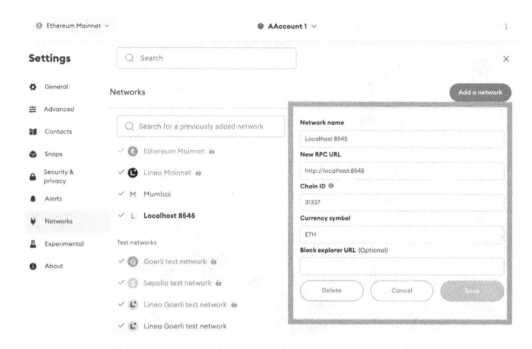

Figure 3.9 – Adding networks in MetaMask

7. Now, let us import two accounts from the local blockchain environment, **Account #0** and **Account #1**. Here, we will use the first two accounts as displayed. These two accounts could be different for you. Use the **Import account** option. The following figure shows you a sample of how the **Import account** option may appear on your screen:

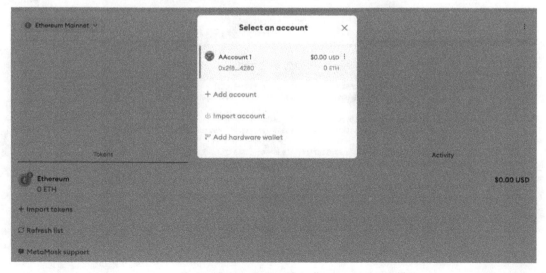

Figure 3.10 – Import account in MetaMask

8. Now, we need the private key of the account that we want to import. As seen in the following figure, there is an input box for the account's private key:

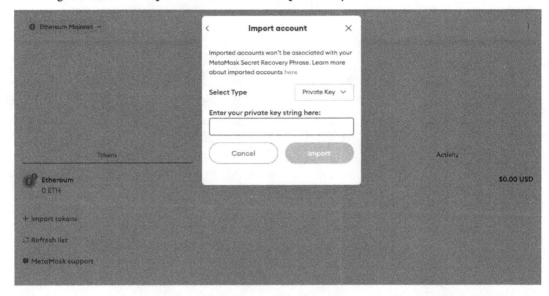

Figure 3.11 – Entering the private key for the account to be imported

9. The following figure shows the Hardhat Private Keys, which shows a list of the accounts, and each account has a Private Key information. Copy the private key for the account we want to import; here, we are using `Account #0`.

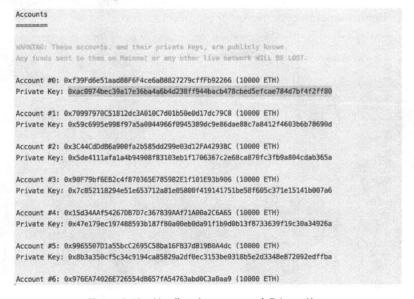

Figure 3.12 – Hardhat Accounts and Private Keys

10. Once you get the private key for the account, paste it into the input field, as shown in the following figure, and click on the **Import** button:

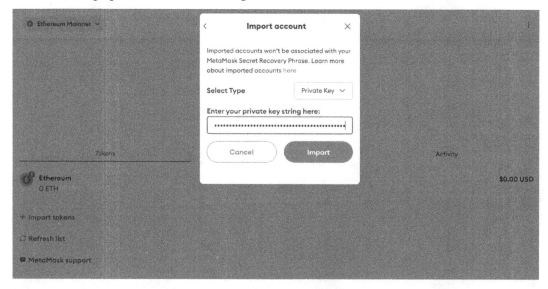

Figure 3.13 – Importing accounts

11. Now, you'll see the account imported into MetaMask, as shown in the following figure. Please take note of the account address to make sure this is the address you imported. Also, the network at MetaMask should point to **Localhost 8545**:

Figure 3.14 – Imported account

12. Now, let us rename this account to a meaningful name so that when we do the transfer transaction, it will be easy to identify and understand it.

13. To rename the account, click on **Account details**. The following figure shows a sample of what the **Account details** screen should look like:

Figure 3.15 – Account details menu

14. The following figure shows the details of the account we want to edit. Use the *edit* option, which is the pencil icon next to **Account 2**, and change the name of the account.

Figure 3.16 – Changing the account name

The following figure shows the new name for the account that we imported and renamed `Account # 0`.

Figure 3.17 – Account details

15. Now, import another account and follow the same steps as previously. Name the account `Account # 1`.

Now, you are ready with the wallet setup, so let us do our very first transaction in Web3 in the next section.

Initiating a transfer transaction

We will do our first transaction with Web3 now by initiating a transfer amount of 2 ETH from `Account # 0` to `Account # 1`. Remember we have to do this transfer only within the local network and you'll use the test ETH to pay for gas or transaction fees:

1. As the very first step, open the MetaMask wallet, switch to the local network, and make sure you are seeing the Hardhat **Account # 0** details. The balance should show 1,000 ETH. There are two ways to initiate a transfer: **Send** or **Receive**. Here, we will use the **Send** option. Make sure you are using localhost as the network and the account points to **Account # 0** to start the transaction.

2. Click on the **Send** option and it will take you to the next step.

3. Now, click on **Transfer between my accounts**; the following figure shows the list of accounts that you can choose from:

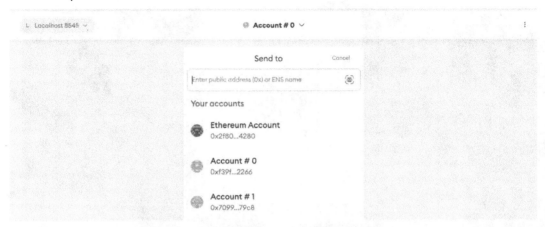

Figure 3.18 – Transferring between accounts

4. Choose **Account # 1**. Enter the amount of ETH to transfer, as shown in the following figure:

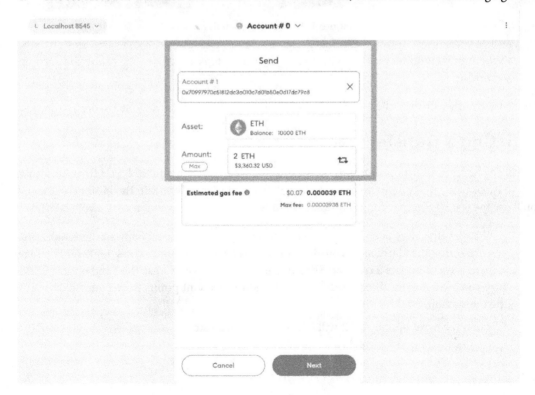

Figure 3.19 – Transfer amount

5. Once you see the confirmation screen, click on **Confirm** and the transfer transaction will be initiated and settled using the locally running blockchain, as shown in the following three figures.

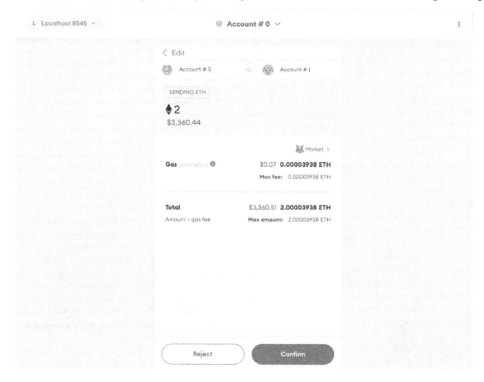

Figure 3.20 – Confirmation of transfer part 1

Figure 3.21 – Confirmation of transfer part 2

Figure 3.22 – Confirmation of transfer part 3

We have successfully transferred 2 ETH from one account to another using a non-custodial wallet and are able to see the balance reduction in one account and the balance increase in the other account.

Next, let us see how things turned out in the locally running blockchain.

Viewing and verifying results

We executed transactions in the previous steps, so now let us see how these transactions reflect in the blockchain and Hardhat local blockchain. Follow these simple steps:

1. Open the Hardhat node and inspect the transaction. You should see something similar to the following figure. This confirms that the transaction happened in the blockchain and was recorded.

```
eth_gasPrice
eth_blockNumber (4)
eth_getCode
eth_estimateGas
eth_blockNumber
eth_estimateGas
eth_blockNumber (6)
eth_getTransactionCount
eth_blockNumber (8)
eth_sendRawTransaction
  Transaction: 0x0e07c7e7a4dbdd418b6ffe9174c11ae4b83c4a4e7c63bb5bf1df44184b1d2f66
  From:        0xf39fd6e51aad88f6f4ce6ab8827279cfffb92266
  To:          0x70997970c51812dc3a010c7d01b50e0d17dc79c8
  Value:       2 ETH
  Gas used:    21000 of 21001
  Block #1:    0xcb6b31e9a51088913cae24e1d65d13c73d1d74fc587a816fc00ee8d78af617b8

eth_blockNumber
eth_getBlockByNumber
eth_getTransactionReceipt
eth_getBalance (3)
```

Figure 3.23 – Confirmation of transaction in the blockchain

2. Here, in this transaction, you will be able to confirm the sender and receiver of the 2 ETH that we transferred. The gas used is **21000**, the gas price is **2375000000**, the gas limit is **21001**, and the block the transaction belongs to is **#1**, the first block that was created as a result of this transaction.

This concludes our first transaction on Web3. Practice a few transactions by importing multiple accounts from Hardhat using their private keys, and initiate multiple transfers. Explore the account balance for these transactions. Verify the block and transaction information on the blockchain and get familiar with everything we discussed in this chapter.

Summary

In this chapter, we learned about MetaMask, a software cryptocurrency wallet used for interacting with the Ethereum blockchain and Dapps. We went through how to install, set up, and use MetaMask, as well as the importance of securely storing your secret backup phrase. We also learned how to connect MetaMask to a local blockchain such as Hardhat by adding a custom RPC network and importing Hardhat accounts. Finally, we learned about the process of transferring tokens between different accounts within MetaMask when using a local Hardhat blockchain.

In the next chapter, we'll jump into the world of smart contracts. We'll start writing and deploying the smart contracts to the locally running blockchain we deployed and take a deep dive into the programming side of smart contracts.

Part 2 –
All about Smart Contracts

Your comprehensive guide to understanding and harnessing the power of smart contracts in the world of blockchain technology. This part begins with an introduction to smart contracts, demystifying their core concepts and highlighting their significance in decentralized systems. As you delve deeper, you'll learn how to write and deploy your very first Solidity smart contract, gaining hands-on experience and practical insights. The chapters place a strong emphasis on smart contract security and access controls, ensuring that you not only create functional contracts but also understand the crucial aspects of keeping them safe and secure, whether you're a newcomer eager to explore the world of smart contracts or a developer looking to enhance your skills.

This section has the following chapters:

- *Chapter 4, Introduction to Smart Contracts*
- *Chapter 5, Creating and Deploying Your First Smart Contract*
- *Chapter 6, Smart Contract Security and Access Controls*

4

Introduction to
Smart Contracts

The chapters will give you a good overview and introduction to smart contracts and also why Ethereum is called a programmable blockchain. You will learn about different language options to write smart contracts, the elements and structures of a smart contract, and the setup and tools required to write smart contracts, which sets the stage for writing your first smart contract in the next chapter.

In this chapter, we're going to cover the following main topics:

- Understanding smart contracts
- Understanding a Hello World smart contract
- Getting started with Hardhat and smart contracts

Understanding smart contracts

A blockchain smart contract can be thought of as a tiny bit of logic or code that can communicate with a blockchain. An easy illustration is a contract that is programmed to automatically split payments between you and another party on the blockchain. You could also refer to those scripting frameworks as contracts, and they are used in implementations such as Bitcoin. Ethereum stands out from other platforms because its smart contracts can be highly intricate, play a vital role in a system, and are permanently stored on the blockchain. These compact pieces of distributed global code are known as smart contracts. In fact, developing blockchain-based applications can become sufficiently challenging.

Smart contracts can be written in a few languages, such as an assembly-like language, which is challenging and requires extremely skilled programming, or in a higher-level language designed specifically for smart programming. **Solidity** is a well-known example of a higher-level language.

Contracts can be deployed in the blockchain, and Solidity code is similar to JavaScript which can be easily deployed into a blockchain. A smart contract code is not very easy to change for updates or upgrades and it has to go through an upgrade process. Also, the code is usually audited before deployed to the blockchain. That is one of its advantages, but it is also a disadvantage because you have to be absolutely certain that your smart contract is error-free, which brings us to the **Ethereum Virtual Machine (EVM)**.

You can think of the EVM as computer code that is used to tune the virtual machine, which runs on every full node in a network. All of the processing on the EVM occurs across the network and is thoroughly verified, so it has everything it needs to function as a computer or information processor.

The EVM is what makes the *Turing Complete* theory so intriguing because it functions like a distributed world computer and has consensus on logic and transaction processing, rather than just transactions and numbers.

However, transaction processing is not free. You need to pay for the processing of these smart contract transactions with gas, which is similar to a charge for a computation transaction. Gas is the transaction fee and consists of a small amount of Ether, set aside to cover the cost of computation carried out on the network.

It serves three primary functions:

- Providing miners and validators with compensation
- Reducing the incidence of spam and abuse, as the rewards of spamming would be offset by the cost of gas
- Preventing the idiom from being programmed into an infinite loop; since the gas for a given process is used up, the loop doesn't last long enough to cause distress to the system

To get a sense of how a smart contract works, we can consider the flow of an example operation. When we use or interact with a smart contract, it's done through transactions – for example, when you send coins to someone else, these transactions are picked up by nodes to validate them. If the transactions are valid and there are enough funds to pay for processing, then the transaction is processed.

A smart contract is executed by the EVM, with the transactions applying any required data input. This process changes the state of a blockchain and gets recorded. Also, smart contracts often engage with other smart contracts allowing for the development of decentralized applications.

We are going to cover smart contract fundamentals in **Solidity**. We'll focus on learning smart contracts in Solidity, the most popular programming language. We'll cover data types, variables in Solidity, and how to write functions. We will also cover some of the nuances of storing data with EVM, smart contract structure, the logging features of Ethereum, and how to use events. We will also go over an example of a smart contract and finish with a deep dive into using tools such as VS Code and Hardhat.

Let us learn some of the basics of Solidity now. This book doesn't cover Solidity in depth, and we recommend learning Solidity in detail if you aim to become a smart contract programmer using Solidity.

Solidity variables and data types

This section provides a comprehensive introduction to types in Solidity. For a statically typed language such as Solidity, all variable types must be specified at compile time. Solidity is compiled into bytecode and executed by the EVM. Solidity can create complex types by combining the elementary types.

As you know, every programming language has its own data types and variable definitions, and most of the time, they are unique to the language.

Solidity is compiled to create bytecode, which is an assembly language and structure. Solidity also has a few value types, such as the following:

Boolean	String literals and types
Integers	Unicode literals
An address	Hexadecimal literals
Contract types	Enums
A fixed-size byte arrays	Under-defined value types
A dynamically sized byte array	Function types
Address literals	Rational and integer literals

Table 1.1 – Solidity data types and literals

We will be covering only the required basic types in this book to get started. For the other complex types, please refer to `https://docs.soliditylang.org/`.

Solidity has several data types and variables that are used to store and manipulate data within a smart contract.

Here are the data types and variables in Solidity:

- **Boolean**: The Boolean data type represents a `true` or `false` value. It can be declared using the `bool` keyword.

- **Integer**: The integer data type represents whole numbers. Solidity has several integer types, including `int` and `uint` (which stand for *signed* and *unsigned* integers, respectively), with different bit sizes.

- **The address**: The `address` data type represents the address of an Ethereum account. It can be declared using the `address` keyword.

- **String**: The string data type represents a sequence of characters. It can be declared using the `string` keyword.

- **Bytes**: The `bytes` data type represents a fixed-length sequence of bytes. It can be declared using the `bytes` keyword, with the number of bytes specified in brackets.

- **Arrays**: Arrays are used to store a collection of elements of the same data type. Both fixed-size and dynamic arrays are supported by Solidity.

- **Mapping**: Mapping is a key-value data structure used to store data in Solidity. It is like a hash table or dictionary in other programming languages.

Solidity also has several variables in addition to these data types, including the following:

- **Constant**: A value that cannot be changed once it has been assigned to a variable

- **Immutable**: Immutable variables are like constants, but they can be assigned a value during contract creation, and that value cannot be changed

- **Variable**: A value that can be changed during the execution of a smart contract that uses variables

- **Storage**: Storage variables are used to store data on the Ethereum blockchain permanently

- **Memory**: Memory variables are used to store data temporarily during contract execution, and they are cleared when the contract is completed

Understanding Solidity data types and variables is important to write efficient and secure smart contracts.

Now, let us do a deep dive into the basic data types and functions.

Boolean

In Solidity, the Boolean data type is used to represent a value that can be either `true` or `false`. It is declared using the "`bool`" keyword.

Here is an example of declaring a `boolean` variable in Solidity:

```
bool isApproved = true;
```

In this example, we declare a boolean variable called `isApproved` and set its initial value to `true`. We can also assign a `boolean` value to a variable using a conditional statement or a function that returns a `boolean` value.

Solidity supports several logical operators that can be used with `boolean` values, such as "`&&`" (logical AND), "`||`" (logical OR), and "`!`" (logical NOT).

Here is an example of using the logical AND operator with `boolean` values in Solidity:

```
bool hasPermission = true; bool isVerified = true; bool canAccess =
hasPermission && isVerified;
```

In this example, we declare two `boolean` variables called `hasPermission` and `isVerified` and set their values to `true`. We then use the logical AND operator to assign the result of the `hasPermission && isVerified` expression to the `canAccess` boolean variable. The value of `canAccess` will be `true`, since both `hasPermission` and `isVerified` are `true`.

Boolean values are commonly used in Solidity smart contracts to represent conditions or states that must be satisfied for a contract to execute a specific operation or function. For example, a smart contract might use a `boolean` variable to track whether a user has authorized a transaction, or whether a condition has been met to release funds.

In Solidity, the `boolean` data type represents a binary value that can be either `true` or `false`. It is useful for expressing logical conditions and making decisions based on those conditions.

Here is an example of declaring and using `boolean` variables in Solidity:

```
pragma solidity ^0.8.0; contract MyContract {   bool public isReady
= false;   bool private isWorking = true;   function startWorking()
public {     isWorking = true;   }   function stopWorking() public
{     isWorking = false;   }   function checkStatus() public view returns
(string memory) {     if (isWorking) {         return "Working";     }
else if (isReady) {         return "Ready";     } else {         return "Not
ready";     }   }}
```

In this example, we declare two `boolean` variables – "`isReady`" as a public variable and "`isWorking`" as a private variable. We also define three functions – "`startWorking`" and "`stopWorking`," which set the "`isWorking`" variable to `true` or `false` respectively, and "`checkStatus`," which returns a string based on the values of the "`isWorking`" and "`isReady`" variables.

We can use `boolean` variables to make decisions based on logical conditions, like so:

```
pragma solidity ^0.8.0; contract MyContract {   uint256 public value =
10;   bool public isGreater = value > 5; }
```

In this example, we declare a boolean variable, "`isGreater`," which is `true` if the "`value`" variable is greater than 5.

Boolean operators such as "`&&`" (and), "`||`" (or), and "`!`" (not) can also be used with `boolean` variables to combine or invert conditions.

Boolean variables in Solidity can only have the `true` or `false` values, and they cannot be assigned to other values or types. Additionally, Solidity does not support short-circuit evaluation for `boolean` operators, which means that all operands of a `boolean` expression may be evaluated even if the result can be determined before all operands are evaluated.

The operators for bool are as follows:

- `!` (logical negation)
- `&&` (logical conjunction – "and")

- | | (logical disjunction – "or")
- == (equality)
- ! = (inequality)

The default value for `bool` is *false*.

Integers

Integers are used to represent whole numbers. Solidity supports both signed and unsigned integer types, with different bit sizes.

Here are the different integer types in Solidity:

- `int`: Integers are signed by default in Solidity. The "`int`" data type is used to represent signed integers with a default size of 256 bits. Integers can also be declared with a specific size, such as "`int8`," "`int16`," "`int32`," "`int64`," "`int128`," and "`int256`."
- `uint`: Unsigned integers are represented by the "`uint`" data type in Solidity. Like the "`int`" data type, the "`uint`" data type can also be declared with a specific size, such as "`uint8`," "`uint16`," "`uint32`," "`uint64`," "`uint128`," and "`uint256`."

Here is an example of declaring an integer variable in Solidity:

```
int count = -10; uint total = 100;
```

In this example, we declare an integer variable called `count` with a value of `-10`, and an unsigned integer variable called "`total`" with a value of `100`.

Solidity supports several arithmetic operators that can be used with integers, such as "+," "-," "*," "/," "%," and "^." It also supports bitwise operators, such as "&" (bitwise AND), "|" (bitwise OR), "<<" (left shift), ">>" (right shift), and "~" (bitwise NOT).

Integers are commonly used in Solidity smart contracts to represent values such as balances, timestamps, and transaction fees. It is important to be careful with integer overflow and underflow, which can occur when an integer value exceeds its maximum or minimum limit. Solidity provides built-in protection against integer overflow and underflow, but it is still important to be aware of these issues when working with integer values.

Solidity has several integer data types, each with a specific range and precision. In general, integers are used to represent whole numbers, both positive and negative.

Here are the integer data types in Solidity:

```
int8: 8-bit signed integer (-128 to 127)
int16: 16-bit signed integer (-32,768 to 32,767)
int32: 32-bit signed integer (-2^31 to 2^31-1)
```

```
int64: 64-bit signed integer (-2^63 to 2^63-1)
int128: 128-bit signed integer (-2^127 to 2^127-1)
int256: 256-bit signed integer (-2^255 to 2^255-1)
uint8: 8-bit unsigned integer (0 to 255)
uint16: 16-bit unsigned integer (0 to 65,535)
uint32: 32-bit unsigned integer (0 to 2^32-1)
uint64: 64-bit unsigned integer (0 to 2^64-1)
uint128: 128-bit unsigned integer (0 to 2^128-1)
uint256: 256-bit unsigned integer (0 to 2^256-1)
```

Here are some examples of using integer data types in Solidity:

```
pragma solidity ^0.8.0; contract MyContract {   int8 public myInt8 =
-128;   uint256 public myUint256 = 123456789;   int128 public myInt128 =
-123456789;      function addInts(int16 a, int16 b) public pure returns
(int16) {     return a + b;   }     function divideInts(uint8 a, uint8
b) public pure returns (uint8) {     require(b != 0, "Cannot divide by
zero");     return a / b;   }}
```

In this example, we declare three integer variables – "myInt8" as int8 with a value of -128, "myUint256" as uint256 with a value of 123456789, and "myInt128" as int128 with a value of -123456789.

We also define two functions – "addInts," which takes two int16 parameters and returns their sum, and "divideInts," which takes two uint8 parameters and returns their quotient. The "divideInts" function also includes a require statement to ensure that the second parameter is not zero, which would result in an error.

Solidity does not support implicit casting between integer types, so explicit casting is required. For example, to cast int8 to int256, we would need to do the following: int256(newInt) = int256(oldInt);.

In addition, arithmetic operations on integers can overflow or underflow if the result is outside the range of the data type, so it's important to carefully consider the ranges of the data types used in a contract.

The operators for int are as follows:

- Comparisons: <=, <, ==, !=, >=, and > (evaluate to bool)
- Bit operators: &, |, ^ (bitwise exclusive or), and ~ (bitwise negation)
- Shift operators: << (left shift) and >> (right shift)
- Arithmetic operators: +, -, unary - (only for signed integers), *, /, % (modulo), and ** (exponentiation)

With these, you will be able to perform shifts, bit operations, comparisons, and arithmetic operations such as additions, subtractions, divisions, multiplications, exponentiation, and modulus.

Address

The address data type is used to represent the address of an Ethereum account or a smart contract on the Ethereum blockchain. It is declared using the address keyword.

An Ethereum address is a 20-byte value that is unique and can be used to send and receive Ether (the token cryptocurrency for the Ethereum network) and other tokens. Ethereum addresses are represented in the hexadecimal format.

Here's an example of declaring an address variable in Solidity:

```
address payable recipient =
0x5B38Da6a701c568545dCfcB03FcB875f56beddC4;
```

In this example, we declare an address variable called "recipient" and assign it the value of an Ethereum address.

Solidity provides several built-in functions that can be used with address values, such as "balance" (which returns the balance of the account in wei), "transfer" (sends Ether from the contract to the specified address), and "send" (sends Ether from the contract to the specified address, and if there is a failure or success, it returns a Boolean value).

Note that there are two types of addresses in Solidity – "address" and "address payable". The "address payable" data type is a subset of the "address" data type that allows you to send Ether, while the "address" data type is used for other purposes, such as storing an Ethereum account address.

Addresses are commonly used in Solidity smart contracts to represent the owner of a contract, the recipient of a payment, or a contract that a function should interact with. It's important to validate and verify addresses to ensure that the intended recipient or contract is being interacted with.

The address data type is used to store Ethereum addresses. An Ethereum address is a 20-byte value that represents a unique location on the Ethereum network. It is represented as a hexadecimal string of 40 characters.

Here is an example of how to declare an address variable in Solidity:

```
address public myAddress;
```

In this example, we declare a public address variable called myAddress.

The address data type has several built-in member functions, including the following:

- balance: Gives the balance of the address in wei (1 ether = 10^{18} wei).

- transfer: Sends ETH from the contract to a different address.

- send: Sends ether to the specified address and returns a Boolean, indicating success or failure

- `call`: Calls a contract method on the specified address.

- `delegatecall`: Calls a contract method on the specified address using the current contract's storage and context

These member functions are also applicable for `address payable`.

Here is an example of how to use some of these member functions in Solidity:

```
pragma solidity ^0.8.0; contract MyContract {   address public
myAddress = 0xAb8483F64d9C6d1EcF9b849Ae677dD3315835cb2;     function
getBalance() public view returns (uint256) {     return myAddress.
balance;   }     function sendEther() public payable {     myAddress.
transfer(msg.value);   }}
```

In this example, we declare a public address variable called `myAddress` with a value of `0xAb8483F64d9C6d1EcF9b849Ae677dD3315835cb2`. We also define two functions – `getBalance`, which returns the balance of `myAddress`, and `sendEther`, which sends ether from the contract to `myAddress`, which is nothing more than `msg.value` specified in the `transfer` function.

Please note that Solidity also supports the address payable data type, which is very similar to the address data type, except that it includes the `transfer` and `send` functions. In Solidity 0.8.0 and later, the address type can also call these functions, but address payable is still commonly used to represent that the address intends to receive ether transfers.

Here is an example of how to declare an `address payable` variable in Solidity:

```
address payable public myAddress;
```

In this example, we declare a public `address payable` variable called `myAddress`.

Here is an example of how to use some of these member functions in Solidity:

```
pragma solidity ^0.8.0; contract MyContract
{   address payable public myAddress =
payable(0xAb8483F64d9C6d1EcF9b849Ae677dD3315835cb2);     function
getBalance() public view returns (uint256) {     return myAddress.
balance;   }     function sendEther() public payable {     myAddress.
transfer(msg.value);   }}
```

In this example, we declare a public `address payable` variable called `myAddress`, with a value of `0xAb8483F64d9C6d1EcF9b849Ae677dD3315835cb2`. We also define two functions – `getBalance`, which returns the balance of `myAddress`, and `sendEther`, which sends ether from the contract to `myAddress`.

With Solidity 0.8.0 and later, the address type can also call the transfer and send functions, so the address payable type is no longer strictly necessary. However, it is still commonly used to show that the address intends to receive ether transfers.

The operators for address are *comparisons* – <=, <, ==, !=, >=, and >.

Let's move on to contract types next.

Contract types

The "contract" data type is used to represent a contract on the Ethereum network. A contract is a collection of business logic, program execution or computation code, data, and state variables that can interact with other contracts and the Ethereum network.

Here's an example of declaring a contract variable in Solidity:

```
contract MyContract {   // contract code}MyContract myContract =
MyContract(address);
```

In this example, we declare a contract called "MyContract" and create an instance of it by passing an Ethereum address to its constructor.

The "contract" data type provides several built-in functions that can be used to interact with other contracts and the Ethereum blockchain, such as "call" (invokes a function in another contract and returns the result), "send" (sends Ether to another contract), and "delegatecall" (invokes a function in another contract but retains the calling contract's storage and context).

Contracts in Solidity can be used to implement smart contracts that automate the execution of transactions and enforce business logic on the Ethereum blockchain. They can also interact with other contracts and external services through various interfaces and protocols.

Solidity contracts are immutable once deployed to the blockchain. This means that any changes to a contract's code or state variables require a new deployment of the contract to the blockchain. Therefore, it's important to thoroughly test and validate a contract before deploying it to the Ethereum network.

Fixed-size byte arrays

Fixed-size byte arrays are a data type used to represent a sequence of bytes with a fixed length. They are declared using the bytesN syntax, where N is the number of bytes in the array.

Here's an example of declaring a fixed-size byte array in Solidity:

```
bytes32 public hash = 0x1234567890123456789012345678901234567890123456
789012345678901234;
```

In this example, we declare a public fixed-size byte array variable called "hash" with a length of 32 bytes, assigning it a value.

Fixed-size byte arrays in Solidity can be used to store and manipulate binary data, such as cryptographic hashes or encoded data. They are often used in smart contracts to represent data structures with a fixed size, such as Merkle trees or binary search trees.

Solidity provides several built-in functions that can be used with fixed-size byte arrays, such as `sha3` (computes the SHA3 hash of a byte array), "`abi.encodePacked`" (packs multiple values into a single byte array), and "`bytes32(uint256)`" (converts an unsigned integer to a 32-byte array).

Fixed-size byte arrays are static and cannot be resized or modified once they are initialized. At compile time, the length of a fixed-size byte array must be known and cannot be changed during runtime.

Operators for fixed-size byte arrays are as follows:

- **Comparisons**: `<=`, `<`, `==`, `!=`, `>=`, and `>` (evaluates to `bool`)
- **Bit operators**: `&`, `|`, `^` (bitwise exclusive or), and `~` (bitwise negation)
- **Shift operators**: `<<` (left shift) and `>>` (right shift)
- **Index access**: If `x` is of type bytes, then `x[k]` for `0 <= k < I` returns the `k` th byte (read-only)

In simpler terms, if we have a variable, `x`, of a specific type called `bytes`, it means that `x` can store a sequence of bytes, and the number, `I`, tells us how many bytes `x` can store.

Now, if we want to access or read a particular byte within this sequence, let's say the byte at position k, we can do that using `x[k]`. This means `x[0]` would give us the first byte, `x[1]` the second byte, and so on, up to `x[I-1]`, which gives us the last byte in the sequence.

In essence, `x[k]` allows us to read a specific byte at a particular position within the sequence of bytes, stored in the x variable.

Dynamically sized byte arrays

Dynamically-size byte arrays are to represent a sequence of bytes with a variable length. They are declared using the syntax bytes and can be resized during runtime using the built-in `push` function, or by assigning a new value to the array.

Here's an example of declaring a dynamic-size byte array in Solidity:

```
bytes public data;
```

In this example, we declare a dynamic-size byte array variable called "`data`."

Dynamic-size byte arrays in Solidity can be used to store and manipulate variable-length binary data, such as input or output data from external contracts or transactions.

Solidity provides several built-in functions that can be used with dynamic-size byte arrays, such as "`length`" (returns the length of the byte array), "`push`" (appends a new byte to the end of the byte array), and "`slice`" (returns a slice of the byte array from a specified start and end position).

It's important to note that dynamic-size byte arrays can be expensive operators in terms of gas consumption and memory usage, especially if they grow to a large size. It's recommended to limit the size of dynamic-size byte arrays in smart contracts and to use other data structures, such as fixed-size byte arrays or mappings, to store and manipulate data whenever possible.

String literals and types

String literals are written with single or double quotes.

In Solidity, string literals are used to represent a sequence of characters or text. They are enclosed in double quotes ("") and can contain any combination of alphanumeric characters, symbols, and whitespace.

Here's an example of a string literal in Solidity:

```
string public message = "Hello, world!";
```

In this example, a public string variable called message is assigned it the "Hello, world!" value.

Solidity has a built-in data type called "string," which is used to represent a variable-length sequence of UTF-8 encoded characters. String variables can be declared using the "string" keyword and can be assigned a value using a string literal, or by concatenating other strings.

Here's an example of a string variable in Solidity:

```
string public name; function setName(string memory _name) public
{   name = _name; }setName("Alice");
```

In this example, we declare a public string variable called "name" and define a function called "setName," which takes a string argument and assigns it to the "name" variable. We then call the "setName" function with the argument Alice, which sets the value of "name" to "Alice".

Solidity provides several built-in functions that can be used with string variables, such as "length" (to get the length of the string), "keccak256" (computes the Keccak-256 hash of the string), and "toLower" (converts the string to lowercase).

String variables can be an expensive operator because they can consume a good amount of gas and memory usage, especially if they are used extensively in smart contracts. It's recommended to limit the size of string variables and to use other data types, such as bytes or fixed-size byte arrays, to store and manipulate binary data whenever possible.

Unicode literals

In Solidity, Unicode literals are used to represent a single Unicode character. They are denoted using the \uXXXX syntax, where XXXX is the Unicode code point in hexadecimal form.

Here's an example of a Unicode literal in Solidity:

```
string public message = "\u0048\u0065\u006c\u006c\u006f, \u0077\u006f\
u0072\u006c\u0064\u0021";
```

In this example, we declare a public string variable called `message` and assign it the `Hello, world!` value, using Unicode literals to represent each character.

Unicode literals in Solidity can be used in string literals and string variables, and they can also be concatenated and manipulated using string functions.

It's important to note that Solidity uses UTF-8 encoding for string variables, which means that Unicode characters outside the ASCII range (0–127) may be represented by multiple bytes. This can affect gas usage and memory usage when working with string variables that contain Unicode characters.

It's recommended to use Unicode literals sparingly and to be mindful of gas and memory usage when working with non-ASCII characters in Solidity.

Hexadecimal literals

In Solidity, hexadecimal literals are used to represent integer values in hexadecimal (base 16) format. They are denoted using the prefix "`0x`", followed by a sequence of hexadecimal digits (0-9, A-F).

Here's an example of a hexadecimal literal in Solidity:

```
uint public number = 0x7B;
```

In this example, we declare a public unsigned integer variable called "`number`" and assign it the value `123` (which is the decimal equivalent of the hexadecimal value `7B`).

Solidity supports several built-in integer data types, including "`uint`" (an **unsigned integer**) and "`int`" (a **signed integer**), which can be declared with a specified number of bits. For example, "`uint8`" is an 8-bit unsigned integer, while "`int256`" is a 256-bit signed integer.

Here's an example of declaring an 8-bit unsigned integer variable in Solidity using a hexadecimal literal:

```
uint8 public value = 0xFF;
```

In this example, we declare a public unsigned integer variable called "`value`" and assign it the maximum value for an 8-bit unsigned integer (which is 255 in decimal or `FF` in hexadecimal).

Hexadecimal literals in Solidity can be used in various contexts, such as to specify function selectors (the first 4 bytes of the Keccak-256 hash of a function's signature) and to specify Ethereum addresses (which are represented as 20-byte hexadecimal values).

Hexadecimal literals can make code more readable and can be useful when working with binary data or low-level operations in Solidity. However, it is also important to understand the potential overflow and underflow issues when working with integer values in Solidity.

Enum

An enum (short for **enumeration**) is a data type that represents a set of named values. Each named value is assigned an integer value, starting from 0 for the first value and incrementing by 1 for each subsequent value.

Here's an example of declaring an enum in Solidity:

```
enum Color {Red, Green, Blue}
```

In this example, we declare an enum called "Color" that contains three named values – Red, Green, and Blue. The integer value of Red is 0, Green is 1, and Blue is 2.

Enums in Solidity can be used to define state variables, function parameters, and return values, and they can also be used with switch statements to control flow.

Here's an example of using an enum in a Solidity function:

```
enum Color {Red, Green, Blue}
function getColorName(Color color) public pure returns (string memory)
{
  if (color == Color.Red) {
    return "Red";
  } else if (color == Color.Green) {
    return "Green";
  } else if (color == Color.Blue) {
    return "Blue";
  } else {
    revert("Invalid color");
  }
}
```

In this example, we define a function called getColorName, which takes a Color parameter and returns the name of the color as a string. We use a switch statement to compare the value of the color parameter to the named values in the Color enum and return the corresponding string value.

Enums in Solidity can also be used with modifiers, events, and struct types, among other features.

Enums in Solidity are not extensible and cannot be modified once they are defined. Additionally, the integer values assigned to the named values in an enum are not guaranteed to be sequential or contiguous, and they may not be used for arithmetic operations.

User-defined value type

A user-defined value type (also known as an opaque value type) is a user-defined data type that is not fully specified at the contract level. Instead, its size and layout are determined by an external entity, such as a compiler or another contract.

Under-defined value types are useful to represent complex data structures that may change over time or may be defined by an external entity. They allow contracts to interact with external systems or other contracts that may use different data layouts or representations.

Here's an example of declaring an under-defined value type in Solidity:

```
pragma solidity ^0.8.0;
struct Account {
  address owner;
  bytes data;
}
interface ExternalContract {
  function getAccountData(address account) external view returns
(bytes memory);
}
contract MyContract {
  ExternalContract externalContract;
  function getAccount(address account) public view returns (Account
memory) {
    bytes memory accountData = externalContract.
getAccountData(account);
    return Account(account, accountData);
  }
}
```

In this example, we define `struct` called "`Account`" that contains an address field for the owner of the account and a bytes field for additional data. We also define an interface for an external contract called "`ExternalContract`," which has a function called "`getAccountData`" that returns the additional data for an account.

In the "`MyContract`" contract, the variable is of type "`ExternalContract`," and "`getAccount`" is a function that retrieves the account data from the external contract and returns it as an `Account` struct.

In this example, the size and layout of the "`data`" field in the `Account` `struct` is determined by the external contract and is not specified in the contract itself. This allows the "`MyContract`" contract to interact with external systems, or other contracts that may use different data layouts or representations.

So, user-defined value types in Solidity should be used with caution, as they can make contracts more complex and may introduce security vulnerabilities. Additionally, they may not be compatible with all Solidity versions or compilers, and they may require additional testing and verification.

Rational and integer literals

Rational and integer literals are used to represent numeric values in contracts. A rational literal represents a decimal number, while an integer literal represents a whole number.

Rational literals

To represent a rational literal in Solidity, we can use the format `<integer> / <integer>` or `<integer>.<integer>`, such as the following:

```
pragma solidity ^0.8.0;
contract MyContract {
  uint256 public ratio = 3 / 2; // ratio == 1
  uint256 public decimal = 0.1 ether; // decimal == 100000000000000000
}
```

In this example, we declare a variable called "`ratio`," which represents the rational number 3 / 2. However, since we are using integer division, the result is rounded down to 1. We also declare a variable called "`decimal`," which represents the decimal number 0.1 ether (where ether is a predefined unit of currency in Solidity).

Integer literals

To represent an integer literal in Solidity, we can use decimal, hexadecimal, or binary notation, such as the following:

```
pragma solidity ^0.8.0;
 contract MyContract {
  uint256 public decimal = 42; // decimal == 42
  uint256 public hex = 0x2a; // hex == 42
  uint256 public binary = 0b101010; // binary == 42
}
```

In this example, we declare three variables that all represent the integer value 42. The first variable uses decimal notation, the second uses hexadecimal notation (where the "`0x`" prefix indicates that the following digits are in hexadecimal), and the third uses binary notation (where the "`0b`" prefix indicates that the following digits are in binary form).

It's important to note that integer literals in Solidity have a maximum size of 256 bits, and also that rational literals may introduce rounding errors when used with integer division. Additionally, Solidity supports various numeric types, such as `uint` and `int`, that have different ranges and sign properties.

Now, let us look at some of the Solidity functions to see how they are defined and how they work.

Solidity functions

Functions are defined the same as they are defined in languages such as JavaScript. However, there are some notable differences.

A function type is a data type that represents the signature of a function. It can be used to declare variables, function parameters, and return values, and it can also be used with function pointers and function callbacks.

Here is an example of declaring a function type in Solidity:

```
pragma solidity ^0.8.0;
contract MyContract {
  function (uint256) internal pure returns (uint256) myFunction;
}
```

In this example, we declare a function type that takes a uint256 parameter and returns a uint256 value. The "function" keyword indicates that this is a function type and specifies the parameter and return types in parentheses.

We also declare a variable called "myFunction" of this function type, using the "internal" visibility modifier to restrict access within the contract.

We can then define a function that matches this signature and assign it to the "myFunction" variable, like so:

```
pragma solidity ^0.8.0;
contract MyContract {
  function (uint256) internal pure returns (uint256) myFunction;
  function myOtherFunction() public {
    myFunction = square;
    uint256 result = myFunction(5);
    // result == 25
  }
  function square(uint256 x) internal pure returns (uint256) {
    return x * x;
  }
}
```

In this example, we define a function called "myOtherFunction," which assigns the "square" function to the "myFunction" variable and then calls it with argument 5. The "square" function matches the signature of the function type, and it is assigned to the variable and called like a regular function.

Function types in Solidity can also include modifiers, visibility specifiers, and error handlers, among other features.

Note that function types in Solidity are not supported by all Solidity versions or compilers and may require additional testing and verification. Additionally, they may introduce additional complexity and security risks, so they should be used with caution.

Solidity storage and memory

In Solidity, variables can be stored either in storage or in memory. Understanding the difference between the two is important to write efficient and secure smart contracts.

Storage refers to the persistent memory on the Ethereum blockchain where the state of the smart contract is stored. Variables declared at the contract level, outside of functions, are stored in storage by default. These variables are written to the blockchain and are available for the lifetime of the contract.

Here is an example of how to declare a variable in storage:

```
pragma solidity ^0.8.0;
contract MyNumberContract {
  uint256 public myMemoryNumber;

  function setMyMemoryNumber(uint256 _numberFromInput) public {
    myMemoryNumber = _numberfromInput;
  }
}
```

In this example, we declare a public `uint256` variable called `myMemoryNumber`, which is stored in the contract's storage. We also define a `setNumber` function, which sets the value of `myMemoryNumber` to the provided input.

Also, note that accessing and modifying variables in storage is expensive, as it requires querying the Ethereum network and writing to the blockchain. Therefore, it is important to be mindful of how frequently storage variables are accessed and modified to ensure that the contract is efficient and cost-effective.

Memory refers to temporary data storage that is cleared when a function call ends. Memory is used to store variables that are only needed during the execution of a function and are not needed after the function ends.

Here is an example of how to declare a variable in memory:

```
pragma solidity ^0.8.0;
contract MyMemoryContract {
  function calculateSum(uint256[] memory _numbers) public pure returns
(uint256) {
    uint256 sum = 0;
    for (uint256 i = 0; i < _numbers.length; i++) {
      sum += _numbers[i];
    }
    return sum;
  }
}
```

In this example, we define a function, `calculateSum`, that takes an array of `uint256` numbers in memory as input, calculates the sum of the numbers, and returns the result. The sum variable is stored in memory because it is only needed during the execution of the function.

Accessing and modifying variables in memory is much faster and less expensive than accessing and modifying variables in storage, as it does not require interacting with the blockchain. Therefore, it is recommended to use memory variables whenever possible to improve the efficiency and cost-effectiveness of the contract.

Solidity contract structure

Solidity contracts are structured using various elements, such as state variables, functions, events, and modifiers. Let us go through each of these elements with examples:

- **Example 1**: A simple contract structure:

```solidity
pragma solidity ^0.8.0;
contract SimpleStructureContract {
    uint256 public myNumberVariable;

    constructor(uint256 _numberInput) {
        myNumberVariable = _numberInput;
    }

    function setNumber(uint256 _numberInput) public {
        myNumberVariable = _numberInput;
    }
}
```

In the preceding example, we define a simple contract, `SimpleStructureContract`, with a state variable, `myNumberVariable`, of type `uint256`. The constructor function is used to set the initial value of `myNumberVariable` when the contract is deployed. The `setNumber` function can be used to update the value of `myNumberVariable`. The "public" keyword in the `myNumberVariable` declaration automatically generates a getter function to read the variable.

- **Example 2**: A contract with an event:

```solidity
pragma solidity ^0.8.0;
contract EventContract {
    event NewNumber(uint256 number);
    uint256 public myNumber;
    constructor(uint256 _number) {
        myNumber = _number;
    }
```

```solidity
    function setNumber(uint256 _number) public {
        myNumber = _number;
        emit NewNumber(myNumber);
    }
}
```

In this example, we define a contract, `EventContract`, with a state variable, `myNumber`, of type `uint256` and an event `NewNumber` that is triggered when the value of `myNumber` is updated. The `emit` keyword is used to trigger the event and pass the updated value of `myNumber` as an argument.

- **Example 3**: A contract with a modifier:

```solidity
pragma solidity ^0.8.0;
contract ModifierContract {
    address public owner;
    constructor() {
        owner = msg.sender;
    }
    modifier onlyOwner() {
        require(msg.sender == owner, "Only the contract owner
can call this function.");
        _;
    }
    function setOwner(address _newOwner) public onlyOwner {
        owner = _newOwner;
    }
}
```

In this example, we define a contract, `ModifierContract`, with a state variable, `owner`, of type `address`, and a modifier, `onlyOwner`, that restricts access to the `setOwner` function to the contract owner. The modifier's require statement checks that the function's caller is the contract's owner. The underscore (_) represents the function code that is modified; in this case, it is the `setOwner` function. Only the contract owner can call the `setOwner` function and update the value of the owner.

A smart contract ABI

An **Application Binary Interface** (**ABI**) is a standardized format used to communicate with smart contracts on Ethereum. It defines how data is encoded and decoded for communication between the contract and external systems, including other contracts, web applications, and mobile applications.

The ABI includes the following information:

- **Function signatures**: A function signature is the combination of the function name and its input parameter types. It is used to uniquely identify a function within a contract.

- **Function input parameters**: The ABI specifies the data types and order of the input parameters required for a function call.

- **Function return values**: The ABI specifies the data types and order of the return values from a function call.

- **Event definitions**: The ABI defines the name and structure of the events emitted by a contract, including the data types of the event parameters.

The ABI is typically represented as a JSON file or a binary file, depending on the specific use case. It is generated automatically by Solidity compilers when a contract is compiled.

Developers use ABI to interact with smart contracts using a variety of tools, such as `web3.js`, `ethers.js`, and other Ethereum development frameworks. An ABI is necessary to create transactions, call functions, and retrieve data from a smart contract.

The **Solidity Smart Contract** ABI is a standardized interface that allows for communication between smart contracts and external systems. It defines how data is encoded and decoded for function calls and event emissions.

Here is an example of a simple smart contract and its ABI:

```
// Simple contract that stores a string value
contract MyContract {
    string public myString;
    function setString(string memory _myString) public {
        myString = _myString;
    }
    function getString() public view returns (string memory) {
        return myString;
    }
}
```

To generate the ABI for this contract, we can use the Solidity compiler. Here is an example of the generated ABI in the JSON format:

```
[    {           "inputs": [               {              "internalType":
"string",                 "name": "_myString",                "type":
"string"                 }       ],
        "name": "setString",
        "outputs": [],
        "stateMutability": "nonpayable",
```

```
            "type": "function"
    },
    {
        "inputs": [],
        "name": "getString",
        "outputs": [
            {
                "internalType": "string",
                "name": "",
                "type": "string"
            }
        ],
        "stateMutability": "view",
        "type": "function"
    },
    {

        "inputs": [],
        "name": "myString",
        "outputs": [
            {
                "internalType": "string",
                "name": "",
                "type": "string"
            }
        ],
        "stateMutability": "view",
        "type": "function"
    }
]
```

This ABI specifies three functions – setString, getString, and myString. The setString function has one input parameter of type string, and no output parameters. The getString function has no input parameters and returns a string. The myString function has no input parameters and also returns string. Additionally, the ABI includes the stateMutability attribute for each function, which indicates whether the function modifies the state of the contract (i.e., it is a nonpayable function) or just retrieves information from the contract (i.e., it is a view function).

To use ABI to interact with the contract, we can use a tool such as web3.js. Here is an example of how to call the setString function using web3.js:

```
const Web3 = require('web3');
const web3 = new Web3('https://sepolia.infura.io/v3/<INFURA_PROJECT_
ID>');
```

```
const abi = <ABI_JSON>;
const contractAddress = '0x123...';
const contract = new web3.eth.Contract(abi, contractAddress);
const newString = 'Hello, world!';
contract.methods.setString(newString).send({from: <MY_ADDRESS>})
    .on('receipt', function(receipt) {
        console.log(receipt);
    });
```

A new instance is created with the code's web3.eth.Contract object, using the ABI and the contract address. It then calls the setString function with the newString value as the input parameter, sending a transaction from the specified address. The on method listens for the event, which includes gas details and the transaction hash. This is just a basic example, but the ABI can be used for more complex interactions with smart contracts.

Solidity events

Solidity smart contract events are a way to emit messages from a smart contract that can be listened to by external applications. Events allow developers to notify external applications about specific actions that occur on the blockchain. In Solidity, events are defined using the event keyword, and they are stored on the blockchain and indexed for faster retrieval.

Here are two examples of **Solidity smart contract events**:

- **Example 1**:

```
pragma solidity ^0.8.0;

contract SimpleEvent {
    event Log(string message, uint256 timestamp);

    function log(string memory message) public {
        emit Log(message, block.timestamp);
    }
}
```

In this example, we define a simple smart contract that has a single event called Log. This event takes in a string message and a timestamp, which are both emitted when the log function is called. This event can be listened to by external applications that are interested in knowing when the log function is called.

- **Example 2**:

```
pragma solidity ^0.8.0;

contract Token {
```

```
    mapping(address => uint256) public balanceOf;

    event Transfer(address indexed from, address indexed to,
uint256 value);

    function transfer(address to, uint256 value) public {
        require(balanceOf[msg.sender] >= value, "Insufficient
balance");
        balanceOf[msg.sender] -= value;
        balanceOf[to] += value;
        emit Transfer(msg.sender, to, value);
    }
}
```

In this example, we define a smart contract called Token, which represents a simple token. This contract has a `balanceOf` mapping that maps addresses to their token balances. Additionally, this contract defines an event called **Transfer**, which is emitted whenever the `transfer` function is called. The `Transfer` event takes from the `from` address, the `to` address, and `value` that was transferred. External applications can listen to this event to keep track of token transfers on the blockchain.

Solidity smart contract events are a powerful feature that enables developers to communicate with external applications, notifying them of specific actions that occur on the blockchain.

Solidity logs

Solidity smart contract logs are messages that are emitted by the smart contract during its execution. These logs are useful for debugging and monitoring the state changes within a smart contract. Logs are stored on the blockchain along with the transaction data, making it possible to access them from any node in the network.

Logs are created using the `emit` keyword and immediately followed by the event name and its parameters. Events are defined in the contract using the `event` keyword and any number of parameters of different variable types.

Here is an example of how to define and emit an event in a Solidity smart contract:

```
contract MyContract {
  event LogMessage(string message);

  function sendMessage(string memory message) public {
    emit LogMessage(message);
  }
}
```

In this example, we defined a `LogMessage` event with a single parameter of type `string`. The `sendMessage` function emits the event with the `message` parameter.

To access the logs, we can use a blockchain explorer or a tool such as `web3.js` to retrieve the logs from the blockchain. Here is an example of how to retrieve the logs for the preceding smart contract using `web3.js`:

```
var MyContract = web3.eth.contract(abi);
var myContractInstance = MyContract.at(address);
var event = myContractInstance.LogMessage();
event.watch(function(error, result){
  if (!error)
    console.log(result.args.message);
});
```

The example shows how an instance is created for a smart contract using its ABI and address. We then define an event listener for the `LogMessage` event and print the `message` parameter when the event is emitted.

Logs can also be used to track state changes within the smart contract. For example, in a voting contract, we can emit a log whenever a vote is cast:

```
contract Voting {
  event VoteCast(address voter, uint indexed candidateId);
   function castVote(uint candidateId) public {
   // record the vote
   //...
    emit VoteCast(msg.sender, candidateId);
  }
}
```

In this example, we emit a `VoteCast` event, with the `voter` parameter set to the address of the voter and the `candidateId` parameter set to the ID of the candidate being voted for. By indexing the `candidateId` parameter, we can instantly search for all votes cast for a particular candidate.

Factory contracts

Solidity factory contracts are a design pattern used in smart contract development to create new contracts dynamically from within a parent contract. This pattern is useful when you need to create multiple instances of a contract with the same code and functionality, but with different state and data.

In this pattern, the parent contract serves as the factory that creates and deploys new child contracts on the blockchain. The parent contract contains the code and logic to create and initialize new child contracts, which are clones of the parent contract.

The benefits of Solidity factory contracts

Solidity factory contracts offer several benefits, including the following:

- **Decoupling**: Factory contracts decouple the creation and management of contracts from the logic of the contracts themselves. This is for the flexibile and modular design of smart contract systems.

- **Dynamic deployment**: Factory contracts enable dynamic deployment of contracts, which means that new instances of a contract can be created on demand as needed.

- **Efficient resource utilization**: By using a factory contract to deploy and manage contracts, the system can utilize resources more efficiently and reduce gas costs.

- **Contract versioning**: Factory contracts can be used to manage different versions of a contract, making it easier to upgrade the contract without affecting the existing instances.

Use cases of Solidity factory contracts

Solidity factory contracts are particularly useful in scenarios where multiple instances of a contract need to be deployed and managed dynamically. Some examples of such scenarios include the following:

- **Token issuance**: A factory contract deploys new instances of a token contract, with each instance representing a different type of token

- **Auctions**: A factory contract deploys new instances of an auction contract, with each instance representing a different auction

- **Identity verification**: A factory contract can be used to deploy new instances of an identity verification contract, with each instance representing a different user

- **Supply chain management**: A factory contract deploys new instances of a supply chain contract, with each instance representing a different product or shipment

A simple factory contract is the simplest type of factory contract. It is used to create new instances using the new keyword. The factory contract can be used to deploy new instances of the contract with different initial parameters.

Here is an example of a factory contract:

```
contract SimpleFactory {
  function createNewContract(uint256 initialData) public returns
(address) {
    return address(new MyContract(initialData));
  }
}
contract MyContract {
  uint256 public data;
```

```
    constructor(uint256 initialData) public {
      data = initialData;
    }
}
```

In this example, we define a simple factory contract called `SimpleFactory`. The `createNewContract` function creates a new instance of `MyContract` with the initial data provided and returns the address of the new contract.

A **proxy factory contract** deploys a contract and a proxy contract that can interact with the deployed contracts. The proxy contract acts as an interface for the deployed contract and can be upgraded without affecting the state of the deployed contract.

Here is an example of a proxy factory contract:

```
contract ProxyFactory {
    event ContractDeployed(address deployedAddress, address
proxyAddress);
    function createProxyContract(bytes memory contractData) public
returns (address) {
      address deployedAddress;
      assembly {
        deployedAddress := create(0, add(contractData, 0x20),
mload(contractData))
      }
      ProxyContract proxy = new ProxyContract(deployedAddress);
      emit ContractDeployed(deployedAddress, address(proxy));
      return address(proxy);
    }
}


contract ProxyContract {
  address public targetContract;
  constructor(address _targetContract) public {
    targetContract = _targetContract;
  }

  function() payable external {
    assembly {
//Implementation here
...
    }
  }
}
```

In this example, we define a proxy factory contract called `ProxyFactory`. The `createProxyContract` function deploys a new contract, using the provided contract data, and then creates a new proxy contract that is linked to the deployed contract. The address of the deployed contract and the address of the proxy contract are emitted in the `ContractDeployed` event.

The `ProxyContract` contract is used to proxy calls to the deployed contract. The `targetContract` variable is set to the address of the deployed contract. The fallback function is used to delegate calls to the deployed contract.

Now, we will move on to see a simple "Hello, World" smart contract and understand how it is structured and coded, using the most basic data types discussed in this section.

Understanding a Hello World smart contract

"Hello World" is quite a simple contract and the best one for beginners to smart contract coding and Solidity. You will find that this example is commonly used by new users to get acquainted with Solidity smart contracts.

Here is an example of a `HelloWorld` smart contract in Solidity, along with a detailed explanation of each line:

```solidity
pragma solidity ^0.9.0;
contract HelloWorld {
    string greeting;
    constructor() {
        greeting = "Hello, World!";
    }
    function greet() public view returns (string memory) {
        return greeting;
    }
}
```

Let us go through each line:

- `pragma solidity ^0.9.0;`: This is a pragma version that specifies which version of Solidity the contract uses. The caret symbol (^) indicates that the contract can use any version of Solidity greater than or equal to `0.9.0`.

- `contract HelloWorld {`: `HelloWorld` is the name of the contract, and the first line mostly starts with a contract definition.

- `string greeting;`: This declares a state variable called `greeting`. It is a `string`-type variable that stores the greeting message.

- `constructor()  {`: This is the constructor that gets called once the contract is deployed. It sets the value of the greeting variable to `"Hello, World!"`.

- `greeting = "Hello, World!";`: The "Hello, World" value is set to the `greeting` variable.

- `function greet() public view returns (string memory)  {`: This declares a function called `greet` that returns a string value. The `public` keyword can be called from outside the contract, and the `view` keyword makes sure it does not modify any state variables.

- `return greeting;`: This line returns the `greeting` variable value.

And that's it! When this contract is deployed to the blockchain, it will store the `"Hello, World!"` message in the `greeting` variable, and anyone can call the `greet` function to retrieve this message.

Here is a variation of the `HelloWorld` smart contract in Solidity, along with a detailed explanation of each line:

```
pragma solidity ^0.8.0; contract HelloWorld {      string
greeting;      constructor(string memory _greeting) {          greeting
= _greeting;      }      function greet() public view returns (string
memory) {          return greeting;      }      function setGreeting(string
memory _newGreeting) public {          greeting = _newGreeting;      }}
```

Let us go through each line:

- `contract HelloWorld  {`: The name and contract definition on the first line.

- `string greeting;`: This declares a state variable called `greeting`. It is a `string`-type variable that will store the greeting message.

- `constructor(string memory _greeting)  {`: This is the constructor that gets called once the contract is deployed. It takes a string parameter, _greeting, which is set to the value of the greeting variable.

- `greeting = _greeting;`: This line sets the initial value of the `greeting` variable to the value passed as the _greeting parameter during contract deployment.

- `function greet() public view returns (string memory)  {`: This declares a function called `greet`, which returns a `string` value. The `public` keyword indicates that it can be called from outside the contract, and the `view` keyword makes sure it does not modify any state variables.

- `return greeting;`: This line returns the `greeting` variable value.

- `function setGreeting(string memory _newGreeting) public  {`: This declares a function called `setGreeting`, which takes a string parameter _newGreeting. The `public` keyword indicates that it can be called from outside the contract.

- `greeting = _newGreeting;`: This line sets the value of the `greeting` variable to the value passed as the _newGreeting parameter when the `setGreeting` function is called.

This smart contract is a variation of the previous example that allows the greeting message to be set and updated using the `setGreeting` function. When this contract is deployed, it stores the initial greeting message passed as a parameter during contract deployment, and anyone can call the `greet` function to retrieve this message. Additionally, anyone can also call the `setGreeting` function to update the greeting message.

Now, let us set up a Solidity smart contract development environment and tools locally with Hardhat, and then we can start writing some contracts.

Getting started with Hardhat and smart contracts

Hardhat is a powerful development tool and framework for building and testing Ethereum smart contracts and **decentralized applications** (**DApps**). It has gained popularity in the Ethereum development community due to its developer-friendly features and robust capabilities.

With Hardhat, developers can perform a wide range of tasks efficiently:

- **Smart contract development**: Hardhat simplifies the creation of Ethereum smart contracts. Developers can write, compile, and deploy contracts using its intuitive interface.

- **Testing**: Hardhat provides a built-in testing environment that makes it easy to write and execute tests for smart contracts. This ensures the reliability and security of your code.

- **Scripting**: You can create custom scripts to automate tasks or interact with your smart contracts, enhancing development and debugging processes.

- **Deployment**: Hardhat streamlines the deployment of smart contracts to various Ethereum networks, from local testnets to the Ethereum mainnet.

- **Integration with other tools**: It seamlessly integrates with other popular tools such as Truffle, allowing developers to migrate projects and leverage their existing knowledge.

- **Plugins**: Hardhat's plugin system allows developers to extend its functionality and customize their development workflow to suit their specific needs.

- **Ethereum network management**: Developers can easily connect to Ethereum networks, manage accounts, and deploy contracts with the help of Hardhat's network management features.

- **Security and auditing**: Hardhat includes various security features and plugins to help developers identify and mitigate vulnerabilities in their smart contracts.

- **Community Support**: Hardhat has an active community and is continuously updated, ensuring that developers have access to the latest features and improvements.

Overall, Hardhat is a versatile and developer-friendly tool that accelerates Ethereum smart contract development, making it an excellent choice for both newcomers and experienced blockchain developers.

Here are the steps to install Hardhat:

1. **Install Node.js**: Hardhat requires Node.js version 16 or later. You can download and install Node.js from the official website: `https://nodejs.org/en/download/`.

2. **Install Hardhat**: Once you have installed Node.js, you can install Hardhat by running the following command in your preferred terminal or Command Prompt:

   ```
   npm install --save-dev hardhat
   ```

   This installs Hardhat globally on your machine.

3. **Verify installation**: After installing Hardhat, you can verify it with the following command:

   ```
   npx hardhat --version
   ```

   This command should display the version of Hardhat you have installed.

4. Now that you have installed Hardhat, you can use it to develop your smart contracts. To create a new Hardhat project, you can run the following commands:

   ```
   mkdir myprojectcd myproject npx hardhat  init
   ```

   `hardhat init` is a command that initializes a new Hardhat project. When you run `hardhat init`, it sets up the basic project structure, creates a `hardhat-config.js` configuration file, and generates some sample contracts and tests.

The following is a breakdown of what happens when you run `hardhat init`:

- **It creates a project structure**: The command sets up the basic project structure, including directories for contracts, migrations, test files, and other important files

- **It generates sample contracts**: `hardhat init` generates sample contracts by default – a `Lock.sol` contract.

- **It generates sample test files**: The command generates sample test files for the sample contracts, including the `Lock.js` and `deploy.js` files

- **It creates a hardhat-config.js file**: `hardhat init` generates a `hardhat-config.js` configuration file that defines the network settings, compilers, and other project-specific settings

Once the project has been initialized, you can use other Hardhat commands to compile, test, and deploy your contracts to the Ethereum network.

You will find this new Hardhat project in the `myproject` directory. Now, you are ready to code your smart contract in the `contracts` folder, using Hardhat to compile, migrate, and test your smart contracts.

Hardhat also provides several useful commands that can help you manage your smart contract development workflow. For example, you can use the `hardhat compile` command to compile your contracts, and the `hardhat test` command to run your test suite.

Here are some of the basic commands in Hardhat and what they are used for:

- `npx hardhat init`: This initializes a new Hardhat project in a directory. It sets up the basic project structure, creates a `hardhat-config.js` configuration file, and generates some sample contracts and tests.

- `npx hadhat compile`: This compiles the contracts in the `contracts` directory and generates the corresponding bytecode and ABI files. The compiled output is saved in the `artifacts` directory.

- `npx hardhat clean`: This cleans the compiled contracts, the `artifacts` folder, and the cache. This command comes in handy when we want to reset a project and start compiling a smart contract from scratch.

- `npx hardhat test`: This runs the tests in the `test` directory. The tests are written in JavaScript and use the Mocha testing framework. The tests are executed against the contracts that have been compiled and deployed to the network.

- `npx hardhat console`: This enables you to interact with deployed contracts. You can use this console to send transactions, read data from a blockchain, and test your contracts.

- `npx hardhat node`: This launches a development blockchain on your local machine. This blockchain is separate from the Ethereum mainnet and is used for testing and development purposes.

These are some of the most common and basic commands in Hardhat. Each command is used for a specific purpose, such as initializing a project, compiling contracts, deploying contracts, running tests, or interacting with contracts on the Ethereum network. By mastering these commands, developers can streamline their development process and build high-quality Ethereum-based DApps.

Summary

This wraps up a long chapter with a lot of Solidity-related topics. We covered various topics related to Solidity programming language and smart contract development. We discussed Solidity data types, including `boolean`, `integer`, `address`, and `byte` arrays, and their usage in smart contract development. We also covered Solidity contract types, including fixed-size and dynamic-size byte arrays, string literals and types, and enumerated types, explaining their definitions and how they are used. We also discussed Solidity storage and memory, including how they differ and how they are used in smart contract development.

Furthermore, we discussed Solidity smart contract events and logs, as well as their importance in debugging and monitoring smart contracts. We also explained how smart contract ABIs are used to interact with smart contracts.

Finally we discussed the importance to use factory contracts like simple factory and proxy factory contracts.

Overall, this chapter provided a comprehensive overview of the Solidity programming language and smart contract development, including its data types, contract types, storage, events and logs, smart contract ABIs, and factory contracts.

In the next chapter, we will take a deep dive into some of the concepts we learned in this chapter, and we will start creating and deploying smart contracts in a blockchain.

5

Creating and Deploying Your First Smart Contract

In this chapter, you will learn to write your first smart contract. The chapter will guide you to set up the development environment and tools required. We will guide you step by step to write your first solidity smart contract. This will be a very simple ERC20 token smart contract, providing an introduction to writing a smart contract and all the basic elements of a smart contract in a practical way. Once the smart contract is written, you will be shown how to compile, deploy, and test them. You'll learn about **Application Binary Interfaces** (**ABIs**), which are essential components that allow your application to interact with and execute functions within a smart contract. They serve as an interpretive layer that facilitates communication between the application and the contract's functions. Finally, we'll see what the verification methods and tools available for smart contracts are.

In this chapter, we're going to cover the following main topics:

- Setting things up to write smart contracts
- Writing your first solidity smart contract
- Compiling and creating ABIs from smart contracts
- Deploying and verifying smart contracts
- Debugging smart contracts

Setting things up to write a smart contract

There are plenty of options when it comes to tooling for smart contracts, such as Remix IDE. In this chapter, and throughout the book we'll use Visual Studio Code, Hardhat, `Node.js`, `Web3.js`, and `Ether.js`.

Here are the basic setups required to write a smart contract using Visual Studio Code, Solidity, Node.js and Hardhat:

1. **Install Visual Studio Code**: Download and install the latest version of Visual Studio Code from the official website.

2. **Install the Solidity extension**: The **Solidity Extension** provides syntax highlighting and other features for Solidity development. To install the Solidity Extension, open **Visual Studio Code**, click on the **Extensions** icon on the left sidebar, search for `Solidity`, and click **Install**.

3. **Install Node.js and npm**: `Node.js` and npm are required to install and manage dependencies for Hardhat and other Ethereum development tools. Download and install the latest version of `Node.js` from the official website.

4. **Install Hardhat**: Hardhat is a development framework for Ethereum-based smart contracts. To install Hardhat, open a terminal window in Visual Studio Code and run the following command:

```
npm install --save-dev hardhat
```

5. **Create a new project**: Use the `npx hardhat init` command to create a new Hardhat project in a directory. This command sets up the basic project structure and generates some sample contracts and tests.

6. **Write the contract code**: Open the contract file in **Visual Studio Code** and write the Solidity code for the contract. The Solidity Extension provides syntax highlighting, code completion, and other helpful features for Solidity development.

7. **Compile the contract**: Use the `npx hardhat compile` command to compile the contract code. The compiled output is saved in the `artifacts` directory.

8. **Test the contract**: Use the `npx hardhat test` command to run the tests in the `test` directory. The tests are written in JavaScript and use the Mocha testing framework. The tests are executed against the contracts that have been compiled and deployed to the network.

9. **Deploy the contract**: Use the `npx hardhat deploy` command to deploy the contract to the Ethereum network. The deployment scripts in the `/scripts` directory will be executed, and they are responsible for deploying the contracts to the network.

These are the basic setups required to write a smart contract using Visual Studio Code. With these setups in place, developers can use Visual Studio Code to write, compile, test, and deploy Ethereum-based smart contracts with ease.

Let us start installing this software straight away.

Installing Visual Studio Code

Visual Studio Code, a widely used open source code editor crafted by Microsoft, is compatible with the Windows, macOS, and Linux operating systems. To guide you through the process, here's how you can install Visual Studio Code on a Windows platform:

1. **Go to the official Visual Studio Code website**: Visit the official Visual Studio Code website at `https://code.visualstudio.com/`.

2. **Download the installation file**: Click on the **Download for Windows** button to download the Visual Studio Code installation file. The download will start automatically.

3. **Run the installation file**: Once the download is complete, locate the downloaded file in your `Downloads` folder or wherever you saved it, and double-click on it to run the installation.

4. **Follow the installation wizard**: The installation wizard will guide you through the installation process. You may be asked to agree to the license terms, choose the installation location, and select additional options, such as creating a desktop shortcut or adding Visual Studio Code to the `PATH` environment variable. Follow the prompts, and click **Next** to proceed.

5. **Complete the installation**: After the installation process concludes, select the **Finish** button to close the installation wizard.

6. **Open Visual Studio Code**: To open Visual Studio Code, go to the **Start** menu and search for `Visual Studio Code`, or double-click on the desktop shortcut if you created one during the installation process.

The following figure shows a sample image of what your Visual Studio Code welcome screen should look like.

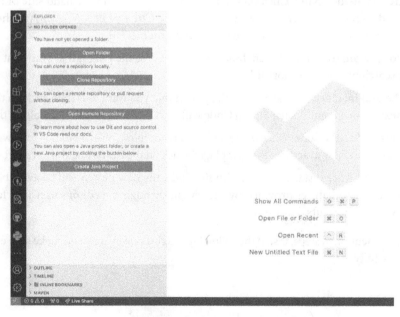

Figure 5.1 – The Visual Studio Code welcome page

That's it! You have successfully installed Visual Studio Code on your Windows machine. You can now start using it to write code for various programming languages, including Solidity for Ethereum-based smart contract development, by installing the appropriate extensions.

> **Web3.js**
>
> Web3.js is a widely used JavaScript library that provides developers with the tools needed to engage with the Ethereum blockchain. It provides a set of APIs that allow developers to read and write data to smart contracts, manage Ethereum accounts, and send transactions on the Ethereum network. `Web3.js` is a vital tool for building **decentralized applications (dApps)** and smart contracts on Ethereum, simplifying the development process and making it easier for developers to build powerful dApps. With its extensive documentation and active developer community, `Web3.js` is an essential resource for any Ethereum developer looking to build on the Ethereum network.

Visual Studio Code extensions

This section provides an introduction to types in Solidity.

Visual Studio Code has a large and active community that develops and maintains various plugins (also known as extensions) to add new features and functionality to the editor. Here are the steps to install a Visual Studio Code plugin:

1. **Open Visual Studio Code**: Open Visual Studio Code on your computer.

2. **Open the Extensions pane**: Click on the Extensions icon on the left-hand side of the Visual Studio Code window. Alternatively, you can use the *Ctrl + Shift + X* keyboard shortcut on Windows or the *Cmd + Shift + X* keyboard shortcut on macOS.

3. **Search for the plugin**: In the **Extensions** pane, search for the plugin that you want to install. You can search by name, author, or keyword.

4. **Install the plugin**: Once you have found the plugin that you want to install, click on the **Install** button next to the plugin. Visual Studio Code will start downloading and installing the plugin.

5. **Restart Visual Studio Code**: Once the installation is complete, Visual Studio Code will prompt you to restart the editor to activate the new plugin. Click on the **Restart** button to restart the editor.

6. **Use the plugin**: After restarting Visual Studio Code, the new plugin will be available for use. You can access the features provided by the plugin through the editor's user interface, or by using keyboard shortcuts.

Following the aforementioned steps, install the following plugins one by one, and make sure everything is installed successfully.

The following figure shows the Hardhat for VS Code plugin; install it, and make sure that all the dependencies are taken care of.

Figure 5.2 – Hardhat for VS Code

The following figure shows the **Hex Editor** plugin; install it, and make sure that all the dependencies are taken care of.

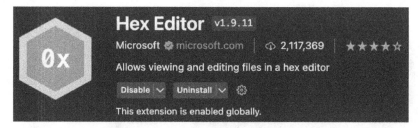

Figure 5.3 – Hex Editor

The following figure shows the **sol-profiler** plugin; install it, and make sure that all the dependencies are taken care of.

Figure 5.4 – sol-profiler

The following figure shows the Solidity Visual Developer plugin; install it, and make sure that all the dependencies are taken care of.

Figure 5.5 – Solidity Visual Developer

The following figure shows the **Solidity Metrics** plugin; install it, and make sure that all the dependencies are taken care of.

Figure 5.6 – Solidity Metrics

The following figure shows the **Solidity Contract Flattener** plugin; install it, and make sure that all the dependencies are taken care of.

Figure 5.7 – Solidity Contract Flattener

The following figure shows the **ETHover** plugin; install it, and make sure that all the dependencies are taken care of.

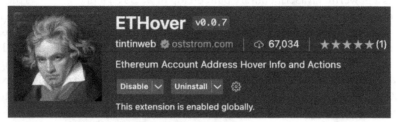

Figure 5.8 – ETHover

The following figure shows the **Solidity Debugger** plugin; install it, and make sure that all the dependencies are taken care of.

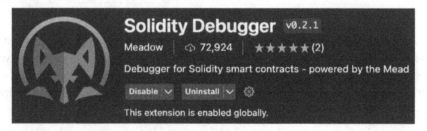

Figure 5.9 – Solidity Debugger

The following figure shows the **solidity** plugin; install it, and make sure that all the dependencies are taken care of.

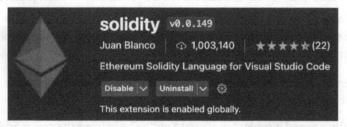

Figure 5.10 – solidity

That's it! You have successfully installed all the Visual Studio Code plugins for smart contract development. You can install and manage multiple plugins to customize the editor according to your needs and preferences. To manage your installed plugins, open the Extensions pane, click on the gear icon, and select **Extensions | Manage Extensions**. From there, you can uninstall, disable, update, and configure your plugins.

Ether.js

`Ether.js` is a powerful JavaScript library built on top of `Web3.js` that simplifies the process of building dApps and smart contracts on the Ethereum network. It provides a streamlined interface to interact with the Ethereum blockchain, allowing developers to easily read and write data to smart contracts, manage Ethereum accounts, and send transactions. Ether.js includes additional features such as transaction signing and contract factories, making smart contract development more accessible and user-friendly. With its intuitive design and extensive documentation, `Ether.js` is an excellent tool for Ethereum developers looking to build powerful and efficient dApps on the Ethereum network.

The Visual Studio Code CLI

Opening a project in Visual Studio Code from the command line can be done using the code **command-line interface (CLI)**. Here are the steps to open a project in Visual Studio Code from the command line:

1. **Install the code CLI**: If you haven't already installed the `code` CLI, you can install it by following the instructions in the Visual Studio Code documentation. In summary, you need to open Visual Studio Code, go to the Command Palette (*Ctrl + Shift + P* on Windows or *Cmd + Shift + P* on macOS), and search for `Shell Command: Install 'code' command in PATH`. Select the option to install the code CLI.

2. **Open the terminal**: Open your Terminal or Command Prompt. You can do this by searching for `Command Prompt` or `Terminal` in the **Start** menu on Windows or by opening the Terminal application on macOS.

3. **Navigate to the project directory**: Navigate to the directory that contains the project you want to open in Visual Studio Code. You can use the `cd` command to change directories.

4. **Open the project**: Type `code .`, and press *Enter*. The `code` command followed by a period (`.`) will open the current directory in Visual Studio Code. If you want to open a specific project folder, replace the period with the path to the folder.

Visual Studio Code will launch and display the contents of the project folder in the editor window. You can now start working on your project.

You have successfully opened a project in Visual Studio Code from the command line using the `code` CLI. This method can be especially useful to automate workflows or integrate with other command-line tools.

Let us write out the first Solidity smart contract now.

Writing your first Solidity smart contract

Now that you have installed all the required tools, you can use them to develop your smart contracts. We will write a simple contract to increase and decrease the count stored in the contract.

To create a new Hardhat project, you can run the following commands:

```
mkdir Counter
cd Counter
npx hardhat init
```

Then, choose the following option in the **Hardhat** menu, and leave all default selections for the prompts:

```
Create a JavaScript project
```

These commands will set up the required folder structure and some skeleton code for you to get started. The following figure shows you what to expect when you open the project in VS Code.

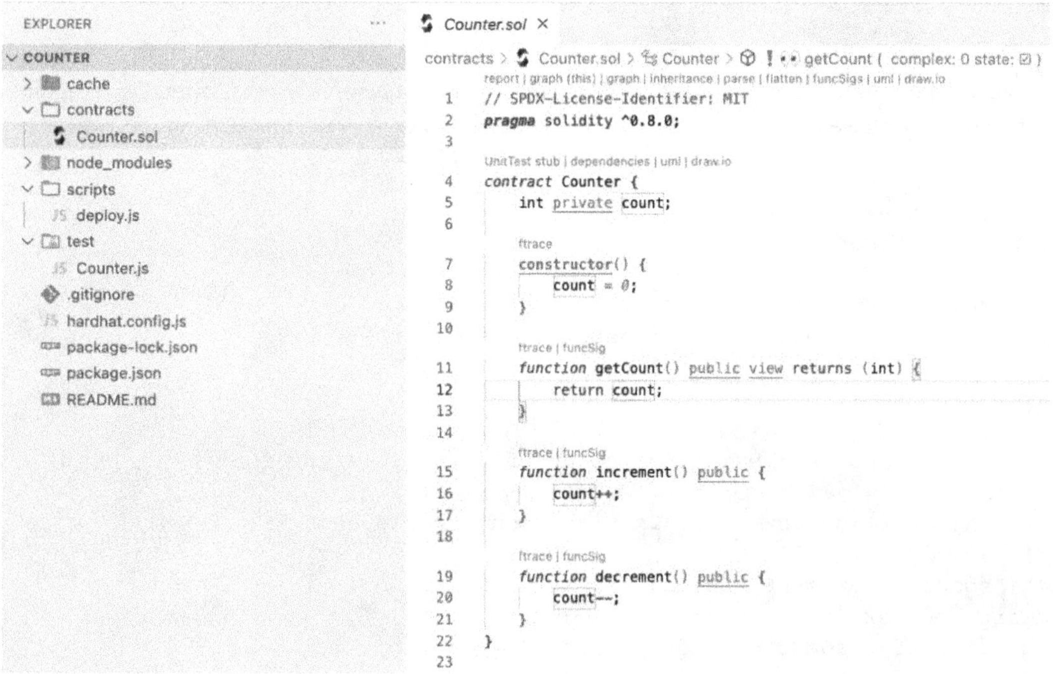

Figure 5.11 – A Hardhat example in VS Code

Your source code will be empty. Now, let us learn what code needs to be placed in these files and folders.

Here is a Solidity smart contract example that allows you to increment and decrement a count stored in the contract:

```
// SPDX-License-Identifier: MIT
pragma solidity ^0.8.0;contract Counter {
int private count;
constructor() {
count = 0;
}
function getCount() public view returns (int) {
return count;
}
function increment() public {
count++;
}
function decrement() public {
count--;
}
}
```

To write unit tests for this contract using Hardhat, you can create a new file called `Counter.js` in the `test` folder of your `Hardhat` project. Here is an example of how to write unit tests for this contract:

```
const { expect } = require("chai");
const { ethers } = require("hardhat");
describe("Counter", function () {
let counter;
beforeEach(async function () {
const Counter = await ethers.getContractFactory("Counter");
counter = await Counter.deploy();
//await counter.deployed();
});
it("should return the initial count of 0", async function () {
const count = await counter.getCount();
expect(count).to.equal(0, "Initial count should be 0");
});
it("should increment the count", async function () {
await counter.increment();
const count = await counter.getCount();
expect(count).to.equal(1, "Count should be 1 after incrementing");
});
it("should decrement the count", async function () {
await counter.decrement();
const count = await counter.getCount();
expect(count).to.equal(-1, "Count should be -1 after decrementing");
});
});
```

To generate the ABIs and bytecode for this contract, you can run the following command in the terminal:

```
npx hardhat compile
```

To deploy this smart contract to the local Hardhat network, you can create a new deploy.js file in the scripts folder of your Hardhat project. For example, you can create a file called `deploy.js` with the following script:

```
const hre = require("hardhat");
async function main() {
const [deployer] = await ethers.getSigners();
console.log("Deploying contracts with the account:", deployer.
address);const contract = await ethers.deployContract("Counter");
console.log("Contract address:", await contract.getAddress());
}
//Deploy
main().catch((error) => {
console.error(error);
process.exitCode = 1;
});
```

You need to set `hardhat-config.js` with the following configuration so that the `migrate` command in the next step deploys the contract to this server:

```
require("@nomicfoundation/hardhat-toolbox");
/** @type import('hardhat/config').HardhatUserConfig */
module.exports = {
solidity: "0.8.19",
};
```

Now, you can run the following command in the terminal to deploy the contract:

```
npx hardhat run scripts/deploy.js
```

The following figure shows a sample of the expected output; some of the data shown could be different for you.

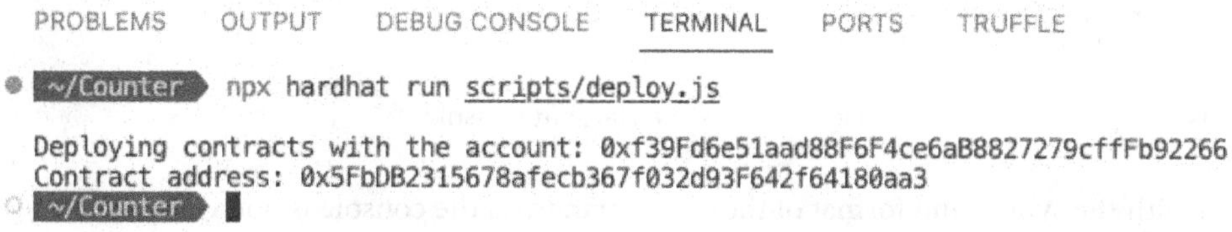

Figure 5.12 – Hardhat deployment

Note the output and some of the details, such as the transaction hash, contract address, block number, amount of gas used, and other attributes in your output.

Now, to test the smart contract after deployment, you can use the Hardhat console. Run the following command in the terminal to open the console:

```
npx hardhat console
```

Then, you can interact with the deployed contract by typing commands such as the following:

```
const counter= await ethers.deployContract("Counter");
await counter.increment();
await counter.getCount(); // returns 1
await counter.decrement();
await counter.getCount(); // returns 0
```

The following figure shows a sample of the Hardhat console and the command to run it:

```
> await contract.getAddress()
'0x5FbDB2315678afecb367f032d93F642f64180aa3'
> await contract.increment();
ContractTransactionResponse {
  provider: HardhatEthersProvider {
    _hardhatProvider: LazyInitializationProviderAdapter {
      _providerFactory: [AsyncFunction (anonymous)],
      _emitter: [EventEmitter],
      _initializingPromise: [Promise],
      provider: [BackwardsCompatibilityProviderAdapter]
    },
    _networkName: 'hardhat',
    _blockListeners: [],
    _transactionHashListeners: Map(0) {},
    _eventListeners: []
  },
  blockNumber: 2,
  blockHash: '0xa565f59c0588125f2e86e99422deda7dc88faffc8fa081d90cb957e70fea61e2',
  index: undefined,
  hash: '0x03b692ad6c78359d1613b8dd726d13a7b8e66904f7b9f20fd7cea6de98fb79c3',
  type: 2,
  to: '0x5FbDB2315678afecb367f032d93F642f64180aa3',
  from: '0xf39Fd6e51aad88F6F4ce6aB8827279cffFb92266',
  nonce: 1,
  gasLimit: 30000000n,
  gasPrice: 1766773941n,
  maxPriorityFeePerGas: 1000000000n,
  maxFeePerGas: 2533547882n,
  data: '0xd09de08a',
  value: 0n,
  chainId: 31337n,
  signature: Signature { r: "0x09b77bd98bff001fb20f81bc90205fdabfc7e28b02d858f194f8aeb592d70022", s: "0x6b2a24aa1
ity: 1, networkV: null },
  accessList: []
}
> await contract.getCount();
1n
> []
```

Figure 5.13 – The Hardhat console

Be careful with the syntax and format of these commands, as the console is not a very user-friendly interface. Play with the console and practice some of these commands; increment the counter to 10, and then decrease it by 5, observing what happens in the console.

You have successfully created, tested, compiled, and deployed a Solidity smart contract using Hardhat.

Compiling and creating ABIs from smart contracts

Compiling a smart contract is the process of converting Solidity code into a format that can be executed on the **Ethereum Virtual Machine (EVM)**. There are several ways to compile a smart contract, including the following:

- **Using the Solidity compiler**: The Solidity compiler is a command-line tool that can compile Solidity code as bytecode. To use the Solidity compiler, download it from the official Solidity website, and run the `solc` command with the appropriate options to compile your contract.

- **Using Remix IDE**: Remix IDE is a web-based IDE that allows you to write, test, and deploy smart contracts. It includes a built-in Solidity compiler that can be used to compile your contract. To use the compiler in Remix, you can simply paste your Solidity code into the IDE, select the appropriate compiler version, and click the **Compile** button.

- **Using Hardhat**: Hardhat is a development environment for building, testing, and deploying smart contracts. It includes a built-in Solidity compiler that can be used to compile your contract. To compile your contract using Hardhat, you can create a new project, add your Solidity code to the `contracts` directory, and run the `npx hardhat compile` command.

Hardhat

Hardhat is a widely used development framework that facilitates the creation and testing of smart contracts on the Ethereum network. It provides a suite of powerful tools and features that make it easy to develop and deploy secure smart contracts quickly and efficiently. With Hardhat, developers can write smart contracts in Solidity or Vyper, test them using Hardhat's built-in testing framework, and deploy them to the Ethereum network using the Hardhat network tool. Hardhat also offers advanced debugging features, including stack traces and console logs, to help developers identify and fix bugs in their code. One of the unique features of Hardhat is its support for multiple Ethereum networks, including local test networks, Mainnet, and popular test networks such as Goerli and Sepolia. This makes it easy for developers to test and deploy their contracts in a variety of different environments. Hardhat also integrates with popular Ethereum development tools, such as Truffle and Remix, and provides a plugin system that allows developers to extend its functionality with custom scripts and plugins. Hardhat is a versatile and powerful development environment for building and testing smart contracts on the Ethereum network. It offers a comprehensive suite of tools and features that make it easy to write, test, and deploy secure and reliable smart contracts.

- **Using the solc-js library**: The `solc-js` library is a JavaScript library that allows you to compile Solidity code from within a JavaScript application. To use `solc-js`, you can install it using NPM, import it into your JavaScript code, and call its `compile` function to compile your Solidity code.

Each of these methods has its advantages and disadvantages, depending on your specific needs and preferences. Some developers prefer to use a web-based IDE, such as Remix, while others prefer to use a command-line tool, such as the Solidity compiler or Hardhat. The choice of compiler will depend on your specific use case and development workflow.

An ABI is a standard interface for interacting with smart contracts on the Ethereum network. There are several techniques to create an ABI for a smart contract:

- **Using the Solidity compiler**: The Solidity compiler generates an ABI, along with the bytecode and other contract-related information. The ABI can be extracted from the compiled output using the `solc` command-line tool. Here is an example command to generate the ABI from a compiled contract:

```
solc --abi MyContract.sol
```

- **Using Hardhat**: Hardhat is a popular development framework for Ethereum. It provides a command-line tool that can compile contracts and generate ABIs. Here is an example command to generate the ABI for a contract named `MyContract`:

```
npx hardhatcompile MyContract
```

- **Using Remix**: Remix is a web-based IDE for Ethereum development. It provides a built-in compiler that can generate an ABI for a contract. Here is how to generate an ABI using Remix:

I.   Open Remix, and navigate to the **Solidity Compiler** tab.

II.   Select the contract you want to generate an ABI for.

III. Click the **Compile** button to compile the contract.

After the contract is compiled, the ABI can be found under the **Compilation Details** section.

- **Manually creating the ABI**: An ABI can be manually created by defining a JSON object that describes the functions, events, and variables of the contract. Here is an example of a simple ABI for a contract that has a single function, named `getCount`:

```
[
  {
    "constant": true,
    "inputs": [],
    "name": "getCount",
    "outputs": [
      {
        "name": "",
        "type": "uint256"
      }
    ],
```

```
        "payable": false,
        "stateMutability": "view",
        "type": "function"
    }
]
```

Creating an ABI for a smart contract is essential to interact with the contract on the Ethereum network. As you have seen, there are several techniques to generate an ABI, including using the Solidity compiler, Hardhat, Remix, or manually creating it using a JSON object.

Deploying and verifying smart contracts

So far, we have used `npx hardhat run scripts/deploy.js` to deploy the smart contract. Now, we will see in detail how `hardhat run` works.

`hardhat run` is a command used to call a JavaScript or a TypeScript to deploy smart contracts on the blockchain. It is part of the Hardhat suite, which is a development framework for Ethereum smart contracts. Hardhat simplifies the deployment process by automating several tasks, such as contract compilation, contract migration, and contract address management.

Here is a step-by-step explanation of how Hardhat deployment works:

1. **Compiling the smart contracts**: Before deploying the smart contracts, they need to be compiled into bytecode, which can be executed by the EVM. Use the Hardhat compiler to compile the smart contracts in the `contracts/` directory.

2. **Creating a deploy script**: The deploy script is usually placed in the `scripts/` directory and has a filename in the `deploy.js` format.

3. **Connecting to the blockchain**: Hardhat uses the local provider to connect to the blockchain. The provider is responsible for handling the communication between the local development environment and the blockchain. The provider can be configured in the `hardhat-config.js` file in the project root directory.

4. **Running the deploy script**: Hardhat deploys the `deploy.js` script using `npx hardhat run deploy - -network localhost`, which deploys the contracts on the blockchain.

5. **Saving the contract addresses**: After a contract is deployed, its address on the blockchain is generated. Hardhat saves the addresses of the deployed contracts in the `artifacts/build-info/` directory. This allows the application to use the contracts on the blockchain.

6. **Testing the contracts**: Once the contracts are deployed, you can test them to make sure they work correctly. Hardhat provides a testing framework that makes it easy to write and run tests for your contracts.

These steps to deploy the contracts in the local development environment are simple and straightforward. However, when we migrate to testnets and mainnets, the process and steps are a little different, and we need ETH to pay for gas costs and have controls in place for failures and fallbacks.

Overall, Hardhat simplifies the process of deploying smart contracts onto the blockchain. It automates several tasks and provides a standard way to deploy contracts.

Now, let us look at how to verify a deployed smart contract. We will use `hardhat verify` for this.

`npx hardhat verify` is a service provided by the Hardhat suite that allows users to verify their smart contracts on Etherscan or BscScan directly from the command line. It requires an API key from Etherscan or BscScan and the contract address to verify the contract.

Here are the steps to use `hardhat verify` to verify a smart contract:

1. **Generate an API key**: To use `hardhat verify`, you need to generate an API key from Etherscan or BscScan. You can create an account on the respective website and generate an API key.

2. **Configure Hardhat**: Once you have installed Hardhat, you need to configure it in your project's `hardhat-config.js` file. You can add the following code to the file

```
Replace <your_etherscan_api_key> and <your_bscscan_api_key>
with the API keys you generated:
require("@nomiclabs/hardhat-waffle");
require("hardhat-etherscan");

const { API_URL, PRIVATE_KEY, ETHERSCAN_API_KEY } = process.env;

/**
 * @type import('hardhat/config').HardhatUserConfig
 */
module.exports = {
  solidity: "0.8.0",
  networks: {
    // Define your networks here
  },
  etherscan: {
    apiKey: ETHERSCAN_API_KEY,
  },
};
```

3. **Deploy your smart contract**: Before you can verify your smart contract, you need to deploy it to the network. You can use the following command:

```
npx hardhat run scripts/deploy.js  --network <network_name>
```

4. Replace `<network_name>` with the name of the network you want to deploy to, such as `Goerli`, `Sepolia`, or `localhost`.

5. **Verify your smart contract**: Once your smart contract is deployed, you can use `hardhat verify` to verify it on Etherscan or BscScan. You can use the following command:

```
npx hardhat verify --network <network_name>  <ContractName>
```

Replace `<ContractName>` with the name of your smart contract and `<network_name>` with the name of the network you deployed to.

This will automatically verify the smart contract on Etherscan or BscScan, using the API key you provided in the `hardhat-config.js` file.

hardhat verify helps ensure that the smart contracts deployed on the blockchain are verified and secure, which increases the trust in the smart contract.

Debugging smart contracts

In this section, we will take a quick overview of the built-in Hardhat debugger and how it can help debug issues easily.

The Hardhat console is a tool used to debug issues or errors in smart contracts during development. It is part of the Hardhat suite, which is a development framework for Ethereum smart contracts. The Hardhat console provides a simple interface for debugging smart contracts and allows developers to step through their code and inspect variables at runtime.

Here is an example of how to use the Hardhat console to analyze an issue in a smart contract:

1. **Install Hardhat**: The Hardhat console is built in, so no other steps are required to enable it. You can install it using the following command:

```
npm install --save-dev hardhat
```

2. **Compile your smart contracts**: Before you can debug your smart contracts, you need to compile them as bytecode. You can use `npx hardhat compile` to compile the smart contracts in the `contracts/` directory:

```
npx hardhat compile
```

3. **Deploy your smart contracts**: Before you can debug your smart contracts, you need to deploy them to a network. You can use Hardhat to deploy the contract, using the following command:

```
npx hardhat run scripts/deploy --network <network_name>
```

4. In our case, since we are using Hardhat and the development server, we will use the following command:

```
npx hardhat run scripts/deploy.js --network localhost
```

5. **Start the Hardhat console**: Once your smart contracts are deployed, you can start the Hardhat console using the following command:

```
npx hardhat console --network localhost
```

6. Now, you can interact with your smart contract using the Hardhat console. For example, to deploy your contract and start debugging, you can run the following:

```
const [deployer] = await ethers.getSigners();
const Counter = await ethers.getContractFactory("Counter");
const counter = await Counter.connect(deployer).deploy();
await counter.deployed();
```

7. **Set breakpoints**: You can set breakpoints in your code by adding `debugger`:

```
function increment() public {
    // ...
    debugger;
    // ...
}
```

When the `debugger` statement is reached, the Hardhat console will pause, and you can inspect variables and step through the code, using commands such as n (next), s (step into), and o (step out).

8. **Inspect variables**: You can inspect the value of variables at runtime using the following command:

```
p <variable_name>
```

Replace <variable_name> with the name of the variable you want to inspect.

By using `hardhat console` and `debugger` to step through the code and inspect variables at runtime, you can identify and fix bugs in your smart contracts more efficiently.

Summary

In this chapter, you first performed all the setup required to write a smart contract in Solidity. You then installed VS Code and its dependencies, along with some useful extensions that will help you in the development process. You wrote your first Solidity smart contract to increment and decrement a counter. You deployed it, tested it, and saw how to debug the code. You also used several Hardhat commands in this chapter. You should now be familiar with the basic tools and the steps involved in creating and deploying smart contracts.

In the next chapter, we will explore the basics of smart contract security and access controls.

6

Smart Contract Security and Access Controls

It is a very complex, cumbersome, and difficult task to write a perfect smart contract that addresses all the best practices and security considerations to be taken care of. To prevent unauthorized use of smart contract functions, it is necessary to implement secure access controls. Access control mechanisms restrict the ability to use certain functions in a smart contract to approved entities, such as accounts responsible for managing the contract. This chapter will introduce you to the concepts of smart contract security, access controls, security tools, audit functions, and common threats to consider when developing smart contracts.

In this chapter, we're going to cover the following main topics:

- Understanding smart contract security
- Understanding smart contract access controls
- Understanding smart contract security tooling and audits

Understanding smart contract security

As a beginner in Solidity and smart contract development, it is crucial to understand and follow basic security requirements. Smart contracts are self-executing agreements with the terms directly written into code, and once deployed on the blockchain, they are immutable. Ensuring the security of smart contracts is vital to prevent hacks, exploits, and loss of funds.

Several high-profile hacks and failures have occurred in the world of smart contracts, primarily due to vulnerabilities in the Solidity code. Here are some notable incidents:

- **The DAO Hack (2016)**: The **Decentralized Autonomous Organization** (**DAO**) was a decentralized venture capital fund built on Ethereum. In June 2016, an attacker exploited a reentrancy vulnerability in the DAO's smart contract, siphoning about 3.6 million ether (worth around $50 million at that time). This ultimately led to a controversial hard fork, creating Ethereum Classic.

- **Parity Wallet Hack (2017)**: In July 2017, the Parity **multi-signature (multisig)** wallet was hacked, leading to a loss of around 150,000 ether (worth around $30 million at that time). The vulnerability was due to a lack of proper access control, allowing the attacker to call the `initWallet` function and gain control of the wallets.

- **Parity Wallet Library Freeze (2017)**: A few months after the first Parity hack, another incident occurred in November 2017. An inexperienced developer accidentally triggered the "self-destruct" function on a shared library used by Parity's multisig wallets. This led to the freezing of around 513,000 ether (worth around $150 million at that time) with no means to recover the funds. This incident highlighted the importance of proper access control and rigorous testing.

- **Bancor Hack (2018)**: In July 2018, the decentralized exchange Bancor experienced a security breach, resulting in a loss of about $13.5 million in various cryptocurrencies. The attackers exploited a vulnerability in the smart contract, allowing them to bypass the access control restrictions and withdraw the funds.

- **Uniswap and Lendf.Me Flash Loan Attacks (2020)**: In early 2020, attackers exploited vulnerabilities in the **decentralized finance (DeFi)** platforms Uniswap and Lendf.Me, stealing around $25 million in total. The attackers used flash loans, which are uncollateralized loans that must be repaid within a single transaction, to manipulate the platforms' pricing oracles and profit from the artificially inflated prices.

These incidents highlight the importance of thorough security audits, rigorous testing, and adherence to best practices in smart contract development. Developers must be vigilant to prevent vulnerabilities and ensure the safety of user funds and the integrity of the platforms they create.

What are the basic security requirements for a smart contract? Let's take a look:

- **Access control**: Ensure that only authorized users can execute specific functions. Use access control patterns such as Ownable and Roles to restrict access.

- **Input validation**: Validate user inputs to prevent unexpected behavior. Implement checks and require statements to ensure input data is within the expected range or format.

- **Error handling**: Use `revert()`, `require()`, and `assert()` statements to handle errors, revert state changes, and provide descriptive error messages.

- **Visibility**: Set appropriate visibility (public, external, internal, or private) for functions and state variables to prevent unauthorized access or modification.

- **SafeMath**: Use the SafeMath library or built-in Solidity functions for arithmetic operations to prevent overflows and underflows.

- **Upgradability**: Plan for upgradability by using a proxy pattern or a similar approach to enable future improvements and bug fixes without breaking the existing contract.

- **Testing and auditing**: Thoroughly test and audit your smart contracts to identify vulnerabilities and ensure their correctness. Consider engaging external security experts for audits.

The consequences of not following security best practices could lead us to the following issues:

- **Loss of funds**: Vulnerable smart contracts can lead to the loss of user funds through hacks or exploits

- **Permanent damage**: As smart contracts are immutable, vulnerabilities in the code cannot be easily fixed, leading to long-term damage to the project's reputation and user trust

- **Legal implications**: Poorly secured smart contracts might result in legal disputes or regulatory scrutiny

Let's look at some common mistakes in writing smart contracts from a security standpoint:

- **Reentrancy**: Calling external contracts without proper checks can lead to reentrancy attacks, where an attacker can repeatedly call a function and drain the contract's funds

- **Integer overflow/underflow**: Failure to handle integer overflows and underflows can lead to unexpected results, potentially benefiting attackers

- **Front-running**: Unprotected functions can be exploited by attackers who monitor the transaction pool and submit transactions with higher gas fees to manipulate the contract's execution order

- **Timestamp manipulation**: Relying on `block.timestamp` for critical logic can be risky as miners have some control over it, leading to potential manipulation

- **Uninitialized storage pointers**: Failing to initialize storage pointers can result in unintended access to other storage slots, potentially causing data corruption or manipulation

- **Inadequate gas usage estimation**: Inaccurate gas estimation can lead to stuck transactions or potential **Denial-of-Service (DoS)** attacks

By understanding and implementing these security best practices, you can minimize the risks associated with smart contract development and create more secure, reliable, and trustworthy applications on the blockchain.

Next, we will look at a couple of these security concerns in detail and see how we can address them in smart contract programs.

Upgradability

Upgradable smart contracts in Solidity are contracts that are designed to allow their code or logic to be updated after they have been deployed on the blockchain. This feature is essential in situations where bugs need to be fixed, optimizations need to be made, or new functionality needs to be added without disrupting the existing contract state or user experience.

Upgrading smart contracts is essential for several reasons:

- **Bug fixes**: Deployed smart contracts may contain bugs or vulnerabilities that were not detected during development or audits. Upgrading allows developers to fix these issues and ensure the contract operates as intended.

- **Enhancements**: Upgrading smart contracts enables the introduction of new features or optimizations, which can enhance the user experience, improve efficiency, or add new functionalities.

- **Regulatory compliance**: Smart contracts might need to be updated to comply with new regulations, rules, or industry standards.

There are several mechanisms to upgrade a smart contract, but here are the two most common ones:

- **Proxy pattern (upgradeable contracts)**: This approach uses a proxy contract to delegate calls to a separate logic contract containing the actual business logic. By updating the logic contract's address in the proxy, developers can upgrade the smart contract without changing the contract's address or state.

- **Separating data and logic**: Another approach involves separating data storage from the contract's business logic. When an upgrade is needed, a new contract can be deployed that interacts with the existing data storage contract, ensuring continuity and minimal disruption to users.

Now, let's look at an example of a contract before and after an upgrade. We will start with the *before the upgrade* scenario:

```
contract SimpleStorage {
    uint256 private data;

    function setData(uint256 _data) public {
        data = _data;
    }

    function getData() public view returns (uint256) {
        return data;
    }
}
```

Now, let's see how this smart contract can be made upgradable using the proxy pattern.

Here's the storage contract:

```
contract SimpleStorageV2 {
    uint256 private data;

    function setData(uint256 _data) public {
```

```
        data = _data;
    }

    function getData() public view returns (uint256) {
        return data;
    }
}
```

Now lets us see how to properly implement the SimpleStorageProxy
contract as a TransparentUpgradeableProxy using the OpenZeppelin
library.

```
import "@openzeppelin/contracts-upgradeable/proxy/transparent/
TransparentUpgradeableProxy.sol";

contract SimpleStorageProxy is TransparentUpgradeableProxy {
    constructor(address _logic, address _admin, bytes memory _data)
TransparentUpgradeableProxy(_logic, _admin, _data) {}
}
```

We must follow these steps to upgrade a smart contract (using the proxy pattern):

1. Develop the new version of the smart contract with the required changes, bug fixes, or new features.

2. Deploy the new version of the smart contract (for example, SimpleStorageV2) to the blockchain.

3. Set up a proxy contract, such as OpenZeppelin's `TransparentUpgradeableProxy`, which will forward calls to the underlying logic contract.

4. Deploy the proxy contract with the initial logic contract (SimpleStorage) and admin address (the account that can trigger upgrades) as parameters.

5. Interact with the proxy contract instead of the logic contract directly. The proxy contract will forward calls to the logic contract, allowing users to interact with the smart contract as if they were directly interacting with the logic contract.

6. When an upgrade is needed, call the upgrade function on the proxy contract (for example, using OpenZeppelin's `upgradeTo` or `upgradeToAndCall` functions) and provide the address of the new logic contract (SimpleStorageV2) as a parameter.

7. The proxy contract will now forward calls to the new logic contract (SimpleStorageV2), effectively upgrading the smart contract while maintaining its state and address.

Note that while this example uses OpenZeppelin's `TransparentUpgradeableProxy`, other proxy patterns can be used to achieve similar results. It is essential to thoroughly test and audit your upgradeable smart contracts to ensure their security and correctness.

> **OpenZeppelin – building secure and reliable smart contracts**
>
> OpenZeppelin is a renowned framework and library for developing secure, high-quality, and reliable smart contracts in the Ethereum ecosystem. Recognized for its focus on security and best practices, OpenZeppelin has become the go-to choice for developers seeking to build **decentralized applications (dApps)** and blockchain projects with confidence. The OpenZeppelin framework offers a rich collection of audited, reusable, and well-tested smart contract components written in Solidity. These components encompass a wide range of use cases, including token standards (ERC20, ERC721, and ERC1155), access control, governance, and upgradeability. By utilizing OpenZeppelin's battle-tested building blocks, developers can reduce the risk of vulnerabilities, save time, and focus on implementing their unique project requirements.

Integer overflow

An integer overflow attack is a type of vulnerability that occurs when an arithmetic operation results in a value that exceeds the maximum (or goes below the minimum) limit of the given integer data type. When an overflow (or underflow) happens, the value wraps around, causing unexpected and unintended consequences in a program, such as smart contracts on a blockchain.

In the context of smart contracts, an integer overflow attack can lead to serious security issues as it can allow an attacker to manipulate the contract's state, exploit vulnerabilities, or cause incorrect calculations. These attacks can result in a loss of funds or compromise the intended functionality of the contract.

Here's a simple example of a smart contract that demonstrates an integer overflow attack:

```
contract IntegerOverflowAttack {//Line 3
    uint256 public counter; //Line 4

    function increment(uint256 value) public { //Line 6
        uint256 oldValue = counter; //Line 7
        counter += value; //Line 8

        assert(counter >= oldValue); // This check can fail due to
integer overflow //Line 10
    }
}
```

The following is a detailed explanation of this program and how an integer overflow attack can happen:

- **Line 3**: Declares the IntegerOverflowAttack contract.
- **Line 4**: Declares a public counter variable of the uint256 type. This variable will be incremented by a value provided in the increment() function.

- **Line 6**: Defines the `increment()` function, which takes a `uint256` argument value. This function is called to increment `counter` by `value`.

- **Line 7**: Stores the old value of `counter` in a local variable called `oldValue`. This is done to compare it with the new value after incrementing.

- **Line 8**: Increments `counter` by the provided `value`. This line is where the integer overflow can occur if the new value exceeds the maximum value of `uint256`.

- **Line 10**: Checks if the new `counter` value is greater than or equal to `oldValue`. If the `counter` value overflows in line 8, this check will fail, and the `assert()` statement will revert the transaction. However, it's important to note that in Solidity 0.8.0 and later, overflow and underflow checks are built-in, and the transaction would revert automatically without this check.

To demonstrate an integer overflow attack, deploy the contract and call the `increment()` function with a sufficiently large value to cause an overflow (for example, `2**256 - 1`). If the contract was written in a Solidity version before 0.8.0 without built-in overflow protection, the `counter` value will overflow and wrap around to a smaller number, causing the `assert()` check to fail and revert the transaction.

tx.origin

`tx.origin` represents the original address that initiated the transaction. In a chain of calls between smart contracts, `tx.origin` remains the same, while `msg.sender` changes to the address of the contract executing the call. Using `tx.origin` for authorization can result in vulnerabilities as it doesn't always represent the immediate caller, making it susceptible to attacks such as phishing or spoofing. The following example shows the vulnerability of the contract and when not to use `tx.orgin`:

```
contract TxOriginVulnerable {
    address public owner;

    constructor() {
        owner = msg.sender;
    }

    function changeOwner(address newOwner) public {
        require(tx.origin == owner, "Only the owner can change
ownership");
        owner = newOwner;
    }
}
```

In the preceding contract, the `changeOwner()` function uses `tx.origin` to check if the caller is the owner. An attacker can create another contract that calls `changeOwner()` on behalf of an unsuspecting victim (the owner), causing a change of ownership to the attacker's desired address:

```
function changeOwner(address newOwner) public {
    require(msg.sender == owner, "Only the owner can change
ownership");
    owner = newOwner;
}
```

To avoid this vulnerability, use `msg.sender` instead of `tx.origin` to ensure you're checking the immediate caller.

Gas limits and DoS attacks

Gas limits in Ethereum transactions determine the maximum amount of gas that can be consumed during the transaction's execution. If a transaction runs out of gas, it is reverted, and the consumed gas is lost. Contracts with functions that consume an unpredictable amount of gas can lead to **DoS** vulnerabilities as malicious users can submit transactions with low gas limits, causing legitimate transactions to be delayed or fail.

The following is an example of a vulnerable contract with an unpredictable gas consumption:

```
contract GasLimitVulnerable {
    mapping(address => uint256) public balances;

    function withdrawAll() public {
        uint256 amount = balances[msg.sender];
        (bool success, ) = msg.sender.call{value: amount}("");
        require(success, "Withdrawal failed");
        balances[msg.sender] = 0;
    }
}
```

In the `withdrawAll()` function, the external call consumes an unpredictable amount of gas. If a malicious contract is used as the recipient, it can have a fallback function with a high gas cost, causing the withdrawal to fail and potentially block other users from withdrawing their funds.

To avoid this vulnerability, use the **checks-effects-interactions** pattern and ensure that state changes are done before external calls:

```
function withdrawAll() public {
    uint256 amount = balances[msg.sender];
    balances[msg.sender] = 0;
    (bool success, ) = msg.sender.call{value: amount}("");
```

```
        require(success, "Withdrawal failed");
}
```

This change ensures that even if the external call fails, the state has already been updated, and the user's balance will not be locked.

Now, let's look at access controls and other interesting aspects of smart contract security.

Understanding smart contract access controls

Access control in Solidity smart contracts is crucial for restricting access to sensitive functionality and preventing unauthorized usage. Implementing strong access control mechanisms can protect your smart contracts from attacks and vulnerabilities.

In this section, we will deep dive into access control with dos and don'ts, followed by examples of bad access controls.

Dos:

- Use well-established access control patterns, such as the Ownable pattern, **role-based access control (RBAC)**, or **access control lists (ACLs)**
- Define modifiers to restrict access to certain functions
- Be explicit in defining access levels for functions and state variables
- Test and audit your access control mechanisms thoroughly to ensure proper restrictions
- Update access controls as needed when adding new functionality or roles

Don'ts:

- Don't rely solely on hardcoded addresses for access control as this can make your contract inflexible and hard to maintain
- Don't make sensitive functions and state variables public or external
- Don't assume that access control is foolproof; always validate user input and handle errors
- Don't use `tx.origin` for access control as it can lead to vulnerabilities

Now, let's look at an example of bad access control in a smart contract. We'll take `tx.origin` and see how we can provide better access control for the contract.

Using `tx.origin` instead of `msg.sender` for access control can lead to vulnerabilities as `tx.origin` always refers to the original sender of the transaction. It can be manipulated by malicious contracts, potentially allowing unauthorized access:

```
contract BadAccessControl {
    address public owner;
```

```
    constructor() {
        owner = tx.origin;
    }

    function sensitiveFunction() public {
        require(tx.origin == owner, "BadAccessControl: Not
authorized");// Sensitive code
    }
}
```

In the preceding example, if a user interacts with a malicious contract that, in turn, calls
sensitiveFunction, tx.origin will still be the user's address, bypassing the access control
and allowing the malicious contract to execute the sensitive code.

Instead, use msg.sender:

```
contract GoodAccessControl {
    address public owner;

    constructor() {
        owner = msg.sender;
    }

    function sensitiveFunction() public {
        require(msg.sender == owner, "GoodAccessControl: Not
authorized");// Sensitive code
    }
}
```

In this second example, we will see how to use overly permissive access control. Using overly permissive
access control can expose sensitive functionality to unauthorized users, potentially causing harm or
enabling attacks:

```
contract BadAccessControl {
    uint256 private sensitiveData;

    function setSensitiveData(uint256 _data) public {
        sensitiveData = _data;
    }

    function getSensitiveData() public view returns (uint256) {
        return sensitiveData;
    }
}
```

In this example, the `setSensitiveData` and `getSensitiveData` functions are publicly accessible, allowing anyone to view and modify the sensitive data. This can be fixed by implementing proper access control via the Ownable pattern, for example:

```
contract GoodAccessControl {
    uint256 private sensitiveData;
    address private owner;

    constructor() {
        owner = msg.sender;
    }

    modifier onlyOwner() {
        require(msg.sender == owner, "GoodAccessControl: Not
authorized");
        _;
    }

    function setSensitiveData(uint256 _data) public onlyOwner {
        sensitiveData = _data;
    }

    function getSensitiveData() public view onlyOwner returns
(uint256) {
        return sensitiveData;
    }
}
```

In this revised example, the `onlyOwner` modifier restricts access to the sensitive functions, ensuring that proper and only required access control is given.

Finally, we will see how to use **multisig**, a security mechanism that requires multiple signatures or approvals to authorize a transaction or perform a specific action. In the context of blockchain, a multisig contract is a smart contract that enforces this requirement.

A multisig contract works by maintaining a list of authorized signers, a threshold for the minimum number of signatures required, and a mechanism to propose, approve, and execute transactions. Each authorized signer can submit a transaction proposal, and other signers can then approve the transaction. Once the number of approvals reaches the threshold, the transaction can be executed.

Multisig contracts offer several advantages. Some of the most common ones are listed here:

- **Enhanced security**: Requiring multiple approvals reduces the risk of single points of failure and mitigates the impact of compromised private keys or insider threats

- **Improved governance**: Multisig contracts can be used to enforce a more decentralized decision-making process among a group of individuals or entities, ensuring that no single party has unilateral control

Now, let's look at some common disadvantages of multisig contracts:

- **Increased complexity**: Implementing and using multisig contracts can be more complex than regular contracts, which may lead to an increased risk of vulnerabilities or user errors
- **Slower operations**: The need for multiple approvals can slow down transaction processing, particularly in cases where prompt action is required

Let's look at a simple multisig contract:

The `MultiSigWallet` contract can be divided into three main blocks: contract variable declarations, constructor functions for transaction management, and functions for transaction execution.

Here's the first block:

```
contract MultiSigWallet {
    uint minApprovers;
    address payable dealProposer;
    address payable beneficiary;
    mapping (address => bool) approvedBy;
    mapping (address => bool) isApprover;
    uint approvalsNum;
```

In this block, we declare the state variables for our contract:

- `minApprovers` is the minimum number of approvers required to execute a transaction
- `dealProposer` is the address that proposed the current deal (initialized in the constructor)
- `beneficiary` is the recipient of the contract's funds if the transaction gets enough approvals
- `approvedBy` keeps track of who has approved the transaction
- `isApprover` checks if an address is an authorized approver
- `approvalsNum` counts the number of approvals received

The second block is the constructor:

```
constructor(
    address[] memory _approvers,
    uint   _minApprovers,
    address payable _beneficiary
) payable {
    require(_minApprovers <= _approvers.length,
```

```
                    "Required number of approvers should be less than or equal to
    the number of approvers");

            minApprovers = _minApprovers;
            dealProposer = payable(msg.sender);
            beneficiary = _beneficiary;

            for (uint i = 0; i < _approvers.length; i++) {
                address approver = _approvers[i];
                isApprover[approver] = true;
            }
        }
```

The constructor is invoked when the contract is deployed. It initializes the approvers, the minimum number of approvers, and the beneficiary. It also checks that the minimum number of approvers is not greater than the number of approvers.

The third block contains transaction management functions:

```
    function approve() public {
        require(isApprover[msg.sender], "Not an approver");
        require(!approvedBy[msg.sender], "Already approved");

        approvalsNum++;
        approvedBy[msg.sender] = true;

        if (approvalsNum == minApprovers) {
            beneficiary.transfer(address(this).balance);
            selfdestruct(dealProposer);
        }
    }

    function reject() public {
        require(isApprover[msg.sender], "Not an approver");

        selfdestruct(dealProposer);
    }
```

In this block, the `approve()` function allows approvers to approve the transaction. If the transaction gets enough approvals, the contract's funds are transferred to the beneficiary and the contract is destroyed. The `reject()` function allows any approver to reject the transaction, which results in the contract being destroyed.

So, can this only be done manually? In the next section, we will cover tooling and audits for smart contracts.

Understanding smart contract security tooling and audits

We will start with tooling first and then move on to auditing. As a beginner, you should be able to distinguish between security and auditing concerns.

A smart contract developer should use tools to ensure their code is free of vulnerabilities for several reasons:

- **Financial implications**: Smart contracts often handle and manage valuable assets, such as cryptocurrencies and tokens. Vulnerable smart contracts can lead to significant financial losses, both for the developer and the users.

- **Immutability**: Once deployed on a blockchain, smart contracts are immutable, meaning they cannot be changed or updated. Any vulnerabilities present in the code will persist, making it crucial to identify and fix issues before deployment.

- **Trust and reputation**: Ensuring that smart contracts are secure is essential for building trust among users and maintaining a good reputation in the industry. Security breaches and loss of funds can damage a project's credibility and discourage future adoption.

- **Complexity and unpredictability**: Writing secure smart contracts can be challenging due to the complexities of blockchain programming and the potential for unintended consequences. Security tools can help identify vulnerabilities that might be difficult to spot through manual code review alone.

- **Compliance with best practices**: Using tools to analyze and optimize smart contract code can help developers adhere to established best practices, improving the overall quality and maintainability of the code.

- **Time efficiency**: Automated security tools can quickly analyze large code bases, making them an efficient way to identify vulnerabilities and other issues. This allows developers to focus on writing better code and resolving issues promptly.

- **Comprehensive analysis**: Security tools use various techniques, such as static and dynamic analysis, fuzzing, and symbolic execution, to thoroughly examine smart contract code. Using multiple tools can provide a more comprehensive analysis and increase the likelihood of detecting vulnerabilities.

Using tools to ensure smart contract security is essential to protect users' assets, maintain trust and reputation, and create high-quality, reliable decentralized applications.

Now, let's look at some of the popular tools for security and auditing a smart contract:

- **MythX (owned by ConsenSys Diligence)**: MythX is a comprehensive security analysis service for Ethereum smart contracts. It uses static analysis, dynamic analysis, and symbolic execution to identify vulnerabilities in your code. It offers integration with popular development environments such as Truffle and Remix and provides an API for custom integrations.

- **Slither (owned by Trail of Bits)**: Slither is a popular open source static analysis framework for smart contracts. It helps find common issues, optimize contracts, and ensure the quality of the code. Slither supports Solidity and has been used by the Ethereum community for years.

- **Remix IDE (owned by Ethereum Foundation)**: Remix is a powerful open source IDE for Solidity development that comes with built-in static analysis tools. These tools can help identify common issues and vulnerabilities in your smart contracts while you are writing them. It also supports plugin development to extend its functionality.

- **Echidna (owned by Trail of Bits)**: Echidna is a property-based fuzzing tool for smart contracts. It tests contracts against custom properties and helps identify vulnerabilities in the code. Echidna is open source and supports Solidity.

- **Manticore (owned by Trail of Bits)**: Manticore is a dynamic binary analysis tool and symbolic execution engine for smart contracts. It can analyze Ethereum contracts and generate inputs that trigger specific code paths, helping to identify potential vulnerabilities in your contracts.

- **Oyente (originally developed by Melonport, now open source)**: Oyente is an open source static analysis tool for Ethereum smart contracts. It uses symbolic execution to detect common vulnerabilities, such as reentrancy, transaction ordering dependence, and timestamp dependency.

- **Securify (developed by ChainSecurity, now open source)**: Securify is an open source, formal verification-based static analysis tool for Ethereum smart contracts. It checks for compliance with a set of predefined security properties and provides an API for integration with other tools.

- **Solhint (owned by Protofire)**: Solhint is an open source linting tool for Solidity code that checks for style, security, and best practices issues. It can be integrated into popular code editors and helps improve code quality during development.

- **Solium (now known as Ethlint, open source)**: Ethlint, formerly known as Solium, is a popular open source linting tool for Solidity code. It enforces style, best practices, and security guidelines, helping developers write cleaner and more secure contracts.

These tools are ordered by their popularity in the industry, but their usefulness may vary, depending on your specific requirements and use cases. It is essential to use multiple tools in combination to ensure the security and quality of your smart contracts.

ConsenSys Diligence – smart contract security and auditing tools

ConsenSys Diligence (`https://consensys.net/diligence/`) stands out as a leading provider of smart contract security and auditing solutions. Their comprehensive suite of tools and services is designed to ensure the highest level of security for your decentralized applications and smart contracts. By leveraging the expertise of their experienced security engineers, ConsenSys Diligence is dedicated to identifying and mitigating risks in the complex world of blockchain technology.

A smart contract audit is a thorough examination of the code, functionality, and security of a smart contract. It aims to identify vulnerabilities, logic flaws, and potential attack vectors to ensure that the contract operates as intended and is free of security risks. Audits are typically performed by security experts or specialized firms.

The following steps are involved in a smart contract audit:

1. **Scoping**: Define the scope of the audit by identifying the contracts, functionality, and specific requirements that need to be reviewed.

2. **Documentation review**: Examine the project's documentation, such as whitepapers and technical specifications, to understand the intended functionality and design of the smart contract.

3. **Manual code review**: Perform a line-by-line analysis of the code to identify potential issues, vulnerabilities, and deviations from best practices.

4. **Automated analysis**: Use tools such as static analyzers, dynamic analyzers, and fuzzing tools to identify vulnerabilities and code quality issues automatically.

5. **Testing**: Conduct unit tests, integration tests, and stress tests to validate the contract's functionality and identify potential edge cases.

6. **Verification**: Verify that the smart contract adheres to the intended design and specifications, and complies with applicable regulations and standards.

7. **Reporting**: Prepare a detailed audit report outlining the findings, recommendations, and remediation steps.

The duration of a smart contract audit depends on the size and complexity of the code base, as well as the audit's scope. It can take anywhere from a few days to several weeks.

Typically, specialized security firms, individual security experts, or in-house security teams perform smart contract audits.

A smart contract should undergo an audit before it is deployed on the mainnet or any production-grade blockchain network, especially if it handles valuable assets or critical functionality.

Some of the popular smart contract audit services include the following:

- ConsenSys Diligence
- Trail of Bits
- Quantstamp
- OpenZeppelin
- CertiK

These firms offer comprehensive audit services, often combining manual code reviews with automated analysis tools to provide a thorough examination of smart contracts.

Summary

In this chapter, we discussed various aspects of Solidity smart contract development, focusing on security and best practices. We covered the importance of adhering to security guidelines and highlighted common mistakes and pitfalls, such as access control, input validation, error handling, visibility, safe math, upgradability, and testing and auditing.

We took a deep dive into access controls, addressing their significance in smart contracts and the potential issues that can arise from bad access control implementations. We also explored popular smart contract hacking incidents and failures, emphasizing the need for vigilance in contract development.

Upgradable smart contracts were examined, discussing their importance and the mechanisms for upgrading them, including the proxy pattern. We also discussed multisig contracts, their functionality, and advantages and disadvantages, and provided a simple multisig contract example.

Furthermore, we delved into smart contract security design considerations for mission-critical contracts in large DeFi networks. We touched on integer overflow attacks and their potential consequences in smart contracts, as well as the relationship between `tx.origin` and gas limits concerning smart contract security vulnerabilities.

Finally, we highlighted ConsenSys Diligence and OpenZeppelin as reputable providers of smart contract security and auditing tools and resources. These platforms offer essential tools, libraries, and frameworks to assist developers in building secure, reliable, and high-quality smart contracts for decentralized applications.

In the next chapter, we will cover core and important developer tools and libraries that are used extensively for Web3 development.

Part 3 –
Writing Your DApps for Web3

This is your essential companion for embarking on a journey into **decentralized application (DApp)** development. This part equips you with the knowledge and tools required to excel in the realm of Web3 development. Beginning with an exploration of developer tooling and libraries tailored for Web3, you'll gain a solid foundation to build decentralized applications. This part then guides you through the process of writing and testing your very first DApp for Web3, providing hands-on experience and practical insights every step of the way.

This section has the following chapters:

- *Chapter 7, Developer Tools and Libraries for Web3 Development*
- *Chapter 8, Writing and Testing Your First dApp on Web3*

Developer Tools and Libraries for Web3 Development

When you are building an application using smart contracts on Ethereum, it's a good idea to test it on a private network first before making it live. Just like how you'd use a local server on your computer for creating websites, you can use a development network to create a local version of the blockchain for testing your app. This chapter will introduce you to the common tools and libraries available to do Web3 development including Ganache, Hardhat, and Testnets. This chapter will also introduce you to how to set up a local development environment. This environment will become the primary environment for all development activities mentioned in this book. We'll create a project in this environment to learn about different topics on Web3 using hands-on methods going forward. You will need some basic programming skills to learn and understand some of these chapters moving forward.

In this chapter, we're going to cover the following main topics:

- Understanding the Web3 development stack
- Understanding Ethereum clients
- Introducing Infra, a node-as-a-service
- Introducing **InterPlanetary File System** (**IPFS**)

Understanding the Web3 development stack

Web3 development involves building **decentralized applications** (**dApps**) that utilize blockchain technology. The development process involves various tools and stacks from frontend to backend, middleware, APIs, and blockchain. We have already seen a number of them in the previous chapters. In this section, we will summarize them into different layers of application development and highlight the tools that fall into each stack. We'll start with the frontend stack.

Frontend stack

A frontend stack is a collection of technologies and tools used to build the user interface of a website or web application. It includes languages such as HTML, CSS, and JavaScript, as well as libraries and frameworks such as React, Angular, or Vue.js, enabling developers to create interactive and visually appealing web experiences. The following are some of the popular libraries that are used in the frontend stack for Web3 development:

- `React.js`: React is a JavaScript library for building user interfaces. It is widely used for building Web3 frontends due to its flexibility, modularity, and scalability.

- `Web3.js`: `Web3.js` is a JavaScript library that's used for interacting with the Ethereum blockchain. It provides a simple and convenient interface for developers to interact with smart contracts, send transactions, and retrieve data from the blockchain.

- `Vue.js`: `Vue.js` is another popular JavaScript library that's used for building user interfaces. It is known for its simplicity, reusability, and flexibility.

The list of libraries mentioned is only a small subset; which frontend stack is chosen depends on the project and the company's standards. Next, we will see a similar set of libraries that are used in the middle tier.

Middle tier stack

The middle tier stack refers to the server-side technology stack for web applications. It handles data processing, business logic, and server-side operations, connecting the frontend and backend components for a complete web application. Let's take a closer look at the popular middle tier stack for Web3 application development:

- **Node.js**: Node.js is a widely used platform for creating server-side applications, and it utilizes JavaScript as its programming language. It provides a robust set of APIs and tools for building Web3 applications.

- **IPFS**: This is a distributed filesystem that allows developers to store and retrieve files in a decentralized manner. It is used as a middleware layer in Web3 development to store and retrieve data in a decentralized way.

These libraries represent just a portion of the available options as the choice of middle tier stacks varies based on project requirements and company preferences. Now, let's explore a similar set of libraries that are commonly used in the backend for Web3 development.

Backend stack

This stack includes Ethereum-based tools and libraries for handling blockchain data and executing smart contracts on the backend. Solidity, a smart contract language, and Hardhat Suite, a framework, act as a good stack for the backend when it comes to Web3 development:

- **Solidity**: We have seen a lot about Solidity so far in this book; it's a high-level language for coding smart contracts. It is similar to JavaScript and is used for writing the backend logic of Web3 applications.

- **Hardhat Suite**: A development framework used for building, testing, and deploying smart contracts. It provides a suite of tools, including coding, testing, and debugging, for Web3 applications.

These are just a portion of available options as the selection often hinges on project-specific needs and a company's established standards. Now, let's explore a similar set of libraries and technologies that are commonly utilized in the **application programming interface** (**API**) stack for Web3 development.

Blockchain API stack

The API layer or stack is a crucial component of modern software architecture. It serves as a bridge between different software systems, enabling them to communicate and share data seamlessly. APIs define how requests and responses are structured, facilitating the integration of diverse applications, services, and platforms. Let's look at the popular API stack for Web3 application development:

- **Infura**: Infura is a popular API provider that offers developers access to Ethereum and IPFS networks without the need for them to run their own nodes. It provides a scalable and reliable infrastructure for building Web3 applications.

- **Alchemy**: Alchemy is another API provider that offers developers access to the Ethereum network. It provides a suite of developer tools, including APIs, SDKs, and analytics, for building Web3 applications.

Infura and Alchemy are a couple of options, but several node providers offer a lot of other services, including APIs as bundles. Now, let's explore a similar set of blockchains that are commonly utilized in the blockchain stack for Web3 development.

Blockchain stack

A blockchain stack or layer is a technology framework that encompasses the various components necessary for building and operating blockchain networks. It includes elements such as consensus algorithms, smart contract languages, node software, and data storage solutions. Collectively, these layers enable the creation of secure, decentralized, and transparent distributed ledger systems. When it comes to blockchains, there are two main choices that many people like:

- **Ethereum**: A decentralized blockchain platform that's used for building smart contracts and decentralized applications. It is the most popular blockchain platform used for Web3 development.

- **Binance Smart Chain** (**BSC**): BSC is another blockchain platform that's used for building decentralized applications. It offers faster transaction times and lower fees than Ethereum.

Web3 development requires a wide range of tools and technologies that span from the frontend to the backend, middleware, APIs, and blockchain. The tools mentioned in this section are just a few of the popular ones that are used in Web3 development. The choice of tools and technologies largely depends on the specific requirements of the Web3 application being built.

Understanding Ethereum clients

Ethereum clients are software implementations of the Ethereum protocol that enable nodes to communicate with the Ethereum network. They are responsible for validating transactions, executing smart contracts, and maintaining the blockchain. There are several different Ethereum clients available, each with its own set of features and capabilities.

We need different Ethereum clients for a few reasons. First, having multiple clients enhances security and decentralization as it minimizes the risk of a single point of failure. Second, different clients may offer different features or performance optimizations that make them better suited for certain use cases.

Here are some of the popular Ethereum clients:

- **Geth**: This is one of the most widely used Ethereum clients. It is written in the Go programming language and is known for its fast syncing capabilities. Geth offers a **command-line interface** (**CLI**) for accessing the Ethereum blockchain, as well as a JavaScript console for running scripts.
- **Parity**: Parity is another popular Ethereum client written in Rust. It offers several advanced features, including built-in support for multisig wallets, and a light client mode that allows users to sync with the network quickly. Parity also offers a **graphical user interface** (**GUI**) for interacting with the Ethereum network.
- **OpenEthereum**: OpenEthereum (formerly known as **Parity-Ethereum**) is a community-driven Ethereum client written in Rust. It offers similar features to Parity, including a light client mode and a GUI, but is maintained by a different team of developers.
- **Besu**: Besu is an Ethereum client written in Java that is maintained by the Hyperledger project. It offers several advanced features, including support for private transactions and a built-in privacy layer. Besu is also known for its high performance and scalability.

Here's a comparison table of some of the key features of these Ethereum clients:

Client Name	Programming Language	Sync Speed	Advanced Features	Community Support
Geth	Go	Fast	No	Large
Parity	Rust	Fast	Multisig wallets, light client mode	Large

Client Name	Programming Language	Sync Speed	Advanced Features	Community Support
OpenEthereum	Rust	Fast	Multisig wallets, light client mode	Medium
Besu	Java	Fast	Private transactions, built-in privacy layer	Medium

Table 7.1 – Ethereum clients

Ethereum clients are software implementations of the Ethereum protocol that enable nodes to communicate with the network. Different clients offer different features and capabilities, which makes them better suited for certain use cases.

Geth is one of the most popular Ethereum clients and allows users to interact with the Ethereum network and execute smart contracts. Here's a brief history of Geth and its different releases:

- **2014**: Geth was first released as an open source project on GitHub by Ethereum co-founder Jeffrey Wilcke. The initial release was version 0.1.0 and supported basic blockchain synchronization, account management, and smart contract execution.

- **2015**: Geth version 1.0.0 was released, which included major improvements to blockchain synchronization and peer-to-peer networking. This release also introduced support for the *Ethereum Yellow Paper* (https://ethereum.github.io/yellowpaper/paper.pdf), which defines the Ethereum protocol.

- **2016**: Geth version 1.4.0 was released, which included support for **Ethereum Name Service** (**ENS**) and Whisper, a peer-to-peer messaging protocol.

- **2017**: Geth version 1.7.0 was released, which included major improvements to the light client protocol, which allows for faster synchronization and reduced storage requirements. This release also introduced support for the Byzantium hard fork, which included several important Ethereum protocol upgrades.

- **2018**: Geth version 1.8.0 was released, which included support for the Constantinople hard fork and several other protocol upgrades. This release also included improvements to the Geth command-line interface and performance optimizations.

- **2019**: Geth version 1.9.0 was released, which included several major improvements to the Ethereum peer-to-peer networking protocol, as well as support for the Istanbul hard fork and other protocol upgrades.

- **2020**: Geth version 1.10.0 was released, which included several performance optimizations and improvements to the Ethereum peer-to-peer networking protocol. This release also included support for the Berlin hard fork and other protocol upgrades.

- **2021**: Geth version was 1.10.12 released, which included several bug fixes and improvements to the Ethereum peer-to-peer networking protocol. Geth continues to be one of the most widely used Ethereum clients, with a large and active development community.

Geth is one of the most popular Ethereum clients and offers several unique features that set it apart from other clients. Here are some of the key features that are unique to Geth:

- **Light client protocol**: Geth has a built-in light client protocol, which allows users to quickly synchronize with the Ethereum network using minimal storage space. This is particularly useful for users who want to interact with the Ethereum network on low-powered devices or with limited storage.

- **CLI**: Geth has a powerful CLI that allows users to interact with the Ethereum network and execute commands directly from the terminal. This makes it easy to automate tasks and build custom scripts to interact with the Ethereum network.

- **Whisper protocol**: Geth supports the Whisper protocol, which is a peer-to-peer messaging protocol that allows users to send and receive encrypted messages on the Ethereum network. This is particularly useful for building decentralized applications that require secure messaging.

- **ENS**: Geth supports ENS, a feature that enables users to associate their Ethereum addresses with easy-to-remember names. With ENS, the challenge of memorizing lengthy and complex Ethereum addresses is eliminated as it provides a simpler domain-like structure.

Geth is written in the *Go* language, which is known for its speed and concurrency features. The Geth source code is available on GitHub, and the project is maintained by a team of developers and contributors from the Ethereum community.

The official Geth website is `https://geth.ethereum.org/`. Here, users can download the latest version of Geth, access the documentation and support resources, and contribute to the development of the project. Geth has come a long way since its initial release in 2014. With each new release, Geth has added important features, performance improvements, and protocol upgrades that have helped make Ethereum more accessible and efficient.

Introducing Infura, a node-as-a-service

Before we jump into Infura, let's understand the requirements to run a node and why we generally prefer a node provider such as Infura for doing Web3 development.

Running an Ethereum node

Running an Ethereum node can be a complex and resource-intensive process that requires significant technical expertise. There are several pitfalls and challenges that users may encounter when running a node.

Here are some examples:

- **Hardware requirements**: One of the main challenges of running an Ethereum node is the hardware requirements. Nodes require significant processing power, storage space, and bandwidth to maintain a copy of the entire blockchain and participate in the network. Users may need to upgrade their hardware or invest in specialized equipment to run a node efficiently.

- **Internet connectivity**: Nodes require a fast and stable internet connection to keep up with the blockchain and communicate with other nodes on the network. Users may encounter connectivity issues, such as dropped connections or network congestion, which can slow down syncing and cause other problems.

- **Software bugs and upgrades**: Ethereum is a rapidly evolving technology, and new versions of the software are released frequently. Upgrading a node can be a complex process that requires careful planning and testing to avoid downtime or other issues. Users may also encounter bugs or other software issues that can cause their nodes to crash or malfunction.

- **Security risks**: Running a node exposes users to several security risks, including hacking attempts, malware infections, and other cyber threats. Users must take appropriate security measures, such as using firewalls, encryption, and secure passwords, to protect their node and the data stored on it.

- **Legal and regulatory risks**: In some jurisdictions, running a node may be subject to legal and regulatory restrictions. Users must be aware of the laws and regulations in their jurisdiction and ensure that they comply with all applicable rules and regulations.

- **Network consensus issues**: Ethereum is a decentralized network, and nodes participate in a consensus process to validate transactions and maintain the blockchain. If a significant number of nodes go offline or fail to agree on the state of the network, it can cause issues such as forked chains or stalled transactions.

Running an Ethereum node can be a challenging and complex process that requires significant technical expertise and resources.

Let's look at some of the advantages of running an Ethereum node:

- **Increased security**: Running your own node allows you to verify the transactions and block yourself, rather than relying on a third-party provider

- **Increased privacy**: Running your own node allows you to keep your transactions private and not expose them to third-party providers

- **Full control**: Running your own node gives you full control over the software and the data stored on the node

- **Access to additional features**: Running your own node can give you access to additional features that are not available through third-party providers

Here are some of the disadvantages of running an Ethereum node:

- **High resource requirements**: Running a node can be resource-intensive and may require significant processing power, storage, and bandwidth

- **Technical knowledge required**: Running a node requires technical knowledge and expertise, as well as the ability to troubleshoot and maintain the software

Here's a step-by-step example of how to run an Ethereum node using Geth, one of the most popular Ethereum clients:

1. Download and install Geth from the official website.

2. Open a command prompt or terminal window and navigate to the directory where Geth is installed. `geth --help` will show you a list of commands that you can use in the CLI:

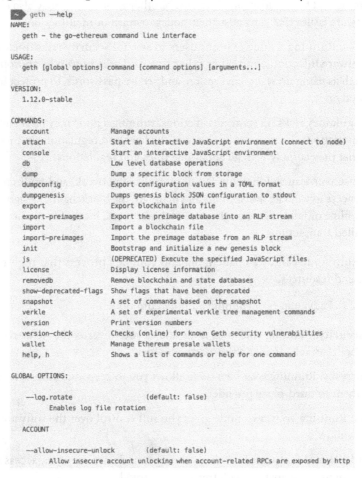

Figure 7.1 – geth --help

3. Start the Geth client by entering the `geth --syncmode full` command in the terminal window. This will start the node in full sync mode, which means that it will download and verify the entire blockchain:

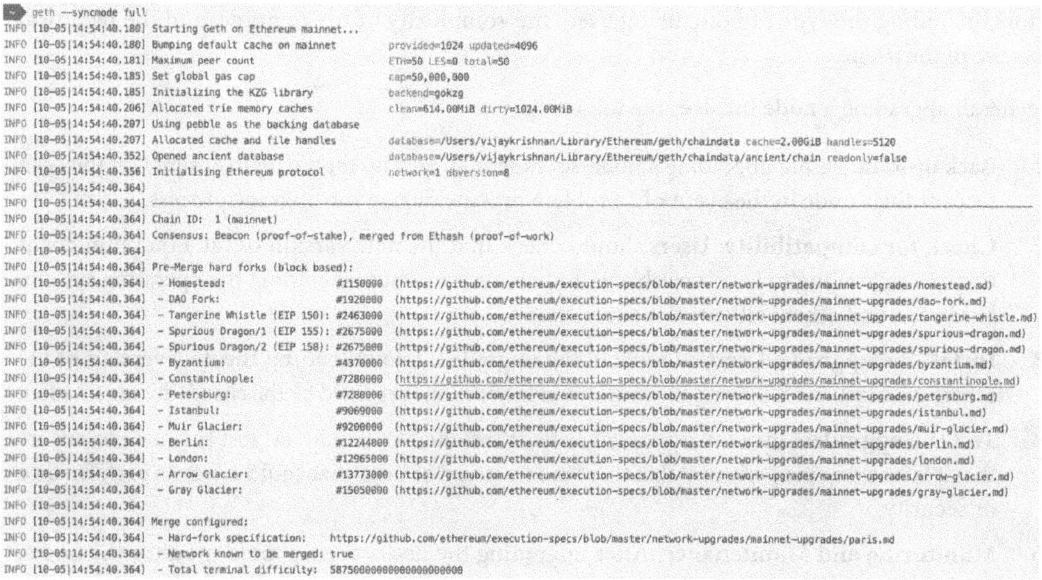

Figure 7.2 – geth --syncmode full

4. Wait for the node to sync with the network. This can take several hours or even days, depending on the speed of your internet connection and the resources available on your computer.

5. Once the node has been fully synced, you can use it to interact with the Ethereum network by running commands in the terminal window or by using a third-party user interface.

6. The hardware requirements for running an Ethereum node depend on the type of node you are running and the resources available on your computer. A full node requires a minimum of 4 GB of RAM, although 8 GB or more is recommended. It also requires a fast internet connection and a significant amount of storage space as the Ethereum blockchain is currently over 1 TB in size. A light node, on the other hand, requires significantly fewer resources and can be run on a low-end computer or even a mobile device.

You do not need to run a node! We will learn how to access Ethereum without running a node ourselves later in this chapter.

Let's say that you managed to run a node and successfully have it up and running for a while. Ethereum goes through multiple updates and upgrades and has a strong roadmap to move into a robust network in the next couple of years. Now, let's understand what process and effort is involved in going through an upgrade process.

Upgrading an Ethereum node

Upgrading Ethereum nodes can be a complex process that requires careful planning and testing to ensure that the node remains stable and secure. The ease of upgrading a node depends on several factors, including the type of node being used, the complexity of the upgrade, and the technical expertise of the user.

In general, upgrading a node involves the following steps:

1. **Back up data**: Before upgrading a node, users should back up their data to ensure that they can recover their node in the event of a problem or issue during the upgrade process.

2. **Check for compatibility**: Users should check that the new version of the Ethereum client they are upgrading to is compatible with their current setup, including the operating system, hardware, and other software dependencies.

3. **Install the upgrade**: Users can install the upgrade by downloading the new version of the Ethereum client and following the installation instructions provided by the client's documentation.

4. **Test the upgrade**: Once the upgrade has been installed, users should test the node to ensure that it is working properly and that there are no issues or bugs that could affect its performance or security.

5. **Monitoring and Maintenance**: After upgrading the node, users should monitor the node's performance and maintain it by applying regular security and software upgrades to keep it up to date and secure.

The ease of upgrading Ethereum nodes can vary depending on the complexity of the upgrade and the user's technical expertise. However, Ethereum clients such as Geth and Parity have made it easy to upgrade nodes by providing easy-to-use tools for installing and upgrading the software.

Upgrading Ethereum nodes can be a complex process that requires careful planning and testing to ensure that the node remains stable and secure. However, with proper preparation and the right tools, upgrading nodes can be straightforward, allowing users to take advantage of the latest security and software upgrades to ensure the stability and security of their node and the Ethereum network.

So, what are the other options to get access to the Ethereum network? *The answer is choosing a node provider.*

A node provider is a service or entity that offers access to blockchain nodes on a network such as Ethereum. These nodes are essential for interacting with the blockchain as they store a copy of the entire blockchain and validate transactions. Node providers enable developers and users to access these nodes through APIs, simplifying the process of building and interacting with blockchain applications without them needing to run their own nodes. Popular node providers include Infura, Alchemy, and QuickNode as they offer reliable access to Ethereum nodes for developers and applications. There are many node providers, also known as **remote procedure call** (**RPC**) providers, who provide an RPC endpoint to access Ethereum. This can be as simple as a URL with an API key and secret to access the network. Let's take a closer look at the most popular node providers:

- **Infura**: Infura (`https://infura.io/`) is a popular RPC node provider for Ethereum that provides a scalable and reliable infrastructure for developers to build and deploy their dApps. Infura offers a free plan that allows developers to connect to the Ethereum network using Infura's API and infrastructure.

- **Alchemy**: Alchemy (`https://www.alchemy.com/`) is another popular RPC node provider for Ethereum that offers a scalable and reliable infrastructure for developers. Alchemy offers a free plan that allows developers to connect to the Ethereum network using Alchemy's API and infrastructure.

- **QuickNode**: QuickNode (`https://www.quicknode.com/`) is a cloud-based Ethereum node provider that offers a range of plans for developers, including free and paid plans. QuickNode provides a fast and reliable infrastructure for developers to build and deploy their dApps.

Next, we will learn about Infura at a very high level and use Infura RPC endpoints for all our exercises going forward.

Infura 101

Infura is a popular Ethereum node provider that offers a scalable and reliable infrastructure for developers to build and deploy their dApps. It provides developers with a simple and easy-to-use API that allows them to connect to the Ethereum blockchain, without the need to set up any nodes or maintain their infrastructure.

The following figure represents a version of the Infura system architecture and how it works. We will not cover the technical aspects of how Infura is built in detail in this book:

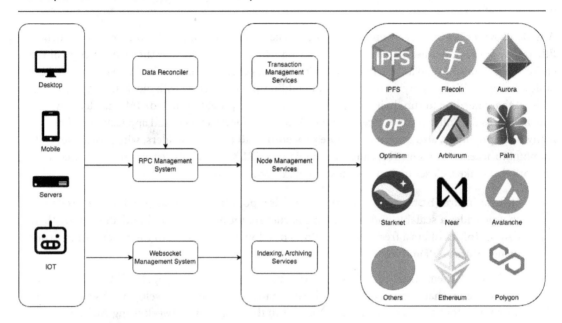

Figure 7.3 – Infura system architecture

In this book, we will learn how to build applications using node providers such as Infura. Now, let's learn how to use Infura and get started with Web3 development.

> **Important note**
> Infura is a self-service **Software-as-a-Service (SaaS)**.

Here is a step-by-step guide on how to use Infura:

1. **Sign up for an Infura account**: To use Infura, you'll need to sign up for an account on the Infura website (`https://app.infura.io/register`). Infura offers a free plan that allows developers to connect to the Ethereum network using Infura's API and infrastructure.

2. **Create a new project**: Once you've signed up for an Infura account, you can create a new project by clicking on the **Create New Project** button on the dashboard. Give your project a name and choose the Ethereum network you want to connect to (such as the main network, Ropsten, or Kovan).

3. **Get your project ID and endpoint**: After creating your project, you'll be provided with a project ID and an endpoint URL that you'll need to use to connect to the Ethereum network. Make note of these as you'll need them later.

4. **Connect to Infura using Web3.js**: To connect to Infura using `Web3.js`, you'll need to create a new instance of the Web3 object and specify the Infura endpoint URL and network ID. Here's an example:

```
const Web3 = require('web3');
const infuraEndpoint = 'https://mainnet.infura.io/v3/
YOUR_PROJECT_ID';
const web3 = new Web3(infuraEndpoint);
```

5. **Interact with the Ethereum network**: Once you've connected to Infura using `Web3.js`, you can use the Web3 API to interact with the Ethereum network. By doing this, you can send transactions, query balances, and interact with smart contracts.

Here is the getting started guide for Infura for your reference: `https://docs.infura.io/infura/getting-started`. Please become familiar with creating projects, identifying API keys and secrets, navigating the dashboard to see the usages and incoming requests that we make using web apps, and so on.

Here are some tips for using Infura effectively:

- Always use HTTPS when connecting to Infura as this provides a secure and encrypted connection

- Keep your Infura project ID and endpoint URL secure as they allow anyone to access your Ethereum account and transactions

- Use the Infura dashboard to monitor your project's usage and performance, and upgrade to a paid plan if necessary.

- Consider using multiple Infura endpoints to improve reliability and redundancy

- Use Infura's documentation and support resources to troubleshoot issues and optimize your usage

For the RPC endpoints, please refer to `https://docs.infura.io/infura/reference/network-endpoints` for the complete list of networks supported by Infura and their endpoints. We will only be using testnets in this book, so please become familiar with the endpoints for the testnets.

Infura is a powerful tool for connecting to the Ethereum network and building decentralized applications. Web3 developers can use Infura to easily connect to the Ethereum network and interact with smart contracts and other Ethereum-based applications. The following figure shows a reference architecture for Infura and how it can be used in traditional AWS service-based implementations:

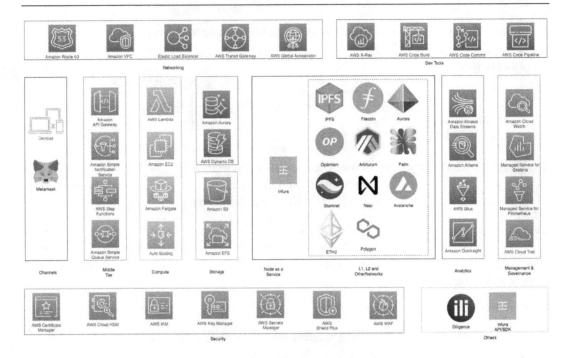

Figure 7.4 – An overview of infura reference architecture with AWS services

At this point, you should have an Infura account, a project or two, and API keys and be ready to start writing some real Web3 applications.

If you want to use any other node/RPC provider, please feel free to use it. All you need is the API key and secret to plug into your code.

> **Important note**
> However, before you move on to the next chapter, you should have an account with Infura, a project created for Ethereum, and an API and secret keys ready and handy.

Introducing IPFS

IPFS is a protocol and network that's developed to facilitate a decentralized way of storing and sharing multimedia content in a distributed filesystem. Initially conceptualized by Juan Benet, it has now evolved into an open source project with contributions from the wider community. IPFS aims to solve some of the limitations of the traditional client-server model of the internet, where web content is hosted on centralized servers. Instead, IPFS allows for a distributed web, where files can be stored and served by any node in the network, making it more resilient to censorship and downtime.

IPFS achieves this by using a content-addressed system, where files are given unique hashes based on their content, rather than their location. When a file is requested, the IPFS network uses the hash to locate and retrieve the file from the nearest node with a copy of it. This means that files are cached locally on nodes, reducing the amount of bandwidth required to serve them and increasing the speed of access.

IPFS has potential applications in various areas, including decentralized file sharing, content delivery networks, and distributed data storage.

Key problems addressed by IPFS

IPFS aims to solve some of the limitations of the traditional client-server model of the internet. Here are some of the key problems that IPFS addresses:

- **Centralization**: The traditional client-server model of the internet is highly centralized, with web content hosted on centralized servers. This makes the internet vulnerable to censorship and downtime.

  IPFS addresses this problem by allowing files to be stored and served by any node in the network, making it more resilient to censorship and downtime.

- **Slow load times**: The traditional client-server model of the internet can lead to slow load times as files must be requested from a centralized server and transmitted over long distances.

  IPFS addresses this problem by using a content-addressed system, where files are given unique hashes based on their content, rather than their location. This means that files are cached locally on nodes, reducing the amount of bandwidth required to serve them and increasing the speed of access.

- **Inefficient data transfer**: The traditional client-server model of the internet can lead to inefficient data transfer as files must be transmitted over long distances and may be duplicated on multiple servers.

  IPFS addresses this problem by allowing files to be distributed across the network and served from multiple nodes, reducing the amount of bandwidth required to transmit them.

IPFS aims to create a more decentralized and efficient internet where files can be stored and served by any node in the network, making it more resilient to censorship and downtime, and reducing load times and inefficient data transfer. These are only a few examples where you can apply or use IPFS. For a detailed explanation of all the benefits, please refer to the product documentation at `https://docs.ipfs.tech/`.

Understanding IPFS use cases

Now, we will see some of the use cases where IPFS comes in handy. There are many potential use cases for IPFS, some of which include the following:

- **Decentralized file sharing**: IPFS can be used for peer-to-peer file sharing, where files are stored and served by any node in the network, rather than centralized servers. This can be useful for sharing large files, such as media files, and can help reduce the load on centralized servers.

- **Content delivery networks** (**CDNs**): IPFS can be used as a decentralized CDN, where files are cached on nodes throughout the network, reducing the amount of bandwidth required to serve them and increasing the speed of access.

- **Distributed data storage**: IPFS can be used for distributed data storage, where files are stored across the network rather than on centralized servers. This can be useful for applications that require high levels of data redundancy and durability.

- **Blockchain-based applications**: IPFS can be used in conjunction with blockchain technology to create dApps that require decentralized storage and content distribution.

- **Offline content sharing**: IPFS can be used for offline content sharing, where files are stored on portable devices and shared between devices using IPFS. This can be useful for scenarios where internet connectivity is limited or unavailable, such as in remote or disaster-stricken areas.

These are just a few use cases; there are many more where IPFS can be very effective and ideal. The adoption of IPFS has significantly grown in the Web3 ecosystem in the last 2 years.

IPFS life cycle

IPFS offers a different life cycle than a regular file management system. The life cycle of data in IPFS can be broken down into several stages, which are as follows:

- **Adding data to IPFS**: The first stage of the IPFS data life cycle involves adding data to the IPFS network. This can be done using the IPFS CLI or an IPFS-enabled application.

  When data is added to IPFS, it is split into blocks, and each block is given a unique content-addressed hash based on its content. These hashes are used to identify and retrieve the data later.

- **Pinning data**: Once data has been added to IPFS, it needs to be pinned to ensure that it is not garbage-collected and removed from the network. Pinning tells the IPFS network to keep a particular block or file in its cache so that it is always available for retrieval.

  Pinning can be done manually using the IPFS CLI, or automatically using an IPFS-enabled application.

- **Retrieving data**: To retrieve data from IPFS, a user or application sends a request to the IPFS network with the content-addressed hash of the desired data.

  The IPFS network then looks for the requested data in its cache or on nearby nodes and retrieves it if available. If the data is not available, the network will search for it on other nodes in the network until it is found.

- **Verifying data**: When data is retrieved from IPFS, it is important to verify its authenticity using the content-addressed hash. This ensures that the data has not been tampered with or corrupted during transmission.

  IPFS uses cryptographic hashing algorithms to ensure that data cannot be tampered with or corrupted without detection.

- **Removing data**: When data is no longer needed, it can be removed from IPFS by unpinning it. This tells the IPFS network that the data is no longer needed and can be garbage-collected.

However, it is important to note that removing data from IPFS does not delete it from the network entirely as other nodes may still have cached copies of the data.

How does IPFS work?

IPFS is a system and network that's built to enable a decentralized approach to storing and sharing multimedia content across a distributed filesystem. Let's see how it works.

Adding data to IPFS

The first step in using IPFS is to add data to the network. This can be done using the IPFS CLI or an IPFS-enabled application.

When data is added to IPFS, it is split into blocks, and each block is given a unique content-addressed hash based on its content. These hashes are used to identify and retrieve the data later.

For example, let's say you want to add a file called example.txt to IPFS. You would use the following command in the IPFS CLI:

```
ipfs add example.txt
```

IPFS would then split the file into blocks and assign each block a content-addressed hash.

Pinning data

Once data has been added to IPFS, it needs to be pinned to ensure that it is not garbage collected and removed from the network. Pinning tells the IPFS network to keep a particular block or file in its cache so that it is always available for retrieval.

Pinning can be done manually using the IPFS CLI, or automatically using an IPFS-enabled application.

For example, to pin the `example.txt` file you added in the previous step, you would use the following command in the IPFS CLI:

```
ipfs pin add <hash>
```

Here, `<hash>` is the content-addressed hash of the file.

Retrieving data

To retrieve data from IPFS, a user or application sends a request to the IPFS network with the content-addressed hash of the desired data.

The IPFS network then looks for the requested data in its cache or on nearby nodes and retrieves it if available. If the data is not available, the network will search for it on other nodes in the network until it is found.

For example, to retrieve the `example.txt` file you added earlier, you would use the following command in the IPFS CLI:

```
ipfs cat <hash>
```

Here, `<hash>` is the content-addressed hash of the file.

Verifying data

When data is retrieved from IPFS, it is important to verify its authenticity using the content-addressed hash. This ensures that the data has not been tampered with or corrupted during transmission.

IPFS uses cryptographic hashing algorithms to ensure that data cannot be tampered with or corrupted without detection.

For example, to verify the integrity of the `example.txt` file you retrieved earlier, you would use the following command in the IPFS CLI:

```
ipfs cat <hash> | shasum -a 256
```

Here, `<hash>` is the content-addressed hash of the file.

Removing data

When data is no longer needed, it can be removed from IPFS by unpinning it. This tells the IPFS network that the data is no longer needed and can be garbage collected.

However, it is important to note that removing data from IPFS does not delete it from the network entirely, as other nodes may still have cached copies of the data.

IPFS works by using a content-addressed system, where files are given unique hashes based on their content, rather than their location. When a file is requested, the IPFS network uses the hash to locate and retrieve the file from the nearest node with a copy of it. This means that files are cached locally on nodes, reducing the amount of bandwidth required to serve them and increasing the speed of access.

In this section, we'll provide some useful information about IPFS. As a beginner, you need to know what IPFS is, how it works, and some basic use cases where you can apply it.

The size of the IPFS network is constantly changing as new nodes join and leave the network. It is believed that, as of August 2021, there were 2 million users, 200,000 nodes, and about 125 TB worth of data being accessed weekly.

It is difficult to give the exact number of files stored in the IPFS network as this is constantly changing. However, you can get an estimate by looking at the number of objects stored in the IPFS network. According to *IPFSStats*, over 25 million objects are stored in the IPFS network as of September 2021.

IPFS is designed to handle files of any size, from small documents to large media files. The size of files stored in the IPFS network varies widely, from a few bytes to terabytes in size.

IPFS nodes are located all over the world. The IPFS network is decentralized, meaning that files can be stored and served by any node in the network. This makes the network more resilient to censorship and downtime.

We will use IPFS in the next few chapters in our coding exercises and examples. Infura has an IPFS service built in as a service. Like creating a project for node access, you will use Infura, create a project for IPFS, and start using IPFS without any setup required.

Before you move on to the next chapter, you should have an account with Infura, a project created for IPFS, and an API and secret keys at hand.

Summary

In this chapter, we got into the core of Web3 development. We learned about the different Ethereum clients and some of the widely used libraries. We also learned about testnets and how to access them. We saw a couple of development frameworks for Web3, including Hardhat, which we are already familiar with and will be using most of the time in this book. However, getting familiar with Hardhat is something I strongly recommend. Then, we learned about node providers and the pros and cons of hosting a node. We also created an account with Infura so that we can use it in our exercises moving forward. Finally, we learned about IPFS, a distributed storage service, and how it made a huge impact on the NFT economy.

While talking about IPFS, we uncovered its purpose and use cases. We also explained the life cycle of data in IPFS and covered the steps involved in adding, pinning, retrieving, verifying, and removing data. Finally, we learned about IPFS gateways, including their advantages and disadvantages, and covered an example of the IPFS public gateway.

In the next chapter, we will start coding our first Web3 application using Hardhat, Infura, MetaMask, VSCode, and React.js.

8

Writing and Testing Your First dApp on Web3

In this chapter, we will cover the essential steps to set up your development environment and create your first **decentralized application (dApp)** using the Hardhat framework.

We will start by guiding you through the process of setting up your development environment, including installing the necessary tools and dependencies. With your environment ready, we'll move on to creating a new Hardhat project, using a pre-built Hardhat template that provides a solid starting point for our dApp.

Once we have our smart contract setup, we'll compile and migrate it to the Ethereum network, making it ready for interaction. Testing is crucial to ensure the integrity and correctness of our smart contract, so we'll also guide you through writing test cases to verify its behavior.

However, a dApp wouldn't be complete without a user interface, right? In the later part of this chapter, we'll walk you through creating a simple web interface that allows users to interact with our smart contract. You'll see how to use simple JavaScript to communicate with the Ethereum network from the browser.

By the end of this chapter, you'll have a fully functional dApp running on your local development environment. So, let's roll up our sleeves and get started on our journey into the exciting world of Web3 development!

In this chapter, we're going to cover the following main topics:

- Compiling, deploying, and testing smart contracts
- Running the Web3 dApp

Technical requirements

Before you dive into creating your ERC20 token, you'll need to ensure that you have the following technical requirements set up and ready:

- **Operating system (OS)**: You can choose any OS that you are comfortable with. The examples in this guide use macOS, but it is flexible to your preference.
- **GitHub CLI**: Make sure you have the **GitHub command-line interface** (**CLI**) installed and access to GitHub. This is essential for version control and collaboration.
- **Visual studio code (VS Code)**: Install VS Code, a popular code editor that makes smart contract development more convenient.
- **Node.js**: Ensure you have Node.js installed. This runtime environment is necessary to run JavaScript-based applications.
- **Node package manager (npm)**: This comes bundled with Node.js. It is used to manage packages and dependencies in your projects.
- **Hardhat**: Install Hardhat, a development environment for Ethereum that simplifies smart contract development and testing.
- **Web browser**: You will need a web browser of your choice. The examples here use Chrome, but you can use your preferred browser.

Once you have confirmed that you have all these technical requirements set up and running smoothly, you are all set to proceed with the next steps to create your ERC20 token.

Configuring and setting up an environment

In this section, we need to ensure that we have all the prerequisites in place and functional for the successful execution of the project. The setup involves two main parts:

- The first part focuses on verifying and ensuring the availability of required tools and software
- The second part involves cloning the pre-coded project to build and run it successfully

> **Note**
> Most of the installation instructions are in *Chapter 3*; please refer to it if you have not completed the setup.

To ensure that you have all the prerequisites set up correctly to run the project successfully, follow these steps:

- **Node.js and npm**: Make sure you have *Node.js* and npm installed on your laptop/desktop.

- **Git CLI**: Install the Git CLI if you don't have it already. On macOS, you can use Homebrew to install Git by running the following command in the terminal:

  ```
  brew install git
  ```

- **Hardhat**: Hardhat should be installed and configured.

- **MetaMask**: Ensure that you have MetaMask installed in your browser.

- **Browser**: You will need a browser of your choice to interact with the project. The examples shown in this chapter use Chrome, but you can use any modern browser such as Safari, Firefox, or Brave.

Once you have all the prerequisites set up, you can proceed to the next part, which is to Git-clone the pre-coded project and build it successfully.

Here's a step-by-step guide on how to access and use the code repository:

1. Use the GitHub CLI, as shown here. The repository you need to clone is at `https://github.com/PacktPublishing/The-Essential-Guide-to-Web3`. If you have already cloned this GitHub repository, you can ignore this step:

   ```
   git clone https://github.com/PacktPublishing/The-Essential-
   Guide-to-Web3
   ```

2. After you've successfully cloned the project, open it in VS Code, and your workspace should resemble the configuration shown in *Figure 10.1*.

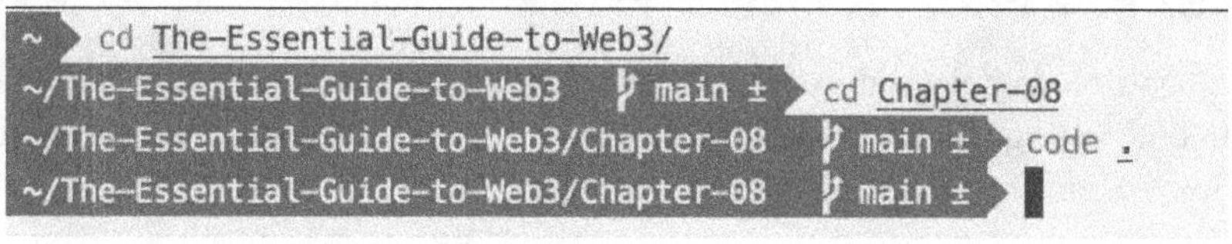

Figure 8.1 – Git checkout and an open project in VS Code

The code will open VS Code with the `project` folder, and it should look as shown in *Figure 8.2*.

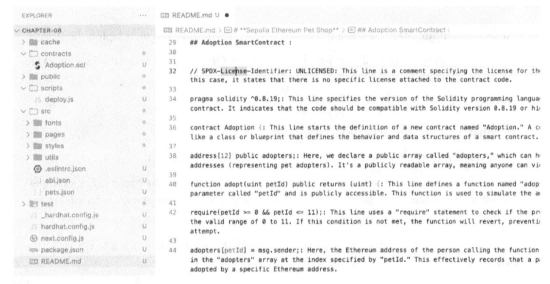

Figure 8.2 – VS Code showing the project structure

Figure 8.2 shows the directory structure that is required for a Hardhat project. Here, you can find a line-by-line explanation of the smart contract code in the README.md file.

This section ensures that all the necessary prerequisites are in place and functional for the smooth execution of the project. It covers the setup of required tools and software, including Node.js, Git, Hardhat, MetaMask, and a compatible web browser. It also guides you through the process of cloning the pre-coded project and successfully building and running it on your MacBook Pro.

Compiling, deploying, and testing the smart contracts

The Git project has already been unboxed for your convenience, and it is now prepared for you to the compilation and testing of smart contracts. Follow the steps outlined as follows to successfully compile and deploy a smart contract on the Hardhat blockchain:

1. Launch VS Code on your computer. Navigate to the project folder that contains the unboxed Hardhat project. The following figure provides an example of how the project folder should look.

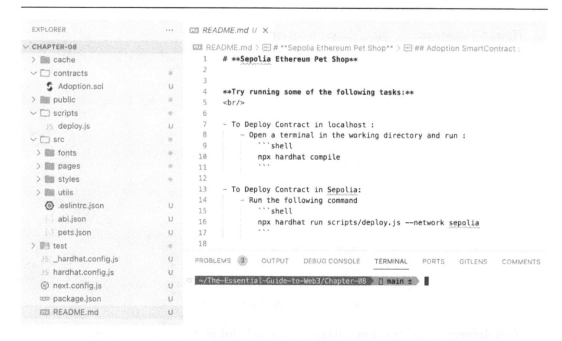

Figure 8.3 – VS Code with the Sepolio Pet Store project

2. Now that you are in the project folder within VS Code, you can proceed to compile and deploy the smart contracts to the Hardhat local blockchain. This process will involve using the Hardhat commands and interacting with the blockchain to simulate the deployment.

3. The project folder in VS Code provides you with an environment to manage and interact with your smart contracts effectively. Remember to refer to the documentation or instructions specific to your project for accurate details on compilation and deployment procedures.

4. Now, run the following command in the terminal window to compile the smart contract:

```
npm install
```

Figure 8.4 shows an example of the expected output.

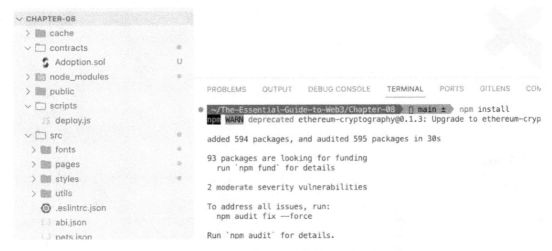

Figure 8.4 – Installing project dependencies

Now, the project dependencies and binaries are installed in the project `root` directory, and we are ready to move on to compiling the smart contracts.

5. Next, run the following command to compile the `Adoption.sol` smart contract.

    `npx hardhat compile` will compile the smart contract and add a new folder, `artifacts/`. This folder holds all the required files for the dApp to use in the next section.

Figure 8.5 – A Hardhat smart contract compiled

6. Now, we have a compiled contract, and the next step is to deploy this contract to the blockchain. We will use a live testnet called **Sepolia** for this purpose.

7. You need to add the following to the `hardhat-config.js` first:

    *   `INFURA_API_KEY`: This variable holds the URL to connect to the Sepolia network via Infura. You can find this URL in your Infura account, which we set up earlier in *Chapter 7*.

    *   `YOUR SEPOLIA PRIVATE KEY`: This is your wallet's private key for Sepolia. Remember, we learned about private keys in *Chapter 3* while using MetaMask wallets. It is crucial to keep your private key safe and never share it in your code or any configurations. If your private key gets exposed, it could lead to the loss of your wallet and the funds within it. So, protect it carefully. Copy your private key from MetaMask and replace the placeholder.

8. Ensure that you have just one `hardhat-config.js` file in your project directory. If there is another file with the same name (`hardhat-config.js`), make sure to rename it to something else. This step is essential to prevent any conflicts or interference with our work on Sepolia.

```js
JS hardhat.config.js > [@] <unknown> > 🧩 solidity
 1  require("@nomicfoundation/hardhat-toolbox");
 2
 3  // Go to https://infura.io, sign up, create a new API key
 4  // in its dashboard, and replace "KEY" with it
 5  const INFURA_API_KEY = "KEY";
 6
 7  // Replace this private key with your Sepolia account private key
 8  // To export your private key from Coinbase Wallet, go to
 9  // Settings > Developer Settings > Show private key
10  // To export your private key from Metamask, open Metamask and
11  // go to Account Details > Export Private Key
12  // Beware: NEVER put real Ether into testing accounts
13  const SEPOLIA_PRIVATE_KEY = "YOUR SEPOLIA PRIVATE KEY";
14
15  module.exports = {
16    solidity: "0.8.9",
17    networks: {
18      sepolia: {
19        url: `https://sepolia.infura.io/v3/${INFURA_API_KEY}`,
20        accounts: [SEPOLIA_PRIVATE_KEY]
21      }
22    },
23  solidity: {
24    version: "0.8.9",
```

Figure 8.6 – The Infura key and wallet private key

Once you have made the required changes and the variables shown in *Figure 8.6*, you need to deploy the smart contract to the **Ethereum Sepolia TestNet**.

9. Run the following command:

```
npx hardhat run scripts/deploy.js --network sepolia
```

This will deploy the smart contract to the Sepolia TestNet. *Figure 8.7* shows an example of the deployment output.

Figure 8.7 – A smart contract to deployed the Sepolia TestNet

Please note the deployer address (this is the wallet address that you configured in the previous step) and the contract address, which is created for you when the deployment is completed. We need this information for use with the dApps in the next section.

10. Let us verify a couple of things here before we move on to run the dApp in the next section. We got a confirmation from the command line that the smart contract was deployed. Let us verify that in the Sepolia TestNet explorer and examine some of the details. Open a new browser at `https://sepolia.etherscan.io/`.

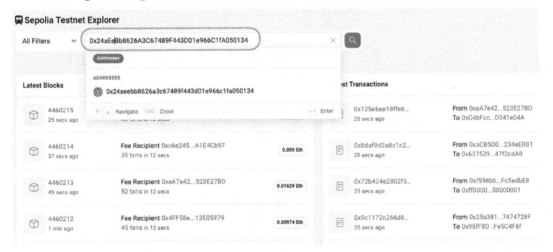

Figure 8.8 – The Sepolia Etherscan page

Search for the contract address, as shown in *Figure 8.8*, and go to the smart contract details page.

11. Pay attention to the data highlighted in *Figure 8.9*. These attributes are very important, and you should understand all of them.

Figure 8.9 – An overview of the smart contract details

In the **Overview** section, **ETH BALANCE** shows zero. This is because we haven't set any initial balance to the smart contract, as this was not in our scope of things to do. In the **More Info** section, you can see the smart contract address and the transaction that created this contract. There is a table at the bottom that shows the **Transactions** section, including **Transaction Hash**, **Block**, and a few other details, including **Txn Fee (Transaction Fee)**. Right above them, there are a few more tabs, including the highlighted tab called **Contract**.

Figure 8.10 – An overview of etherscan smart contract details

Figure 8.9 shows a sample of the **Contract** tab. You can also see the contract code here. If you are not able to see it, that means you have not verified the contract, which is a separate step and not part of this exercise. Refer to the *Deploying and verifying smart contracts* section in *Chapter 5*.

12. The last step is to log in to MetaMask and prepare it so that when we run the dApp, we get the desired results.

Figure 8.11 – MetaMask account details

As shown in *Figure 8.11*, choose the **Sepolia** TestNet, the corresponding account we used to deploy the smart contract, and also make sure there is enough **SepoliaETH (ETH)** to pay the gas fee.

Now, we are ready to launch the dApp, make a few transactions, and verify them in Etherscan in the next section.

Running the Web3 dApp

Now, we have come to the last step in the exercise of our goal to launch a dApp and create a Web3 application, end to end. Let us jump right into it:

1. Open your VS Code editor and locate the `index.js` file. Within this file, you'll need to update the `contractAddress` variable to reflect the contract that we deployed in the previous section. *Figure 8.12* provides an example.

```
src > pages > JS index.js > ...
  1    import Head from 'next/head'  5.5k (gzipped: 2k)
  2    import Image from 'next/image'  14.3k (gzipped: 5.5k)
  3    import styles from '../styles/Home.module.css'
  4    import {ethers} from 'ethers'  458.4k (gzipped: 189.6k)
  5    import { useEffect, useState } from "react";  4.2k (gzipped: 1.8k)
  6
  7    import nftAbi from "../abi.json"
  8    import pets from "../pets.json"
  9
 10    const contractAddress = "0x24aEeBb8626A3C67489F443D01e966C1fA050134" //sepolia
 11

PROBLEMS  3    OUTPUT    DEBUG CONSOLE    TERMINAL    PORTS    GITLENS    COMMENTS

~/The-Essential-Guide-to-Web3/Chapter-08    main ±
```

Figure 8.12 – Changing the contract address in the dApp

This will ensure that the dApp will use the correct contract to call and return the expected values from the contract and complete our exercises.

2. Next, let us start our dApp from the command line:

```
npm run dev
```

This command will deploy and run a dApp (web app) and the URL will be published as shown in *Figure 8.13*:

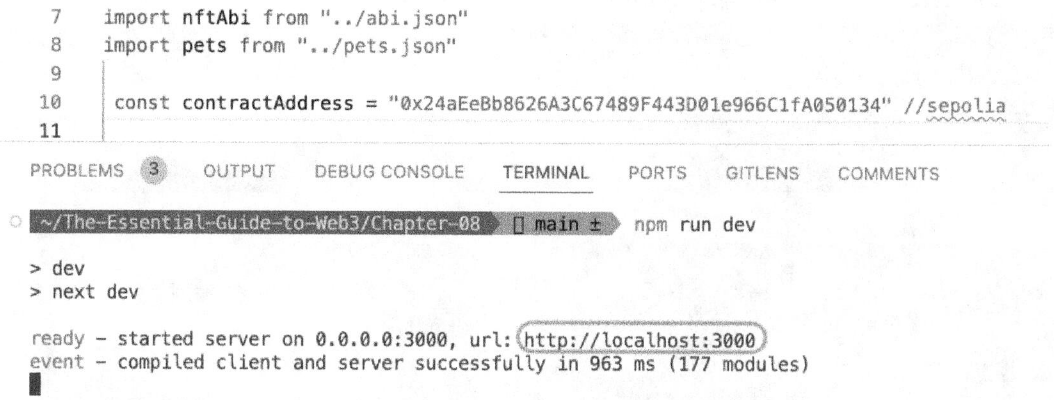

```
  7    import nftAbi from "../abi.json"
  8    import pets from "../pets.json"
  9
 10    const contractAddress = "0x24aEeBb8626A3C67489F443D01e966C1fA050134" //sepolia
 11

PROBLEMS  3    OUTPUT    DEBUG CONSOLE    TERMINAL    PORTS    GITLENS    COMMENTS

~/The-Essential-Guide-to-Web3/Chapter-08    main ±    npm run dev

> dev
> next dev

ready - started server on 0.0.0.0:3000, url: http://localhost:3000
event - compiled client and server successfully in 963 ms (177 modules)
```

Figure 8.13 – Starting the dApp from the command line

Note the published URL, which is http://localhost:3000. Open this URL in a new window.

3.   Now, we have launched our Pet Shop dApp. The next step is to interact with the smart contract and make some pet adoptions. First, click the **Connect Wallet** button to connect to MetaMask.

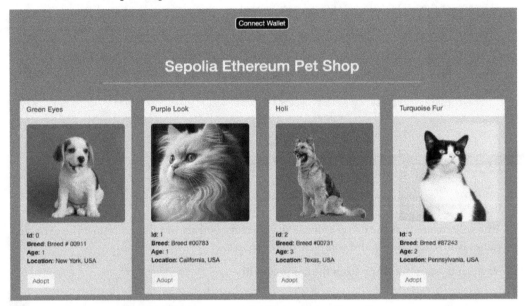

Figure 8.14 – The Sepolia Ethereum Pet Shop dApp

This should result in connecting to MetaMask, and the wallet address should be displayed on the screen, as shown in *Figure 8.15*.

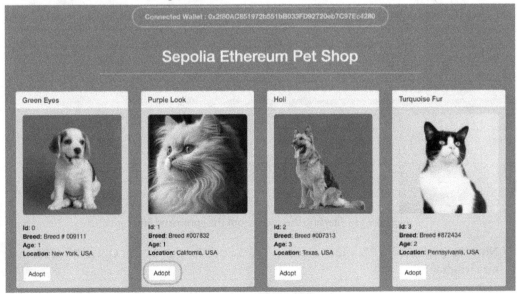

Figure 8.15 – Connected to the wallet

Also, note that the **Adopt** button is now enabled, as shown in *Figure 8.15*. Open MetaMask, and make sure you are connected to the correct address and the Sepolia TestNet, as shown in *Figure 8.16*.

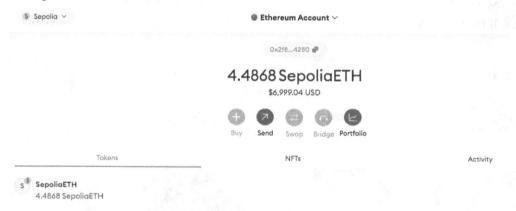

Figure 8.16 – Verifying the MetaMask setup

Now, we are all set to play with the Sepolia Ethereum Pet Shop dApp, make a few transactions, and complete the exercise and our chapter.

4.   Let's select a pet from the browser that you'd like to adopt and experience how the dApp interacts with the live blockchain. Once you click on the **Adopt** button, MetaMask will open a modal window, displaying a preview of the transaction that will be submitted to the Sepolia TestNet.

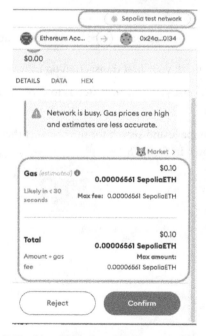

Figure 8.17 – MetaMask showing a transaction preview

Pay close attention to the highlighted sections in *Figure 8.17*. This step ensures that we post the transaction to the correct network and pay the appropriate gas fees.

5.   Once you've reviewed this information, proceed by clicking the **Confirm** button.

6.   If the transaction executes successfully, you should observe the **Adopt** button changing to **Adopted**, as illustrated in *Figure 8.18*.

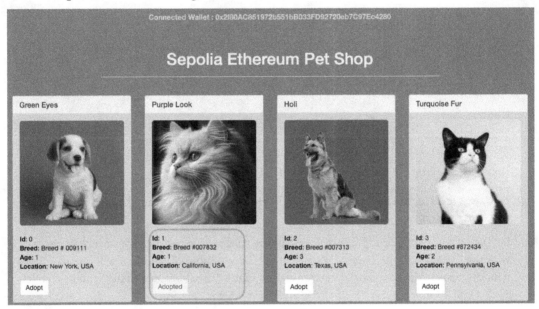

Figure 8.18 – A pet adopted, and the transaction is successful

Congratulations! This may mark your first transaction on Ethereum, the first of many to come.

However, we're not finished just yet! Our next step is to explore Sepolia and see the details of this blockchain transaction.

7.   Open the Sepolia Etherscan page and search for the contract that we deployed. It should look something like what is shown in *Figure 8.19*.

Figure 8.19 – An overview of sepolia Etherscan showing the transaction

This solidifies the transaction's success, confirming that we have created a dApp capable of generating and submitting transactions to the Sepolia TestNet. We have also successfully signed the transaction through MetaMask.

8. As a final step, let's explore how to query the smart contract using Etherscan, confirming that the pet we adopted is indeed stored on the blockchain. To do this, navigate to the **Contract** tab and click on the **Read Contract** button. You'll notice a **Connect to Web3** button; click on it and establish a connection with MetaMask. Ensure that you use the same account that was utilized to initiate the transaction. Refer to *Figure 8.20* for a visual reference.

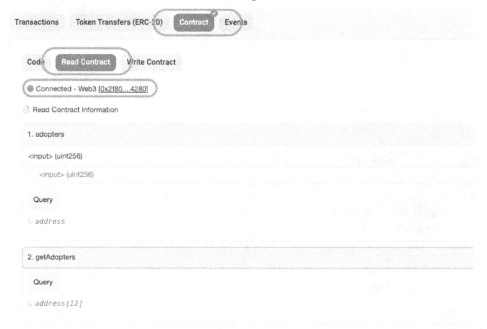

Figure 8.20 – Connecting to a smart contract via Etherscan

Now, you have the ability to query the smart contract directly from the live Sepolia TestNet. This enables you to retrieve information about the adopters and verify whether the pet has indeed been adopted and recorded on the blockchain.

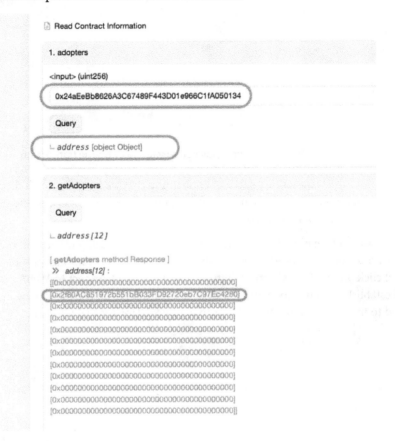

Figure 8.21 – Querying a contract via Etherscan

Figure 8.21 provides compelling evidence that the initial query targeting `adopters` has successfully returned an `address` object. This result, while promising, can be further refined and utilized through programming for more precise parsing. This outcome serves as a solid confirmation that our query is indeed operational and capable of returning a list of addresses belonging to **adopters**.

Subsequently, when we executed the `getAdopters` query, it returned a set of 12 *addresses*. In *Figure 8.21*, we can see that with address[1] index value corresponding to pet ID 2, which we selected for adoption, we have obtained the associated address.

With this successful sequence of actions, we have established a seamless end-to-end transaction journey from our dApp to the Sepolia testnet, and we can confidently assert that we have effectively verified the results.

Summary

In this chapter, we embarked on a journey to set up our development environment and create our very first **dApp**) using the Hardhat framework. We began by configuring our development environment, ensuring that we had all the necessary tools and dependencies installed.

Once our environment was primed, we ventured into creating a new Hardhat project. We kicked off the project with the help of a pre-built Hardhat template, offering a solid foundation for our dApp development endeavors. With our smart contract set up, we took the crucial steps of compiling and deploying it to the Ethereum network, thereby making it ready for interaction.

However, a dApp is not complete without a user interface. Hence, we dedicated the latter part of the chapter to crafting a simple web interface that would enable users to interact with our smart contract. We harnessed the power of JavaScript to communicate seamlessly with the Ethereum network straight from the browser.

Finally, we achieved a fully operational dApp, running smoothly in our local development environment. This marked our initiation into the exciting realm of Web3 development. In the next chapter, we embark on an enlightening journey into the realm of tokenization, unraveling its intricacies and exploring its diverse applications.

Part 4 –
Fungible Tokens

This part introduces you to the fascinating world of tokenization. It begins with a comprehensive overview of tokenization, helping you understand its fundamental concepts and importance in various blockchain ecosystems. As you dive deeper into the chapters, you'll embark on a practical journey to create your very first fungible token. This hands-on experience empowers you to grasp the intricacies of token creation, from concept to implementation. This part provides the knowledge and guidance needed to become proficient in creating and managing tokens in the blockchain space.

This section has the following chapters:

- *Chapter 9, Introduction to Tokenization*
- *Chapter 10, Creating Your First Token*

9

Introduction to Tokenization

A token represents the ownership of something. A majority of blockchain use cases start with a token. Fungible tokens are all identical and cannot be distinguished from each other; currencies are an example of fungible tokens. **Non-fungible tokens** (NFTs) are all unique. They're adapted to represent legal documents, luxury goods, pieces of art, and so on, whereas hybrid tokens are a mix of both as they introduce token classes. A class can be tranches of a pool of securities, a container on a ship, and so on. Adopting a modular strategy provides the necessary adaptability to meet the needs of both conventional stakeholders and crypto-oriented audiences, thereby facilitating the merging of **decentralized finance** (DeFi) and **centralized finance** (CeFi) into a tangible reality.

In this chapter, we will discuss the possibilities of creating a real-world asset with tokens, creating new business models with tokens, and looking at examples of digital assets with decentralized finance.

In this chapter, we're going to cover the following main topics:

- What is tokenomics?
- Common token standards in Ethereum
- Tokenizing real-world assets

What is tokenomics?

Token economics, also known as **tokenomics**, is a concept in the field of cryptocurrencies and blockchain technology that refers to the study and design of economic systems that govern the creation, distribution, and management of digital tokens within a decentralized ecosystem. Token economics aims to create a well-balanced, sustainable, and incentivized structure for participants in a blockchain network or a **decentralized application** (dApp).

Some of the key aspects of token economics are as follows:

- **Token supply**: The total number of tokens that can ever exist and the schedule for their creation, such as fixed supply, inflationary, or deflationary models

- **Token distribution**: The process and methods by which tokens are allocated to different stakeholders in the ecosystem, such as **initial coin offerings** (**ICOs**), token sales, airdrops, mining, or staking rewards

- **Token utility**: The various use cases and functionalities of the token within the ecosystem, such as governance rights, access to services, payment for goods or services, or as a medium of exchange

- **Incentive mechanisms**: The strategies used to encourage the desired behavior from participants in the network, such as rewarding users for providing computing power, validating transactions, or maintaining the security and stability of the network

- **Governance**: The decision-making processes and structures that determine the future development and management of the ecosystem, including voting rights, proposal systems, and dispute-resolution mechanisms

Understanding and designing effective token economics is crucial for the success of any blockchain-based project as it helps create an environment that is secure, stable, and attractive to both investors and users.

Token supply

Token supply refers to the total number of tokens or coins in a particular blockchain or decentralized ecosystem. It plays a critical role in determining the scarcity and value of cryptocurrency. This token supply can be divided into various categories, each with its unique characteristics and implications for the project's tokenomics. We'll cover these in the following subsections.

Fixed supply

A fixed supply model involves a predetermined number of tokens that will ever be created. Once the supply cap is reached, no more tokens can be minted or created. This scarcity can lead to an increase in the token's value as demand grows while supply remains constant.

For example, Bitcoin is the most famous example of a fixed-supply cryptocurrency, with a maximum supply of 21 million coins. The supply of Bitcoin is released through a process called mining, where miners are rewarded with newly minted bitcoins for validating transactions and maintaining the network's security.

Inflationary supply

An inflationary supply model involves the continuous creation of new tokens, increasing the total supply over time. This approach can help maintain the incentives for participants in the network, such as miners or validators, as the rewards do not run out. However, the increase in token supply may lead to a decrease in the token's value over time if the demand for the token does not grow at the same pace.

Ethereum, in its **proof-of-work (PoW)** implementation, had an inflationary supply. Although there was no fixed cap on the total number of **Ether (ETH)** that could be created, the issuance rate was gradually reduced through adjustments in the mining rewards.

Deflationary supply

In a deflationary supply model, the total number of tokens in circulation decreases over time. This can happen through various mechanisms, such as token burning (removing tokens from circulation permanently) or implementing deflationary monetary policies. The reduction in token supply can create scarcity, which may lead to an increase in the value of the remaining tokens if the demand remains strong or grows.

Binance Coin (BNB) employs a deflationary model through token burning. Binance, the company behind BNB, periodically burns a portion of the BNB tokens based on their trading volume, effectively reducing the total supply. This approach aims to create scarcity and potentially increase the value of the remaining BNB tokens.

Dynamic supply

Some projects use dynamic supply models, which involve adjusting the token supply based on certain factors, such as market demand or the achievement of specific milestones. This flexibility can help maintain the balance between supply and demand, ensuring the token's stability and value.

Ampleforth (AMPL) is a cryptocurrency with a dynamic supply model. Its supply expands and contracts based on market demand, aiming to maintain a stable value by adjusting the supply according to a price target. This is achieved through a process called "rebase," which periodically adjusts the token balances of AMPL holders.

Each token supply model has its pros and cons, and the choice depends on the project's goals, target market, and desired economic incentives. A well-designed token supply strategy can contribute to the long-term success and sustainability of a blockchain or decentralized ecosystem.

Token distribution

Token distribution refers to the methods by which tokens are allocated to different stakeholders within a blockchain or decentralized ecosystem. The distribution process can significantly impact the project's overall success, adoption, and decentralization. Let's delve deeper into various token distribution methods and provide examples for each.

ICOs or token sales

ICOs are fundraising events where a project sells a portion of its tokens to early investors in exchange for capital, typically in the form of cryptocurrencies such as Bitcoin or ETH. The funds that are raised are often used for project development, marketing, and operations.

Ethereum conducted an ICO in 2014, raising around 31,500 bitcoin (worth about $18 million at the time) by selling ETH tokens to early investors. This capital helped the Ethereum project develop its platform and become one of the leading blockchain networks.

Airdrops

Airdrops involve distributing tokens to users or holders of another cryptocurrency for free or as a reward for participating in specific activities. Airdrops can help boost the awareness and adoption of a new token, as well as incentivize holding or using the associated platform.

OmiseGo (OMG) conducted an airdrop in 2017, distributing 5% of its total OMG token supply to Ethereum holders. This distribution helped increase awareness of the OmiseGo project and gave Ethereum users an incentive to explore and use the OmiseGo platform.

Mining or PoW rewards

In a PoW consensus algorithm, miners compete to solve complex mathematical problems, validating transactions and securing the network. As a reward, miners receive newly minted tokens and transaction fees, contributing to the token's distribution.

For example, Bitcoin uses a PoW consensus mechanism, where miners are rewarded with newly created bitcoins for solving mathematical problems and validating transactions. This process not only secures the network but also distributes new bitcoins to participants.

Staking or proof-of-stake rewards

In a **proof-of-stake (PoS)** consensus algorithm, users lock up or "stake" their tokens to help validate transactions and secure the network. In return, they receive a portion of newly minted tokens or transaction fees as rewards, based on their staked amount.

Cardano (ADA) uses a PoS consensus mechanism called Ouroboros. Users who stake their ADA tokens are rewarded with additional ADA, contributing to the token's distribution while incentivizing users to secure the network.

Developer allocations

A portion of the token supply is sometimes reserved for the project team, advisors, or partners. These allocations can serve multiple purposes, such as funding ongoing development, compensating team members for their efforts, or forming strategic partnerships.

In the case of the EOS ICO, 10% of the total token supply was allocated to the project's development team. This allocation provided funding for the ongoing development and maintenance of the EOS platform.

Grants and community programs

Some projects allocate tokens to fund grants or community programs, encouraging developers and users to contribute to the ecosystem by building applications, creating content, or participating in various activities.

The Graph, a decentralized protocol for indexing and querying data from blockchains, has a community treasury. This treasury funds grants, ecosystem development, and community engagement initiatives, helping grow and strengthen The Graph's ecosystem.

Token distribution methods can vary significantly between projects, with each approach presenting unique advantages and challenges. A well-designed token distribution strategy can promote decentralization, incentivize participation, and ensure the long-term sustainability of a project.

Token utility

Token utility refers to the various use cases and functionalities that a token offers within a blockchain or decentralized ecosystem. It's a crucial aspect of tokenomics as it can drive the demand, adoption, and value of the token. Different projects offer different utilities for their tokens, depending on their goals and target markets. Let's look at some common token utilities and provide some examples.

Governance rights

Tokens can grant holders the right to participate in decision-making processes that affect the ecosystem, such as voting on proposed changes, updates, or new features. This utility can incentivize users to be more involved in the project, fostering a sense of ownership and responsibility.

MakerDAO's governance token, MKR, allows holders to vote on proposals related to the Maker Protocol, such as adjusting stability fees, collateral parameters, or adding new collateral types is a perfect example.

Access to services

Tokens can be used to access specific services, features, or content within a dApp or platform. This utility can create demand for the token as users need to acquire and spend the token to access these services.

For example, **Filecoin (FIL)** is a decentralized storage network where users can pay with FIL tokens to rent storage space from other users or offer their storage capacity in return for FIL tokens.

Payment for goods or services

Tokens can function as a medium of exchange within an ecosystem, allowing users to pay for goods or services provided by other users or third parties.

For example, **Basic Attention Token** (BAT) is a digital advertising token that can be used by advertisers to purchase ad space and by users to tip content creators within the Brave browser ecosystem.

Staking or collateral

Tokens can be staked or used as collateral to secure a network, participate in consensus mechanisms, or access certain financial services, such as lending or borrowing.

In the **Aave protocol**, a decentralized lending platform, users can deposit tokens as collateral to borrow other cryptocurrencies. Aave's native token, AAVE, can also be staked to secure the platform and earn staking rewards.

Network fees

Some projects require users to pay network fees in their native tokens for specific activities or transactions, such as sending tokens, interacting with smart contracts, or using dApps. These fees can be used to incentivize network validators or fund future development.

Ethereum requires users to pay gas fees in ETH for transactions and smart contract interactions. These fees are paid to miners or validators for processing the transactions.

Store of value or unit of account

Tokens can serve as a store of value, allowing users to hold and transfer wealth within the ecosystem, or act as a unit of account, measuring the relative value of goods or services.

For example, Bitcoin is often considered a store of value due to its fixed supply and wide adoption, with some users referring to it as "digital gold."

Liquidity provision and rewards

Tokens can be used to provide liquidity to **decentralized exchanges** (DEXs) or other platforms, with users earning rewards in the form of transaction fees or additional tokens.

For example, **Uniswap**, a DEX, allows users to provide liquidity by depositing pairs of tokens into liquidity pools. In return, users receive LP tokens, which represent their share of the pool and can be redeemed for a portion of the trading fees generated by the DEX.

Token utility is a crucial aspect of any blockchain or decentralized project. By offering valuable use cases and functionalities, a project can drive demand, adoption, and long-term success for its token and ecosystem.

Token incentive mechanisms

Token incentive mechanisms are strategies that are used to encourage the desired behavior of participants in a blockchain or decentralized ecosystem. These mechanisms can promote network security, stability, and user engagement, contributing to the overall success and sustainability of the project. Let's look at some common token incentive mechanisms and provide examples of each.

Mining or PoW rewards

In a PoW consensus algorithm, miners compete to solve complex mathematical problems, validating transactions and securing the network. As a reward for their efforts, miners receive newly minted tokens and transaction fees. This mechanism incentivizes miners to provide computing power and maintain the network's security.

Bitcoin uses a PoW consensus mechanism, where miners are rewarded with newly created bitcoins for solving mathematical problems and validating transactions. This process secures the network and distributes new bitcoins to participants.

Staking or PoS rewards

In a PoS consensus algorithm, users lock up or "stake" their tokens to help validate transactions and secure the network. In return, they receive a portion of newly minted tokens or transaction fees as rewards, based on their staked amount. This mechanism encourages users to hold and stake tokens, contributing to network security and stability.

Cardano (ADA) uses a PoS consensus mechanism called **Ouroboros**. Users who stake their ADA tokens are rewarded with additional ADA, incentivizing them to secure the network and validate transactions.

Liquidity provision rewards

Some **DeFi** platforms offer rewards for users who provide liquidity to DEXs or other protocols. These rewards can come in the form of transaction fees or additional tokens and serve to incentivize users to contribute liquidity, promoting the smooth functioning of the platform.

Uniswap, a DEX, rewards users who deposit pairs of tokens into liquidity pools with a portion of the trading fees generated by the platform. These users also receive LP tokens, representing their share of the pool, which can be redeemed for the underlying assets.

Governance rewards

Some projects offer rewards for participating in governance, such as voting on proposals or contributing to the development and management of the ecosystem. These rewards can come in the form of additional tokens or other benefits, incentivizing users to be more involved and take responsibility for the project's success.

For example, **MakerDAO** rewards MKR token holders who participate in governance by voting on proposals related to the Maker Protocol, such as adjusting stability fees or collateral parameters. This incentive mechanism encourages active involvement in the decision-making process.

Token-based incentive programs

Projects may offer token-based incentives for various activities, such as referring new users, creating content, or completing tasks within the ecosystem. These incentives can drive user engagement, adoption, and growth.

We already saw that BAT rewards users for viewing ads and engaging with content within the Brave browser ecosystem. Users can earn BAT tokens, which can be used to tip content creators or be redeemed for other goods and services.

Network fee redistribution

Some projects redistribute a portion of the network fees that are collected from users to other participants, such as validators, stakers, or token holders. This mechanism can incentivize users to contribute to the network's security or hold tokens as they can receive a share of the network's revenue.

Ethereum 2.0, which employs a PoS consensus mechanism, rewards validators with a portion of the transaction fees generated on the network. This incentive mechanism encourages users to stake their ETH and contribute to the network's security and stability.

Token incentive mechanisms play a vital role in the success and sustainability of blockchain and decentralized projects. By incentivizing users to participate, contribute, and engage with the ecosystem, these mechanisms can drive adoption, growth, and long-term value for the token and the project.

Token governance

Token governance refers to the decentralized decision-making process within a blockchain or decentralized ecosystem, where token holders can influence the project's development, direction, and policies. Governance is a crucial aspect of decentralized projects as it promotes transparency, fairness, and community involvement.

Let's look at some common token governance models and examples.

Direct voting

In a direct voting model, token holders can vote on proposals related to the project's development, updates, or new features. The weight of a user's vote is typically proportional to the number of tokens they hold, which means that users with more tokens have a larger influence on the decision-making process.

MakerDAO uses a direct voting model for its governance token, **MKR**. Token holders can vote on proposals related to the Maker Protocol, such as adjusting stability fees and collateral parameters, or adding new collateral types. The weight of each user's vote is proportional to the amount of MKR they hold.

Delegated voting

In a delegated voting model, token holders can delegate their voting power to other users or entities, who then vote on their behalf. This model allows users who may not have the time, expertise, or interest to participate directly in governance to still have a say in the project's direction.

Compound, a DeFi lending platform, uses a delegated voting model for its governance token, COMP. Token holders can delegate their voting power to other users, who then vote on proposals related to the platform's development, updates, or new features.

Liquid democracy

Liquid democracy combines elements of both direct and delegated voting. In this model, token holders can either vote on proposals directly or delegate their voting power to other users. Delegates can, in turn, delegate their accumulated voting power to others, creating a flexible and dynamic voting system.

Polkadot uses a liquid democracy model for its governance token, **DOT**. Token holders can either vote directly on proposals or delegate their voting power to other users, who can also delegate their voting power further down the line. This system enables a more nuanced and adaptable governance process.

Governance through decentralized autonomous organizations (DAOs)

DAOs are decentralized organizations that use blockchain technology and smart contracts to manage their operations, decision-making processes, and resources. Token holders can participate in governance by submitting proposals, voting on decisions, and allocating resources within the DAO.

The Kyber Network, a decentralized exchange and liquidity protocol, transitioned to a DAO-based governance model in 2020. Token holders of **Kyber Network Crystal** (**KNC**) can participate in the KyberDAO, voting on proposals related to the protocol's development, updates, and fee structure.

Multi-layered governance

Some projects employ multi-layered governance models, which combine different governance mechanisms or involve multiple decision-making entities within the ecosystem. These models can provide a more robust and flexible governance process, catering to various needs and preferences within the community.

Tezos, a blockchain platform with a focus on formal verification and secure smart contracts, employs a multi-layered governance model. Token holders can participate in different stages of the governance process, such as proposing, discussing, and voting on protocol upgrades. The process includes multiple rounds of voting and testing before a proposed upgrade is implemented.

Token governance is a critical aspect of decentralized projects as it enables community members to have a say in the project's direction and decisions. By fostering a sense of ownership and responsibility, token governance models can contribute to the long-term success and sustainability of a blockchain or decentralized ecosystem.

Common token standards in Ethereum

Ethereum, as a platform, supports the creation and use of several types of tokens. Tokens built on Ethereum usually follow specific standards that define a set of rules and functions that make them compatible with existing wallets, exchanges, and dApps. Let's look at some of the most common Ethereum token standards.

ERC-20

The **Ethereum Request for Comments 20 (ERC-20)** standard is a widely adopted token standard on the Ethereum network. ERC-20 tokens are fungible, meaning that each token is interchangeable with another of the same type. They follow a predefined set of rules and functions, ensuring compatibility with a wide range of wallets, exchanges, and dApps.

Here are some examples of ERC-20 tokens:

- **Chainlink (LINK):** A decentralized oracle network token used to connect smart contracts with off-chain data
- **BAT:** A digital advertising token used to reward users for their attention within the Brave browser ecosystem
- **USD Coin (USDC):** A stablecoin pegged to the US dollar that's used in various DeFi applications for lending, borrowing, and trading

The ERC-20 standard defines a set of six functions and two events that a smart contract must implement to be considered ERC-20 compliant. Here is a simplified example of an ERC-20 token smart contract:

```solidity
// SPDX-License-Identifier: MIT
pragma solidity ^0.8.7;


// Import the ERC-20 interface from OpenZeppelin, a library of secure
and audited smart contract code
import "@openzeppelin/contracts/token/ERC20/ERC20.sol";


// Define the BookToken contract, which inherits from the ERC20
contract
contract BookToken is ERC20 {
    // The constructor function is executed once when the contract is
deployed
    // It sets the name and symbol of the token and mints all initial
tokens to the address that deploys the contract
    constructor(uint256 initialSupply) ERC20("Book", "BOK") {
        _mint(msg.sender, initialSupply);
    }
}
```

In this example, we are using the `OpenZeppelin` Contracts library, which provides a secure and audited implementation of the ERC-20 standard:

- `pragma solidity ^0.8.7;`: This line specifies the Solidity compiler version required for the smart contract. The caret symbol (`^`) indicates that the contract is compatible with any version greater than or equal to 0.8.0 but less than 0.9.0.

- `import "@openzeppelin/contracts/token/ERC20/ERC20.sol";`: This line imports the ERC20 contract from the `OpenZeppelin` Contracts library, which provides a secure, audited, and well-tested implementation of the ERC-20 standard.

- `contract BookToken is ERC20 { ... }`: This line defines the `ExampleToken` contract, which inherits from the imported ERC20 contract. This means that the `ExampleToken` contract will inherit all the functions and properties of the ERC20 contract, making it compliant with the ERC-20 standard.

- `constructor(uint256 initialSupply) ERC20("Book", "BOK") { ... }`: This line defines the constructor function for the `ExampleToken` contract. The constructor function is called only once when the contract is deployed. In this case, it takes an argument, `initialSupply`, which represents the initial supply of tokens. The `ERC20("BookToken", "BOK")` part is a call to the constructor of the parent ERC20 contract, setting the token's name to `"BookToken"` and the symbol to `"BOK"`.

- `_mint(msg.sender, initialSupply);`: This line calls the _mint function, which is an internal function provided by the ERC20 contract. The _mint function creates new tokens and assigns them to the specified address. In this case, the `msg.sender` address (the address deploying the contract) receives `initialSupply` of tokens.

This simple example demonstrates the creation of an ERC-20-compliant token using the `OpenZeppelin` Contracts library. This contract can be deployed to the Ethereum network, and users can interact with it to transfer, approve, and manage their **BookToken (BOK)** balances.

Now, let's look at the six functions and two events that are required to call a contract ERC-20 compliant. These functions and events provide a standardized way for wallets, exchanges, and other smart contracts to interact with the token.

Here are the six functions:

- `totalSupply()`: This function returns the total token supply. It is a constant function that does not modify the state of the blockchain, and it does not cost any gas to call.

  Example:

  ```
  function totalSupply() public view returns (uint256);
  ```

- `balanceOf(address _owner)`: This function returns the token balance of a specific address (`_owner`). It is a constant function, meaning it does not modify the state of the blockchain and does not cost any gas to call.

  Example:

  ```
  function balanceOf(address _owner) public view returns (uint256
  balance);
  ```

- `transfer(address _to, uint256 _value)`: This function transfers a specific amount (`_value`) of tokens from the message sender's address to the specified recipient address (`_to`). It returns a Boolean value indicating whether the transfer was successful. This function modifies the state of the blockchain, so it consumes gas.

  Example:

  ```
  function transfer(address _to, uint256 _value) public returns
  (bool success);
  ```

- `approve(address _spender, uint256 _value)`: This function allows the message sender to approve another address (`_spender`) to withdraw a specified amount (`_value`) of tokens from the sender's balance. It returns a Boolean value indicating whether the approval was successful. This function modifies the state of the blockchain, so it consumes gas.

  Example:

  ```
  function approve(address _spender, uint256 _value) public
  returns (bool success);
  ```

- `allowance(address _owner, address _spender)`: This function returns the number of tokens that an owner (`_owner`) has allowed another address (`_spender`) to withdraw from their balance. It is a constant function, meaning it does not modify the state of the blockchain and does not cost any gas to call.

  Example:

  ```
  function allowance(address _owner, address _spender) public view
  returns (uint256 remaining);
  ```

- `transferFrom(address _from, address _to, uint256 _value)`: This function allows a third party (`_spender`) to transfer a specified amount (`_value`) of tokens from one address (`_from`) to another (`_to`). `_spender` must have an allowance (previously set by the `approve` function) to do so. It returns a Boolean value indicating whether the transfer was successful. This function modifies the state of the blockchain, so it consumes gas.

  Example:

  ```
  function transferFrom(address _from, address _to, uint256 _
  value) public returns (bool success);
  ```

Here are the two events:

- `Transfer(address indexed _from, address indexed _to, uint256 _value)`: This event is emitted when a token transfer occurs. It includes the sender address (`_from`), the recipient address (`_to`), and the amount of tokens transferred (`_value`). Events allow clients to efficiently track token transfers without scanning the entire blockchain.

  Example:
  ```
  event Transfer(address indexed _from, address indexed _to,
  uint256 _value);
  ```

- `Approval(address indexed _owner, address indexed _spender, uint256 _value)`: This event is emitted when an approval occurs. It includes the owner's address (`_owner`), the approved spender's address (`_spender`), and the number of tokens approved for withdrawal (`_value`).

These interfaces make it easy to launch a token and also ensure some of the best practices and security concerns with tokenization. With these standards in place, it hardly takes any time for a developer to implement an ERC20 token smart contract and take it into production.

ERC-20 is the widely used token standard with Ethereum. The whole concept of tokenization evolved from the ERC-20 standard. In this section, we learned about the core functions and implementations of fungible tokens with ERC-20. Now, let's look at the NFT standards.

ERC-721

The ERC-721 standard defines rules for creating NFTs on the Ethereum network. Unlike ERC-20 tokens, each ERC-721 token is unique and cannot be directly replaced by another. ERC-721 tokens are often used to represent digital collectibles, art, or other digital assets with individual characteristics and value. A well-known example of ERC-721 tokens is *CryptoKitties*, a blockchain-based virtual game that allows users to collect, breed, and trade unique digital cats. We will do a deep dive into ERC-721 in the next chapter.

ERC-1155

The ERC-1155 standard is a more advanced and flexible token standard that combines the benefits of both fungible (ERC-20) and non-fungible (ERC-721) tokens. ERC-1155 tokens can represent multiple types of assets within a single contract, allowing developers to create and manage a wide range of digital items more efficiently. This standard is particularly useful for gaming platforms, where various types of assets (such as in-game currency, items, or characters) need to coexist and be managed simultaneously. We will do a deep dive into ERC-1155 in the next chapter.

ERC-777

The ERC-777 standard is an improved and backward-compatible version of the ERC-20 standard, offering additional functionality and security features. ERC-777 tokens support advanced token interactions, allowing users to approve and transfer tokens in a single transaction, reducing complexity and gas costs. They also offer better protection against accidental token loss by implementing a token-receiving function that can reject tokens sent in error.

Some of the key features of ERC-777 tokens are as follows:

- **Advanced token interactions**: ERC-777 tokens support sending and receiving tokens in a single transaction, reducing complexity and gas costs compared to ERC-20 tokens

- **Better protection against token loss**: ERC-777 implements a token-receiving function that can reject tokens sent in error, preventing accidental token loss

- **Compatibility with ERC-20**: ERC-777 tokens are backward-compatible with ERC-20 tokens, which means they can interact with existing wallets, exchanges, and dApps

These are only some of the features ERC-777 offers. For more details and to find the full feature list, please refer to the Ethereum EIP documentation.

Examples of ERC-777 tokens are relatively scarce compared to ERC-20 tokens, but some projects have started adopting the standard:

- **Aventus (AVT)**: A blockchain-based protocol that aims to improve the event ticketing industry by offering a more transparent and secure ticketing process

- **Kleros (PNK)**: A decentralized dispute resolution platform that uses the ERC-777 standard for its native token, allowing users to participate in the platform's arbitration process

Here's a simplified example of an ERC-777 token smart contract:

```
import "@openzeppelin/contracts/token/ERC777/ERC777.sol";
contract ExampleToken is ERC777 {
    constructor(address[] memory defaultOperators, uint256
initialSupply) ERC777("ExampleToken", "EXT", defaultOperators) {
        _mint(msg.sender, initialSupply, "", "");
    }
}
```

This example also uses the `OpenZeppelin` Contracts library, which provides a secure and audited implementation of the ERC-777 standard:

- `import "@openzeppelin/contracts/token/ERC777/ERC777.sol";`: This line imports the ERC777 contract from the `OpenZeppelin` Contracts library, which provides a secure, audited, and well-tested implementation of the ERC-777 standard.

- `contract ExampleToken is ERC777 { ... }`: This line defines the `ExampleToken` contract, which inherits from the imported ERC777 contract. This means that the `ExampleToken` contract will inherit all the functions and properties of the ERC777 contract, making it compliant with the ERC-777 standard.

- `constructor(address[] memory defaultOperators, uint256 initialSupply) ERC777("ExampleToken", "EXT", defaultOperators) { ... }`: This line defines the constructor function for the `ExampleToken` contract. The constructor function is called only once when the contract is deployed. In this case, it takes two arguments – `defaultOperators`, which is an array of addresses that have default control over all tokens, and `initialSupply`, which represents the initial supply of tokens. The `ERC777("ExampleToken", "EXT", defaultOperators)` part is a call to the constructor of the parent ERC777 contract, setting the token's name to `"ExampleToken"`, the symbol to `"EXT"`, and the default operators for the token.

- `_mint(msg.sender, initialSupply, "", "");`: This line calls the `_mint` function, which is an internal function provided by the ERC777 contract. The `_mint` function creates new tokens and assigns them to the specified address.

The ERC-721 standard has indeed revolutionized the realm of blockchain by enabling the creation of NFTs on the Ethereum blockchain. It has provided a standardized set of rules and functions that all NFTs must adhere to, facilitating developers to launch their unique tokens with ease.

ERC-721 is vital in the Ethereum ecosystem, simplifying the process of minting unique tokens that can represent ownership or proof of authenticity over a vast range of tangible and intangible assets. Each token minted under the ERC-721 standard is unique, distinguishing it from other tokens, even those in the same collection. This uniqueness is what makes these tokens non-fungible.

The introduction of the ERC-721 standard has significantly expanded the scope of tokenization, allowing the creation of tokens that can represent unique assets, such as digital art, collectibles, real estate, and much more. The standard has also addressed the complexities and security concerns associated with tokenizing unique assets.

Now that we have explored the fundamentals and applications of the ERC-721 standard for NFTs, let's discover another standard, ERC-223.

ERC-223

The ERC-223 standard is another improved version of the ERC-20 standard, focusing on addressing the issue of lost tokens. In the ERC-20 standard, if a user accidentally sends tokens to a smart contract that is not designed to handle them, the tokens are lost forever. ERC-223 tokens include a `tokenFallback` function that prevents tokens from being lost in such situations by checking if the receiving contract can handle ERC-223 tokens before executing the transfer.

Although the ERC-223 standard is not as widely adopted as ERC-20 or ERC-777 standards, some projects have utilized the ERC-223 token standard, such as **ChainZilla (ZILLA)**, a company that offers blockchain development and deployment services, utilizing the ERC-223 standard for its native token.

Here is a simplified example of an ERC-223 token smart contract:

```
import "./ERC223/ERC223.sol";
contract ExampleToken is ERC223 {
    constructor(uint256 initialSupply) {
        _name = "ExampleToken";
        _symbol = "EXT";
        _decimals = 18;
        _totalSupply = initialSupply;
        _balances[msg.sender] = initialSupply;
    }
}
```

In this example, we assume that the ERC223 contract has been implemented separately, following the ERC-223 standard, and is imported into the `ExampleToken` contract.

- `import "./ERC223/ERC223.sol";`: This line imports the ERC223 contract, which provides a secure, audited, and well-tested implementation of the ERC-223 standard.

- `contract ExampleToken is ERC223 { ... }`: This line defines the `ExampleToken` contract, which inherits from the imported ERC223 contract. This means that the `ExampleToken` contract will inherit all the functions and properties of the ERC223 contract, making it compliant with the ERC-223 standard.

- `constructor(uint256 initialSupply) { ... }`: This line defines the constructor function for the `ExampleToken` contract. The constructor function is called only once – when the contract is deployed. In this case, it takes one argument, `initialSupply`, which represents the initial supply of tokens.

- `_name = "ExampleToken";`: This line sets the name of the token to `"ExampleToken"`.

- `_symbol = "EXT";`: This line sets the symbol of the token to `"EXT"`.

- `_decimals = 18;`: This line sets the number of decimals for the token to `18`, which is a common choice for most tokens.

- `_totalSupply = initialSupply;`: This line sets the total supply of the token to the initial supply provided during the contract deployment.

- `_balances[msg.sender] = initialSupply;`: This line assigns the entire initial supply of tokens to the address that deploys the contract (`msg.sender`).

This simple example demonstrates the creation of an ERC-223-compliant token using a custom implementation of the ERC-223 standard. This contract can be deployed to the Ethereum network, and users can interact with it to transfer, approve, and manage their **ExampleToken** (**EXT**) balances. The contract also includes the `tokenFallback` function to prevent accidental token loss when sending tokens to incompatible contracts.

These are some of the most common Ethereum token standards, each serving different purposes and offering unique features for developers and users. By providing these standards, Ethereum has enabled the creation of a vast ecosystem of tokens and digital assets that can be seamlessly integrated with various wallets, exchanges, and dApps.

Now, let's learn about tokenizing real-world assets, one of the most looked-upon topics for the adoption of Web3 and blockchain.

Tokenization

You have probably heard of the term **digital assets**. In Ethereum, tokenization is a simple way to create digital assets. Your tokens are a kind of digital asset. In simple terms, making traditional assets such as money, real estate, and creative work into digital tokens on the web is how you turn them into digital assets in the Web3 world. It involves creating a business model around these tokens to use them in the digital economy. Theoretically, you can tokenize anything that has a physical or virtual form in this world.

Tokenization refers to the process of digitally representing ownership of physical or non-physical assets on a blockchain network. Ethereum, with its versatile and robust platform for creating smart contracts, has emerged as a popular choice for asset tokenization.

Tokenization is the process of converting rights to an asset into a digital token on a blockchain. For example, valuable commodities such as real estate, artwork, precious metals, or company shares can be tokenized and represented as digital tokens on the Ethereum blockchain. Each token represents a specific share or ownership in each asset, with the ownership details transparently and immutably recorded on the blockchain.

Tokenizing real-world assets – examples

Consider high-value artwork. Tokenizing such an asset enables the ownership to be fractionally divided among numerous stakeholders, each holding a token representing a fraction of the artwork's total value. The tokens are easily tradable, and owners can sell their tokens to other parties without intermediaries, reducing costs and increasing speed.

Real estate, one of the most lucrative investment assets globally, can also benefit from tokenization. An owner can tokenize a property, dividing it into numerous tokens, each representing a fraction of the property's total value. Investors can then buy these tokens, owning a fraction of the property, and enjoy returns from its future appreciation or rental income.

This has opened up new opportunities in finance and investment, making it easier for individuals and organizations to issue, trade, and manage assets. Here are the key benefits of tokenization:

- **Accessibility**: Tokenization democratizes access to high-value asset investments. Fractionalizing ownership lowers the entry barrier, enabling small investors to participate.
- **Liquidity**: Tokenizing assets increases their liquidity. Typically, selling high-value assets is a lengthy process, but with tokens, owners can sell fractions of their assets quickly and easily, enhancing liquidity.
- **Transparency**: The use of blockchain technology ensures transparency and immutability. Every transaction involving token transfers is recorded, reducing the risk of fraud.
- **Cost-effective**: Tokenization can reduce or eliminate the need for intermediaries, cutting down transaction costs significantly.

While tokenization offers enormous potential, it's also important to consider the challenges and risks involved, such as regulatory uncertainties or the technological complexity of managing digital tokens. However, as the technology matures and regulations catch up, tokenization is set to revolutionize various industries, from finance to real estate, fine art, and beyond.

Now, let's see how we can leverage tokenization to create new business models.

Creating new business models through tokenization

Tokenization opens numerous innovative business models. One such model is fractional ownership, where multiple investors can own a portion of a high-value asset. This model enables individuals to participate in lucrative markets that were previously only accessible to wealthy investors or large corporations.

Companies can also raise capital by issuing security tokens, representing shares of company stock, and bypassing traditional fundraising methods. These tokens can be traded in a secondary market, providing liquidity for investors.

Furthermore, tokenization can create new possibilities in the sharing economy. For instance, a group of people can tokenize and collectively own a vacation home and smart contracts could manage the time-sharing of the property.

Tokenizing digital assets involves converting the rights to a digital asset into a digital token on a blockchain. Digital assets include things such as music, art, photographs, and domain names, among other things.

Let's take the example of digital art, a field that has garnered substantial attention recently with the rise of NFTs. A digital artist can tokenize their artwork and sell it on an NFT marketplace.

Here are the steps in detail:

1. **Create the artwork**: First, the artist creates digital artwork. This artwork is a digital asset, existing in a digital format and possessing value.

2. **Tokenization**: Next, the artist decides to tokenize the artwork. They do this by minting an NFT that represents the artwork on a blockchain that supports NFTs, such as Ethereum. This NFT is unique and carries information about the artwork, such as its origin, ownership, metadata, and the artist's signature. The NFT now represents the digital rights to the artwork.

3. **List the artwork on a marketplace**: The artist can then list the NFT for sale on a marketplace that supports NFT transactions, such as *OpenSea* or *Rarible*. They set a price for the NFT, and potential buyers can view the listing.

4. **Sale and ownership transfer**: When a buyer purchases the NFT, the ownership of the digital token is transferred to the buyer. The transaction is recorded on the blockchain, confirming the transfer of ownership. The buyer now owns the digital rights to the artwork.

5. **Secondary market**: After the initial sale, the NFT can be resold or traded on the secondary market. Every time it's sold, the blockchain records a new transaction, creating an immutable history of ownership.

The benefit of this process is that it allows digital artists to maintain ownership and control over their work while also profiting from its sale. Tokenizing digital art also brings much-needed transparency to the art world, with clear, immutable records of ownership and provenance. It is an excellent example of how tokenization can add value to digital assets, enabling creators to monetize their work in new ways and providing buyers with proof of ownership and authenticity.

Now, let's look into the financial world and how tokenization could revolutionize the way banks and financial institutions do business.

Tokenizing financial instruments such as bonds involves converting the rights to an asset into a digital token on a blockchain. This process is often referred to as **security tokenization** because these financial instruments are typically considered securities under most jurisdictions.

Let's use the example of a corporate bond to illustrate this process:

1. **Create the bond**: A corporation issues a bond as a means of raising capital. This bond is a financial instrument, representing a loan made by an investor to the corporation.

2. **Tokenization**: Next, the corporation decides to tokenize the bond. This involves creating digital tokens on a blockchain network, each representing a fraction of the total value of the bond. This process may involve a technology platform specialized in security tokenization, which helps ensure that the tokenization process complies with applicable securities laws and regulations.

3. **List the bond on a security token exchange**: Once tokenized, the bond tokens can be listed on a regulated security token exchange. Potential investors can then purchase these tokens. The listing price would typically represent the face value of the bond, divided by the number of tokens.

4. **Trade and ownership transfer**: When an investor purchases the bond tokens, the ownership of the tokens transfers to the investor, and this transaction is recorded on the blockchain. The investor now owns a portion of the bond.

5. **Interest payments and redemption**: The terms of the bond (such as interest payments and redemption) can be programmed into a smart contract associated with the token. This means that interest payments can be automatically paid to the token holders' digital wallets when due, and the tokens can be automatically repurchased by the corporation when the bond matures.

The advantage of this approach is that it allows for fractional ownership of bonds, potentially making it easier for a larger pool of investors to invest in bonds. Additionally, tokenization can increase liquidity in the bond market as token holders may be able to sell their tokens more easily than traditional bondholders. Lastly, the use of blockchain technology can also bring increased transparency and efficiency to the bond market as transactions are recorded on a transparent ledger, and the use of smart contracts can automate certain processes.

However, it is important to note that tokenizing bonds and other financial instruments is a complex process that needs to comply with a variety of securities laws and regulations. Furthermore, as this is a new and evolving field, various technological and operational challenges need to be overcome.

Now, let's move into the wild world of Web3. We have learned most of the basics required to be a beginner in the Web3 ecosystem.

Let's go to kindergarten! Yes, let's use **do it yourself (DIY)** toys to understand tokenization.

This section will let you visualize how a tokenization project works and help you relate to something that you are used to in your daily life and investments. We are going to use a DIY toy set to understand tokenization. A simple marble toy set will help you understand and appreciate the various aspects of tokenization. With this, you could start associating the work that you do in your organization or a side project, which could be a potential candidate for tokenization.

We are using a marble-based DIY toy model to create a token business. Here, marbles are the tokens and all the DIY toy pieces are various business assets or instruments that will help us build new business models. When the marbles run through these business models, we create investment and earning opportunities. Based on the route the marble takes from the top to the bottom and the various components it goes through, the output differences. This is similar to a financial system – when the tokens are created and traded via different business models, investors get different results in terms of yield, interest, dividend, and so on. With concepts such as fractional ownership and the ability to invest, a diverse portfolio could result in a solid return, though there are always risks associated, irrespective of any investment model.

The following figure summarizes the high-level steps that are involved in creating and launching a token or a tokenization business:

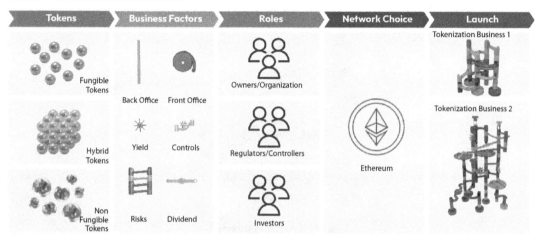

Figure 9.1 – Steps involved in creating a token business

Let's look at all the ingredients that are shown in the preceding figure and understand how they all come together to create a new business using tokens.

We learned a lot about tokens in this chapter and earlier chapters. In this context, token(s) can be one or a combination of fungible tokens, hybrid tokens, or NFTs. First, let's look at fungible tokens:

Figure 9.2 – Fungible tokens

Fungible tokens, as an asset class, are an excellent example of gold, bonds, cash, funds, and other fungible real-world assets that we want to tokenize. We create ERC-20 tokens in Ethereum to get them into a digital asset.

Hybrid tokens are asset classes where you can combine two or more fungible assets and tokenize them into a digital asset class. In the following figure, we are combining a few fungible assets to create a hybrid token asset. We can also create a hybrid token using fungible tokens and NFTs:

Figure 9.3 – Hybrid tokens

Each layer represents a token layer and how different asset classes can be combined to form a hybrid token type. When you start adding fungible and non-fungible into a mix, it becomes even more interesting and attractive for investors to take part in the tokenization program.

The third ingredient is a non-fungible *asset class*. Anything from art, music, movies, media, and so on can fall into the non-fungible category. The following figure represents an NFT asset class; the marbles are of varied sizes and colors and each possesses unique properties:

Figure 9.4 – NFTs

Any combination of these fungible and non-fungible asset classes can be combined to create a new token class. If it makes sense for the buyer, seller, or trader to invest, these possess excellent value in terms of investments and returns for the creators and how they perform in their life cycle.

Now, let's move on to the second set of ingredients, which is nothing but business components and factors just like DIY toys, and how they each have a certain function when put together. Remember that a simple component in the DIY toy system can be used in a few variations. This is how business factors and attributes can also be used in creating different business models. The following figure summarizes a list of various components that are involved in creating a DIY toy system for the marbles to flow in and out:

Figure 9.5 – Business components

Using these business components and factors, we can create simple to medium and complex business models. When we relate this to real-world business scenarios, the risks are also assessed based on the model types, how easy and attractive these investment proposals are, and how early we could expect returns.

Next, we will investigate the common people and roles that are usually associated with this business process from start to finish.

Individuals, owners, and organizations are the first category. They are the brains behind these new financial and business models. Second, regulators are anything that involves gain, returns, interests, and dividends that are subject to regulation in today's world, so they play a key role in assessing these new instruments and deciding and flagging risks associated with them. Lastly, the most key role is investors, who perform tokenization or create a new financial model to become successful.

The choice of a blockchain network is critical and it has its advantages and disadvantages. Some do not support tokenization, some have limitations on token standards, and so on. Ethereum is the ultimate choice in today's world for launching a new token play.

Next, we'll cover the model itself, which consists of a few of the ingredients we discussed previously. This become a new recipe for success in the tokenization world. The following figure represents three different models with three different approaches and many different outcomes when you roll the tokens (the marbles). These tokens follow a certain path, business model, or pattern and are monitored by the respective playing parties (regulators, owners, and investors). When this happens, we get different results and outcomes:

Figure 9.6 – Tokenization business models. Creating these models
could be challenging, similar to how it is in real life

If these models are created by different age groups, they would differ in terms of style, thinking, and purpose. This applies to the tokenization side as well; a matured and solid structure around the business process and workflows creates a strong model.

At this point, I hope you have a clearer understanding of tokenization. However, we only discussed this topic at a high level. There are lots of other factors to consider and when it comes to regulatory standards, a lot of the fancy models that look very attractive don't make it. It comes down to managing risk and managing it effectively.

With that, we can dive into the wild world of Web3. We have learned most of the basics that are required to be a beginner in the Web3 ecosystem.

Summary

In this chapter, we explored the concept of tokenization, where rights to a real-world or digital asset are converted into digital tokens on a blockchain. Tokenization democratizes access to investments, improves liquidity, and ensures transaction transparency.

We saw various examples of tokenization, such as fractionalizing high-value artwork or property and tokenizing digital art into NFTs. We also discussed how tokenization enables small investors to participate in markets that are typically reserved for wealthier individuals or larger organizations. We also explored how businesses can tokenize their assets, whether they're physical, digital, or financial, to create new opportunities and business models.

In the case of financial instruments such as bonds, we saw how they can be tokenized, making them more accessible and liquid, with transactions recorded transparently on a blockchain. However, we also highlighted that the tokenization process must comply with various securities laws and regulations, which presents a significant challenge in this nascent field. By exploring these topics, we gained valuable insights into tokenomics, Ethereum tokens, and smart contract development and testing processes.

In the next chapter, we will create our first token using ERC-20 standards. This will be a hands-on chapter, so get ready to create your first Ethereum-based token.

10

Creating Your First Token

The ERC-20 token specification is the widely accepted standard for Ethereum tokens, making it the go-to choice for most Ethereum contracts in use today. In this chapter, you'll learn how to create your own Ethereum token by following this established ERC-20 standard. This is a short chapter but an exciting one.

In this chapter, we're going to cover the following main topics:

- Writing your first ERC-20 token smart contract
- Deploying and testing the ERC-20 token smart contract

Technical requirements

Before you dive into creating your ERC-20 token, you'll need to ensure that you have the following technical requirements set up and ready:

- **Operating system (OS)**: You can choose any OS that you are comfortable with. The examples in this guide use MacOS, but it is up to your preference.

- **GitHub CLI:** Make sure you have the **GitHub command line interface** (**CLI**) installed and access GitHub. This is essential for version control and collaboration.

- **Visual Studio Code** (**VS Code**): Install VS Code, a popular code editor that makes smart contract development more convenient.

- **Node.js**: Ensure you have Node.js installed. This runtime environment is necessary for running JavaScript-based applications.

- **Node Package Manager** (**npm**): This comes bundled with Node.js. It is used for managing packages and dependencies in your projects.

- **Hardhat**: Install Hardhat, a development environment for Ethereum that simplifies smart contract development and testing.

- **Web browser**: You will need a web browser of your choice. The examples here use Chrome, but you can use your preferred browser.

Once you have confirmed that you have all these technical requirements set up and running smoothly, you are all set to proceed with the next steps to create your ERC-20 token.

Writing your first ERC-20 token smart contract

Creating your first token on the Ethereum network can be an exciting and rewarding experience. By following these simple steps, you can have your own custom token up and running in no time.

Here are the steps, but you should already be familiar with them from *Chapter 8*:

1. **Choose a token standard**: Select a token standard that suits your needs, such as ERC-20. ERC-20 is suitable for fungible tokens (tokens with equal value).

2. **Write the smart contract**: Using the Solidity programming language, write a smart contract that implements the chosen token standard. This contract will define the token's properties, such as name, symbol, and total supply, as well as its functionalities.

3. **Test the smart contract**: Before deploying the contract to the Ethereum network, test it on a local development environment or a testnet. This step helps identify and fix potential bugs and issues in the contract.

4. **Deploy the smart contract**: Once the contract has been thoroughly tested, deploy it to the Ethereum mainnet using a wallet such as MetaMask and a deployment platform such as Remix, Truffle, or Hardhat.

5. **Interact with the token**: After deploying the contract, interact with your token using a wallet or a **decentralized application** (**dApp**) to perform actions such as transferring tokens or approving allowances.

By following these steps, you will create a token on the Ethereum network that can be traded, held, and used in various applications. Always ensure to follow best practices and consult with experienced developers to ensure the security and functionality of your token.

To make the learning process smoother, we've already prepared the smart contract for you in a GitHub repository.

Here's a step-by-step guide on how to access and use it:

1. Use the GitHub CLI as follows. The repository you need to clone is here. If you have already cloned this GitHub repository, you can ignore this step:

```
https://github.com/PacktPublishing/The-Essential-Guide-to-Web3
git clone https://github.com/PacktPublishing/The-Essential-
Guide-to-Web3
```

2. After you've successfully cloned the project, open it in VS Code. Your workspace should resemble the configuration shown in *Figure 10.1*:

Figure 10.1 – Git checkout and open project in VS Code

3. The code. will open VS Code with the project folder and it should look like *Figure 10.2*:

Figure 10.2 – VS Code showing the project structure

Figure 10.2 shows the directory structure that is required for a Hardhat project. Here, you can find a line-by-line explanation of the smart contract code in the README.md file.

In summary, this contract creates a simple **ERC-20** token called MySimpleToken with the symbol STKN and an initial total supply of 1 million tokens. It inherits the functionality of the ERC-20 standard from the **OpenZeppelin** library and allows the contract creator to mint and manage these tokens.

Now, let's build the project first, compile the contract, test it, and deploy it into the Hardhat local blockchain environment:

1. Open a terminal in VS Code and start executing the following commands one by one:

```
npm install
```

2. This will set up the runtime requirements for the project, including all Node.js dependencies, Hardhat binaries, etc. Now you are ready to run the hardhat commands to compile, test, and deploy the smart contract code.

Now run the following:

```
npx hardhat compile
```

You should see a message stating that the smart contract has been successfully compiled and a new `artifacts` directory with all the binaries that got created by Hardhat with the `hardhat compile` command. This `artifacts` directory is essential for implementing scripts or programs that implement and calling the smart contract in the next section.

Now that we have a contract and we already ready to launch our own token let us deploy the contract and start testing it and mint and transfer some tokens.

Deploying and testing the ERC-20 token smart contract

You are already familiar with the steps to test a smart contract, but here is another method of testing the `MySimpleToken` contract.

The tests for the `MySimpleToken` smart contract are in the `test` folder and a file named `MySimpleToken.test.js`, which contains the following test cases:

- Test case 1 to create a token with a name
- Test case 2 to create a token with a symbol
- Test case 3 to check that tokens have the correct number of decimals
- Test case 4 to check whether the token has a valid total supply
- Test case 5 to check if users are able to query account balances
- Test case 6 to transfer the right amount of tokens to/from an account
- Test case 7 to see if the smart contract emits a transfer event with the right arguments
- Test case 8 to allow for allowance approvals and queries
- Test case 9 to emit an approval event with the right arguments
- Test case 10 to allow an approved sender to transfer tokens to the owner (60 ms)
- Test case 11 to emit a transfer event with the right arguments when conducting an approved transfer (53 ms)
- Test case 12 to allow allowance to be increased and queried (39 ms)
- Test case 13 to emit an approval event when allowance is increased

- Test case 14 to allow allowance to be decreased and queried (38 ms)

- Test case 15 to emit an approval event when allowance is decreased

These extensive test cases provide thorough validation of the `MySimpleToken` smart contract, ensuring its functionality and reliability in various scenarios. Now, let us get to the steps for running these test cases:

1. Run the following command to see if the unit test works and all test cases pass:

    ```
    npx hardhat run
    ```

    Figure 10.3 shows an example output of the test cases after you run the `npx hardhat run` command:

```
 ~/The-Essential-Guide-to-Web3/Chapter-10    main ±   npx hardhat test


MySimpleToken
  ✔ Test case 1 to create a token with a name
  ✔ Test case 2 to create a token with a symbol
  ✔ Test case 3 to check that Token a valid decimal
  ✔ Test case 4 to check whether Token has a valid total supply
  ✔ Test case 5 to check if able to query account balances
  ✔ Test case 6 to transfers the right amount of tokens to/from an account
  ✔ Test case 7 to see if the smart contact emits a transfer event with the right arguments
  ✔ Test case 8 to allow for allowance approvals and queries
  ✔ Test case 9 to emits an approval event with the right arguments
  ✔ Test case 10 to allows an approved spender to transfer from owner (60ms)
  ✔ Test case 11 to emit a transfer event with the right arguments when conducting an approved transfer (54ms)
  ✔ Test case 12 to allow allowance to be increased and queried (39ms)
  ✔ Test case 13 to emits approval event when alllowance is increased
  ✔ Test case 14 to allow allowance to be decreased and queried (39ms)
  ✔ Test case 15 to emits approval event when allowance is decreased


15 passing (2s)
```

Figure 10.3 – Hardhat test cases

2. Now that all the unit tests have been passed and confirmed, we can move on to deploying them into a local blockchain network. To deploy into the Hardhats local blockchain, no other configuration changes are required, but you need to first start the blockchain node by opening a new terminal window, making sure you are in the project directory, and running the following command:

    ```
    npx hardhat node
    ```

3. This command will bring up a local blockchain node with 20 default accounts that you can use for testing purposes. *Figure 10.4* shows a sample local Hardhat running in the same project folder:

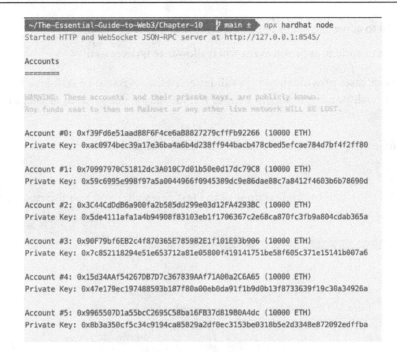

Figure 10.4 – Hardhat local blockchain

4. Now we have everything we need to deploy the smart contract to the blockchain. Run the following command from your VS Code terminal window:

```
npx hardhat run scripts/deploy.js --network localhost
```

Figure 10.5 shows the deployed contract. Please note the highlighted information in the image.

Figure 10.5 – Hardhat local blockchain

> **Important note**
>
> Note down the owner of the contract, which is usually the first address from the Hardhat blockchain. Also note down the `MySimpleToken` contract address. In this case, it is `0x5FbDB2315678afecb367f032d93F642f64180aa3`.

5. Now let us look at the blockchain node window to confirm whether the contract was deployed. *Figure 10.6* shows the deployment on the blockchain node window:

```
eth_accounts
eth_chainId
eth_call
  WARNING: Calling an account which is not a contract
  From: 0xf39fd6e51aad88f6f4ce6ab8827279cfffb92266
  To:   0x5fbdb2315678afecb367f032d93f642f64180aa3

eth_accounts
eth_chainId
eth_accounts
eth_blockNumber
eth_chainId (2)
eth_estimateGas
eth_getBlockByNumber
eth_feeHistory
eth_sendTransaction
  Contract deployment: MySimpleToken
  Contract address:    0x5fbdb2315678afecb367f032d93f642f64180aa3
  Transaction:         0x152ac8a114c52cc3681516acf7d19fe0d7eb847ac33575796659203cc6848fce
  From:                0xf39fd6e51aad88f6f4ce6ab8827279cfffb92266
  Value:               0 ETH
  Gas used:            1172081 of 1172081
  Block #1:            0xe759f59c910d317415b73a38089c70407f5412c8779974111c46114bb6ae7511
```

Figure 10.6 – MySimpleToken deployed

Pay attention to the highlighted section of *Figure 10.6*; it displays information about the transaction we created for the deployment of the smart contract `MySimpleToken`. You will also see that the contract address is the same as the one we got from the command line. Also note the from address, the gas used, and the block information. This confirms that we successfully deployed the contract to the blockchain node.

6. Next, we will start interacting with the smart contract running in the blockchain node.

    Now run the following command:

    ```
    npx hardhat run scripts/interact.js --network localhost
    ```

7. The interact.js script calls the smart contract MySimpleToken, invokes various methods/functions, and displays output using console.log statements. The following figure shows a sample of the output created by the interact.js script file:

```
~/The-Essential-Guide-to-Web3/Chapter-10    main ±    npx hardhat run scripts/interact.js —network localhost

Getting the My Simple Token Contract...

---------------------------------------------------
List of all ERC20 public functions called via Hardhat
---------------------------------------------------
The smart contract created the Token with Name: SimpleToken
The smart contract created the Token with Symbol: STKN
The smart contract created the Token with Decimals: 18
Smart Contract has a total supply of the STKN: 1000000.0
Smart contract owner at 0xf39Fd6e51aad88F6F4ce6aB8827279cffFb92266 has a STKN balance of 1000000.0
```

Figure 10.7 – interact.js script prints token information

Figure 10.7 shows a sample output of the interact.js which prints the token name, token symbol, decimals, total supply and smart contract token balance.

- The smart contract named SimpleToken uses the symbol STKN and has 18 decimal places for its tokens. There is a total supply of 1,000,000.0 STKN. The owner of this smart contract, whose address is 0xf39Fd6e51aad88F6F4ce6aB8827279cffFb92266, currently holds a balance of 900,100.0 STKN tokens. These outputs provide information about the attributes and initial state of the ERC-20 token contract, as well as the balance of the contract owner's STKN tokens.

- Now, if you look at the next section of the console.log statements, it prints interactions for all transfer functions between accounts and inquiring account balances and sets an approved number of tokens for spending.

```
---------------------------------------------------
An account transfer from one account to another
---------------------------------------------------
Initiating a transfer...
Transferring 100000 STKN tokens to 0x70997970C51812dc3A010C7d01b50e0d17dc79C8 from 0xf39Fd6e51aad88F6F4ce6aB8827279cffFb92266
Transfer completed
Balance of owner (0xf39Fd6e51aad88F6F4ce6aB8827279cffFb92266): 900000.0 STKN
Balance of recipient (0x70997970C51812dc3A010C7d01b50e0d17dc79C8): 100000.0 STKN

---------------------------------------------------
Set spending limits for accounts with 10000 tokens
---------------------------------------------------
Setting allowance amount of spender over the caller's STKN tokens...
This example allows the contractOwner to spend up to 10000 of the recipient's STKN token
Spending approved

---------------------------------------------------
An  transfer from one account to another
---------------------------------------------------
Getting the smart contract owner spending allowance over recipient's STKN tokens...
contractOwner Allowance: 10000.0 STKN

---------------------------------------------------
Transfer 100 Tokens from one account to another
---------------------------------------------------
contracOwner transfers 100 STKN from recipient's account into own account...
New owner balance (0xf39Fd6e51aad88F6F4ce6aB8827279cffFb92266): 900100.0 STKN
New recipient balance (0x70997970C51812dc3A010C7d01b50e0d17dc79C8): 99900.0 STKN
Remaining allowance: 9900.0 STKN
```

Figure 10.8 – interact.js script prints token transfer information

The output provided in *Figure 10.8* describes a series of actions and transactions involving a smart contract that manages STKN tokens.

Let's go through a summary of each section in *Figure 10.8*:

- **An account transfer from one account to another**: The transfer is initiated and successfully executed, resulting in the movement of 100,000 STKN from the sender to the recipient

  Following the transfer, the sender's balance is 800,100.0 STKN, while the recipient's balance stands at 199,900.0 STKN.

- **Set spending limits for accounts with 10000 tokens**: An allowance of 10,000 STKN is established for the recipient's account, permitting the contract owner to expend this amount.

  It is confirmed that the spending approval has been successfully granted, indicating that the contract owner now has permission to spend up to 10,000 STKN tokens from the recipient's account.

- **A transfer from one account to another**: The smart contract owner queries the spending allowance over the recipient's STKN.

  It's revealed that the contract owner has an allowance of 10,000 STKN to spend from the recipient's account.

- **Transfer 100 tokens from one account to another**: The contract owner initiates a transfer of 100 STKN from the recipient's account to their own account.

  The transfer is successful, resulting in a new balance of 800,200.0 STKN for the contract owner and 199,800.0 STKN for the recipient.

  The remaining allowance for the contract owner to spend from the recipient's account is 9,900.0 STKN.

In summary, these outputs demonstrate token transfers, allowance settings, and balance adjustments within the smart contract. The contract owner can spend tokens from the recipient's account, subject to the approved allowance amount. The balances are updated accordingly after each transaction.

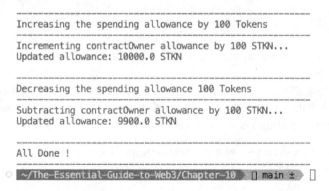

```
------------------------------------------------
Increasing the spending allowance by 100 Tokens
------------------------------------------------
Incrementing contractOwner allowance by 100 STKN...
Updated allowance: 10000.0 STKN

------------------------------------------------
Decreasing the spending allowance 100 Tokens
------------------------------------------------
Subtracting contractOwner allowance by 100 STKN...
Updated allowance: 9900.0 STKN

------------------------------------------------
All Done !
------------------------------------------------
~/The-Essential-Guide-to-Web3/Chapter-10    [] main ±   []
```

Figure 10.9 – interact.js script prints token spending information

The provided *Figure 10.9* outputs describe actions related to adjusting the spending allowance within a smart contract managing STKN. Here's a summary of each section:

- **Increasing the spending allowance by 100 tokens:** The contract owner increases their allowance by 100 STKN tokens. The updated allowance after the increase is 10,000.0 STKN.

- **Decreasing the spending allowance by 100 tokens:** The contract owner reduces their allowance by 100 STKN tokens. The updated allowance after the decrease is 9,900.0 STKN.

These outputs demonstrate the ability of the contract owner to adjust their spending allowance within the smart contract. The allowance can be both increased and decreased, allowing fine-grained control over the amount of tokens that can be spent from the recipient's account by the contract owner.

```
eth_chainId
eth_getTransactionByHash
eth_chainId
eth_call
  Contract call:       MySimpleToken#allowance
  From:                0xf39fd6e51aad88f6f4ce6ab8827279cfffb92266
  To:                  0x5fbdb2315678afecb367f032d93f642f64180aa3

eth_chainId
eth_estimateGas
eth_feeHistory
eth_sendTransaction
  Contract call:       MySimpleToken#decreaseAllowance
  Transaction:         0xb3af38c4cbea86ac1b359c07aa96e1e4f59003f711c17278ef6dd93b340be8a4
  From:                0x70997970c51812dc3a010c7d01b50e0d17dc79c8
  To:                  0x5fbdb2315678afecb367f032d93f642f64180aa3
  Value:               0 ETH
  Gas used:            30122 of 30122
  Block #6:            0xfc8ee7505931f57b16beb527eb5234ad9f19f7f621fefbce155257c473708f2b

eth_chainId
eth_getTransactionByHash
eth_chainId
eth_call
  Contract call:       MySimpleToken#allowance
  From:                0xf39fd6e51aad88f6f4ce6ab8827279cfffb92266
  To:                  0x5fbdb2315678afecb367f032d93f642f64180aa3
```

Figure 10.10 – Hardhat blockchains show confirmation of transactions

Finally, let's confirm that all these transactions have been recorded on the blockchain. You can check this by using the blockchain node window, which is illustrated in *Figure 10.10*. Here, you'll find details about each transaction, including gas usage, transaction hash, and block information.

Now that we've acquired the skills to deploy on local networks, it's time to take the next step and deploy on a live testnet. This real-world experience will help us learn more. Our next task is to deploy the MySimpleToken contract to the **Sepolia** testnet. We'll not only deploy it but also interact with the contract to understand how it functions.

Deploying into the Ethereum Sepolia testnet

We have two testnets to choose from: **Goerli** and **Sepolia**. We're going with Sepolia because Goerli is nearing its **End of Life** (**EOL**) (`https://github.com/eth-clients/goerli`) in January 2024.

To deploy on testnets, we'll need to make some adjustments to our project. Here is a summary of the changes required:

- A new `hardhat.config.js` with the required changes for deploying into Sepolia testnet.

  Here is the link to the Hardhat page: `https://hardhat.org/tutorial/deploying-to-a-live-network`.

- A MetaMask wallet address, including a private key.

- A new deploy script, `sepolia-deploy.js`, for deploying into Sepolia testnet.

- A new script to interact with Sepolia testnet `interact-sepolia.js`.

- Sepolia ETH to pay the gas fee.

All the changes are already available in the same project with different files named and qualified as **Sepolia**. The following image presents the Hardhat configuration changes for Sepolia:

```
JS hardhat.config.js > [●] <unknown> > solidity
1    require("@nomicfoundation/hardhat-toolbox");
2
3    // Go to https://infura.io, sign up, create a new API key
4    // in its dashboard, and replace "KEY" with it
5    const INFURA_API_KEY = "KEY";
6
7    // Replace this private key with your Sepolia account private key
8    // To export your private key from Coinbase Wallet, go to
9    // Settings > Developer Settings > Show private key
10   // To export your private key from Metamask, open Metamask and
11   // go to Account Details > Export Private Key
12   // Beware: NEVER put real Ether into testing accounts
13   const SEPOLIA_PRIVATE_KEY = "YOUR SEPOLIA PRIVATE KEY";
14
15   module.exports = {
16     solidity: "0.8.9",
17     networks: {
18       sepolia: {
19         url: `https://sepolia.infura.io/v3/${INFURA_API_KEY}`,
20         accounts: [SEPOLIA_PRIVATE_KEY]
21       }
22     },
23   solidity: {
24     version: "0.8.9".
```

Figure 10.11 – Hardhat configuration changes for Sepolia

In *Figure 10.11*, we can see two important variables that need to be defined:

- INFURA_API_KEY: This variable holds the URL for connecting to the Sepolia network via Infura. You can find this URL in your Infura account, which we set up earlier in *Chapter 7*.

- YOUR SEPOLIA PRIVATE KEY: This is your wallet's private key for Sepolia. Remember, we learned about private keys in *Chapter 3* while using MetaMask wallets. It's crucial to keep your private key safe and never share it in your code or any configurations. If your private key gets exposed, it could lead to the loss of your wallet and the funds within it. So, protect it carefully.

Ensure that you have just one hardhat-config.js file in your project directory. If there's another file with the same name (hardhat-config.js), make sure to rename it to something else. This step is essential to prevent any conflicts or interference with our work on Sepolia.

Deploying contracts to the network should be simple and straightforward. You need a script, an account (wallet address) with enough balance to pay for the gas fee and you are ready to deploy your token to the Sepolia testnet.

Follow these steps to deploy the smart contract:

1. Deploy the MySimpleToken contract to the Sepolia testnet:

    ```
    npx hardhat run scripts/deploy-sepolia.js --network sepolia
    ```

    This step will deploy the smart contract to the Sepolia network and you should see the contract/token address and the account used to deploy the smart contract.

Figure 10.12 – Contract deployed to Sepolia

Figure 10.12 displays the confirmation of the smart contract deployment on the Sepolia network. Take note of the account and the token address.

2. Next, open a new browser window or tab and visit https://sepolia.etherscan.io/. In the search box on this website, enter the token address you just noted. You should see a screen like in *Figure 10.13*:

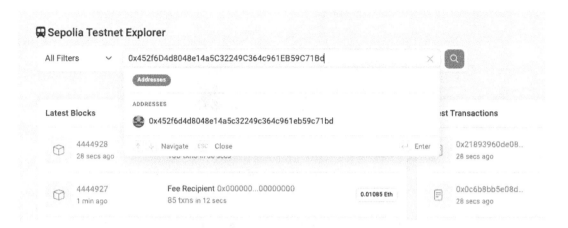

Figure 10.13 – Contract deployed to Sepolia testnet

The image confirms the successful deployment of the contract into a live testnet! Congratulations on this achievement.

3. To proceed, navigate to the contract page and explore its different sections. Pay close attention to specific fields, as highlighted in *Figure 10.14*:

Figure 10.14 – Contract page at Sepolia TestNet

4. Now let us query and interact with the contract deployed in the Sepolia testnet. We will use the `interact-sepolia.js` script. Replace the actual contract address in place of `<< CONTRACT-ADDRESS >>` and run the following command:

```
npx hardhat run scripts/interact-sepolia.js --network sepolia
```

```
~/The-Essential-Guide-to-Web3/Chapter-10    main ±    npx hardhat run scripts/interact-sepolia.js --network sepolia
Getting the My Simple Token Contract...

----------------------------------------------------------------
List of all ERC20 public functions called via Hardhat from Sepolia
----------------------------------------------------------------
The smart contract created the Token with Name: SimpleToken
The smart contract created the Token with Symbol: STKN
The smart contract created the Token with Decimals: 18
Smart Contract has a total supply of the STKN: 1000000.0
Smart contract owner at 0x2f80AC851972b551bB033FD92720eb7C97Ec4280 has a STKN balance of 1000000.0

----------------------------------------------------------------
All Done !
----------------------------------------------------------------
```

Figure 10.15 – Querying the MySimpleToken contract from the Sepolia testnet

The previous screenshot provides evidence that we can successfully interact with the deployed smart contract in Sepolia. You can also find detailed token information on the Sepolia Etherscan page. This marks the completion of our practical journey in creating, deploying, and testing a token in real-time, both on a local network and the testnet.

If you find it difficult to follow or feel there are too many steps to test a smart contract, you could use Remix IDE to simplify these steps. The reason we are taking the longer route is to make sure you learn the basics and that when you run into issues, you can go back to the code and the steps to debug them. With Remix IDE, you can complete this section for deploying and testing in 10 minutes. We will not be covering how to use Remix IDE in this book, but here is a link to the documentation page for Remix (`https://remix-ide.readthedocs.io/en/latest/`)

Remix IDE: A versatile development environment for Ethereum smart contracts

Remix IDE stands out as a go-to tool for Ethereum smart contract development. It's an open source web-based **integrated development environment** (**IDE**) that simplifies the creation, testing, debugging, and deployment of Ethereum smart contracts.

Remix IDE's user-friendly interface facilitates Solidity smart contract coding, supporting the latest Solidity compiler to ensure compliance with Ethereum standards. It excels in testing and debugging, with a robust framework for unit tests, transaction simulations, and contract interaction using JavaScript VM or custom Ethereum nodes such as Ganache.

Furthermore, Remix IDE streamlines deployment by seamlessly integrating with MetaMask, allowing developers to deploy smart contracts directly to Ethereum networks, including the mainnet and various testnets. Whether you're new to smart contract development or an experienced pro, Remix IDE offers an efficient and comprehensive platform for crafting decentralized applications on Ethereum.

Now you should be hands-on enough and ready to get immersed in the non-fungible world. Yes, that is where we are heading next.

Summary

We covered various topics related to Ethereum tokens and smart contract testing. The key takeaways are that we learned about the six functions and two events required for an ERC-20-compliant smart contract and provided explanations and examples for each. We covered the process of creating an ERC-20 token contract, which is fungible in nature, with decent complexity (`MySimpleToken`) and we provided step-by-step instructions for testing its various methods using the Hardhat. Throughout the conversation, we provided detailed explanations, examples, and code snippets to help illustrate the concepts and guide users in creating, deploying, and testing token contracts. Overall, this discussion offers a solid foundation for understanding tokenomics, Ethereum tokens, and smart contract development and testing.

In the next chapter, we will cover non-fungible token standards in detail.

Part 5 –
Non-Fungible Tokens

This part provides a comprehensive journey through the world of **non-fungible tokens** (**NFTs**), starting with an exploration of NFT standards. Gain a deep understanding of the various standards and protocols that underpin the NFT ecosystem, enabling you to navigate this exciting space with confidence. As you progress through the chapters, you'll embark on a practical journey to create your very first NFT. This hands-on experience equips you with the skills and knowledge needed to mint, manage, and interact with NFTs effectively. Additionally, this part delves into the essential tooling, **software development kits** (**SDKs**), and APIs required to build and interact with NFTs in various blockchain ecosystems.

This section has the following chapters:

- *Chapter 11, Non-Fungible Token Standards*
- *Chapter 12, Creating Your First Non-Fungible Token*

Non-Fungible Token Standards

This chapter introduces two important **non-fungible token** (**NFT**) standards, ERC-721 and ERC-1155. Both these standards are very important in the NFT ecosystem. Most NFTs issued today are based on these two standards. We'll also discuss the application of these standards and how they differ.

In this chapter, we're going to cover the following main topics:

- Understanding NFT standard ERC-721
- Understanding NFT standard ERC-1155
- Other important NFT token standards

Technical requirements

For this chapter, you will require Solidity.

Please make sure you've met this chapter's technical requirements and that you've completed the required setup before proceeding.

Introduction to NFT standards

There are several popular ERC standards for NFTs on the Ethereum blockchain, including ERC-721, ERC-1155, and ERC-998:

- *ERC-721* is the original NFT standard and is used for creating unique, one-of-a-kind tokens that cannot be exchanged for each other. Each ERC-721 token has a unique identifier, making it ideal for creating digital art, collectibles, and other unique assets.

- *ERC-1155* is a more versatile standard that allows for the creation of both fungible and non-fungible tokens within the same contract. This makes it ideal for creating games and other applications that require both types of tokens.

- *ERC-998* is a newer standard that allows for the creation of complex tokens that can contain other tokens. This makes it possible to create more complex assets, such as collections of ERC-721 tokens.

The key difference between NFT standards and fungible token standards (such as ERC-20) is that NFTs represent unique assets, while fungible tokens represent interchangeable assets. Fungible tokens can be exchanged for each other on a one-to-one basis, whereas each NFT is unique and cannot be exchanged for each other in the same way.

Now, let's start understanding the most popular NFT standard, ERC-721.

Understanding NFT standard ERC-721

ERC-721 is an NFT standard on the Ethereum blockchain that defines a set of rules that a smart contract must follow to enable the creation and management of unique digital assets. ERC-721 tokens are unique, one-of-a-kind assets that cannot be exchanged with each other on a one-to-one basis, making them ideal for creating digital art, collectibles, and other unique assets.

Each ERC-721 token has a unique identifier called a token ID, which is stored on the blockchain and cannot be duplicated or altered. This allows for ownership and provenance of the asset to be tracked and verified on the blockchain.

Here are some examples of ERC-721 tokens:

- *CryptoKitties*, a popular blockchain-based game where each CryptoKitty is an ERC-721 token with a unique appearance and set of attributes
- *NBA Top Shot*, a blockchain-based platform where users can buy, sell, and trade unique moments from NBA games as ERC-721 tokens

An ERC-721-based smart contract is designed for creating digital assets and is often used for NFTs. In this example, we'll explore how to build and interact with such a contract, enabling the creation and ownership of one-of-a-kind digital items on the Ethereum blockchain.

Here's an example of an ERC-721-based smart contract:

```solidity
pragma solidity ^0.8.0;
import "@openzeppelin/contracts/token/ERC721/ERC721.sol";
contract MyNFT is ERC721 {
    constructor() ERC721("MyNFT", "NFT") {}
    uint256 public tokenCounter;
    struct NFT {
        string name;
        string metadata;
    }
    mapping (uint256 => NFT) public myNFTs;
```

```
     function mintNFT(string memory _name, string memory _metadata)
public returns (uint256) {
         uint256 tokenId = tokenCounter;
         myNFTs[tokenId] = NFT(_name, _metadata);
         _safeMint(msg.sender, tokenId);
         tokenCounter++;
         return tokenId;
     }
}
```

Let's go over this ERC-721-based smart contract line by line:

- `import "@openzeppelin/contracts/token/ERC721/ERC721.sol";`: This imports the ERC-721 contract from the `OpenZeppelin` library.

- `contract MyNFT is ERC721 {`: This declares a new contract called `MyNFT`, which extends the ERC-721 contract.

- `constructor() ERC721("MyNFT", "NFT") {}`: This is the constructor function that sets the name and symbol for the NFT.

- `uint256 public tokenCounter;`: This declares a public variable called `tokenCounter`, which will keep track of the total number of tokens that have been minted.

- `struct NFT { string name; string metadata; }`: This defines a new struct called `NFT`, which will store the `name` and `metadata` details of each NFT.

- `mapping (uint256 => NFT) public myNFTs;`: This declares a public mapping called `myNFTs`, which will map each token ID to its corresponding NFT struct.

- `function mintNFT(string memory _name, string memory _metadata) public returns (uint256) {`: This is the function that allows users to mint a new NFT. It takes two string arguments, `name` and `metadata`, and returns the new NFT's `tokenId`.

- `uint256 tokenId = tokenCounter;`: This sets the `tokenId` variable to the current value of `tokenCounter`.

- `myNFTs[tokenId] = NFT(_name, _metadata);`: This creates a new NFT struct with the provided name and metadata, and maps it to `tokenId` in the `myNFTs` mapping.

- `_safeMint(msg.sender, tokenId);`: This mints the actual tokens from the contract to the owners.

Now, let's look at the transfer and burn functions of the contract. Please note that these functions are part of the same program and are not shown in this example to reduce the complexity of the code:

```
function transferNFT(address to, uint256 tokenId) public {
    require(_isApprovedOrOwner(msg.sender, tokenId), "Not
authorized");
```

```
    _safeTransfer(msg.sender, to, tokenId, "");
}
```

Let's go over this example line by line:

- `function transferNFT(address to, uint256 tokenId) public {`:
  This line defines the start of the `transferNFT` function. It takes two parameters: `to`,
  which is the address to which the NFT will be transferred, and `tokenId`, which is the
  unique identifier of the NFT to be transferred.

- `require(_isApprovedOrOwner(msg.sender, tokenId), "Not authorized");`: This line uses a require statement to ensure that the sender of the
  transaction is either the owner of the NFT (according to ERC-721 ownership rules) or
  an approved address. If this condition is not met, the function will revert, preventing
  unauthorized transfers.

- `_safeTransfer(msg.sender, to, tokenId, "");`: Here, the `_safeTransfer`
  function from ERC-721 is used to safely transfer the NFT from the sender (`msg.sender`)
  to the specified recipient (`to`) with the given `tokenId`. The empty string, `""`, is used for
  additional data (it's not used in this case).

Now, let's investigate the `burnNFT` function:

```
function burnNFT(uint256 tokenId) public {
  require(_isApprovedOrOwner(msg.sender, tokenId), "Not authorized");
  _burn(tokenId);
  delete myNFTs[tokenId];
}
```

Let's go over this example line by line:

- `function burnNFT(uint256 tokenId) public {`: This line defines the start
  of the `burnNFT` function, which takes one parameter, `tokenId`, representing the unique
  identifier of the NFT to be burned.

- `require(_isApprovedOrOwner(msg.sender, tokenId), "Not authorized");`: Similar to the `transferNFT` function, this line uses a `require`
  statement to ensure that the sender of the transaction is either the owner of the NFT or
  an approved address. If this condition is not met, the function will revert, preventing
  unauthorized burns.

- `_burn(tokenId);`: This line invokes the `_burn` function provided by ERC-721, which
  destroys (burns) the NFT associated with the given `tokenId`. After this line, the NFT no
  longer exists on the blockchain.

- `delete myNFTs[tokenId];`: This line deletes the corresponding NFT metadata from
  the `myNFTs` mapping, effectively removing any reference to the NFT's name and metadata.

These functions ensure that only authorized individuals can transfer or burn NFTs while adhering to ERC-721 ownership rules, and also handle the removal of associated metadata in the case of burning an NFT.

Now that we have a contract and are ready to launch a token, we can deploy the contract and start testing it and mint, transfer, and burn some tokens.

Next, we'll start understanding the other most popular NFT standard, ERC-1155.

Understanding NFT standard ERC-1155

ERC-1155 is a token standard on the Ethereum blockchain that allows for the creation of both fungible and non-fungible tokens within the same contract. This standard was introduced to improve efficiency and reduce gas costs by allowing multiple tokens to be minted or transferred in a single transaction.

ERC-1155 tokens are identified by a unique ID, and each ID can represent either a single NFT or a collection of fungible tokens. This makes it ideal for creating game assets, where players can own unique items as well as currency that can be used to purchase in-game items.

Here are some examples of ERC-1155 tokens:

- *Enjin Coin*, which is used to purchase and trade gaming assets on the Enjin Marketplace
- *ChainGuardian*, a blockchain-based game where players can collect both unique heroes and in-game currency as ERC-1155 tokens

Now, let's look at an example of a smart contract for ERC-1155. This Solidity smart contract represents a collection of game assets following the ERC-1155 standard. These assets can include digital items such as GOLD, SILVER, and BRONZE. The contract allows the owner to mint new assets and burn existing ones. Each asset is associated with a unique ID and can be accessed via a URL pattern specified in the contract constructor. Additionally, the contract inherits functionality from the ERC1155 and Ownable OpenZeppelin contracts for added security and ownership control. Let's look at the contract in more detail.

Here's an ERC-1155-based smart contract example:

```
pragma solidity ^0.8.0;
import "@openzeppelin/contracts/token/ERC1155/ERC1155.sol";
import "@openzeppelin/contracts/access/Ownable.sol";
contract MyGameAssets is ERC1155, Ownable {
    constructor() ERC1155("https://website.com/assets/{id}.json") {}
    uint256 public constant GOLD = 0;
    uint256 public constant SILVER = 1;
    uint256 public constant BRONZE = 2;
    function mint(address account, uint256 id, uint256 amount, bytes
memory data) public onlyOwner {
```

```
            _mint(account, id, amount, data);
    }
    function burn(address account, uint256 id, uint256 amount) public
{
        require(msg.sender == account || msg.sender == owner(), "not
authorized");
        _burn(account, id, amount);
    }
}
```

Let's go over this ERC-1155-based smart contract line by line:

- `import "@openzeppelin/contracts/token/ERC1155/ERC1155.sol";`: This imports the ERC1155 contract from the OpenZeppelin library.

- `import "@openzeppelin/contracts/access/Ownable.sol";`: This imports the Ownable contract from the OpenZeppelin library, which provides an owner-only access control mechanism.

- `contract MyGameAssets is ERC1155, Ownable {`: This declares a new contract called MyGameAssets, which extends both the ERC1155 and Ownable contracts.

- `constructor() ERC1155("https://website.com/assets/{id}.json") {}`: This is the constructor function that sets the base URI for the token metadata.

- `uint256 public constant GOLD = 0;`: This declares a constant variable called GOLD, which is set to 0 and represents the ID of the gold token.

- `uint256 public constant SILVER = 1;`: This declares a constant variable called SILVER, which is set to 1 and represents the ID of the silver token.

- `uint256 public constant BRONZE = 2;`: This declares a constant variable called BRONZE, which is set to 2 and represents the ID of the bronze token.

- `function mint(address account, uint256 id, uint256 amount, bytes memory data) public onlyOwner {`: This is the function that allows the contract owner to mint new tokens. It takes four arguments – account to receive the tokens, the token's ID, amount of tokens to mint, and optional data to include in the mint event.

- `_mint(account, id, amount, data);`: This is a function provided by the ERC1155 contract that mints the tokens and assigns them to the specified account.

- `function burn(address account, uint256 id, uint256 amount) public {`: This function allows users to burn (that is, destroy) their tokens. It takes three arguments: account, which specifies the account that owns the tokens, the token's ID, and amount of tokens to burn.

- `require(msg.sender == account || msg.sender == owner(), "not authorized");`: This requires that the transaction's `sender` be either the account that owns the tokens or the contract owner.

- `_burn(account, id, amount);`: This is a function provided by the ERC1155 contract that burns the tokens.

As you can see, ERC-1155 appears to be very similar to the ERC-721 methods and functions, but its core functionality is quite different. At this point, you should have a fair understanding of when you will use ERC-721 versus ERC-1155 while writing smart contracts for NFTs.

In the next section, we will look at other NFT standards that play an important role in creating and maintaining digital assets.

Understanding NFT standard ERC-998

ERC-998 is a token standard on the Ethereum blockchain that allows for the creation of complex tokens that can contain other tokens. This standard enables the creation of tokens with hierarchical ownership structures, where a token can contain other tokens that represent sub-assets.

ERC-998 tokens are identified by a unique ID and can contain a mixture of fungible tokens and NFTs. This makes it ideal for creating more complex assets, such as collections of ERC-721 tokens.

Here are a few examples of ERC-998 tokens:

- The Mokens project, which uses ERC-998 to create **multi-token contracts (mokens)** that can contain other tokens and assets

- The Ocean Blue project, which allows users to create and trade tokens representing seashells, each of which can contain pearls and other seashells as ERC-998 sub-tokens

Let's go over an example of an ERC-998-based smart contract. In this example, we will create a Token721 contract that represents a collection of ERC-721 tokens. The code is divided into a few sections here:

```
pragma solidity ^0.8.0;
import "@openzeppelin/contracts/token/ERC721/ERC721.sol";
interface Token998 {
    function transferFromParent(address from, address to, uint256
tokenId) external;
}
```

Let's look at this section of code and see what it does.

Here, `interface Token998 {function transferFromParent(address from, address to, uint256 tokenId) external;}` declares an interface for the ERC-998 contract that will be used to transfer tokens between the parent and child contracts.

Now, let's look at the second section of code:

```
contract Token721 is ERC721 {
    uint256 public totalSupply;
    mapping (uint256 => address) public owners;
    mapping (address => uint256[]) public ownedTokens;
    Token998 public parentToken;
    constructor(string memory name, string memory symbol, Token998
_parentToken) ERC721(name, symbol) {
        parentToken = _parentToken;
    }
```

Let's look at this code in more detail:

- `contract Token721 is ERC721 {`: This declares a new contract called `Token721`, which extends the `ERC721` contract

- `Token998 public parentToken;`: This declares a public variable called `parentToken`, which will hold a reference to the parent ERC-998 contract

- `Constructor(string memory name, string memory symbol, Token998 _parentToken) ERC721(name, symbol) { parentToken = _parentToken; }`: This is the constructor function that sets the token's name and `symbol`

Now, let's look at the third section of the code:

```
function mint(address to, uint256 tokenId) public {
    _mint(to, tokenId);
    totalSupply++;
    owners[tokenId] = to;
    ownedTokens[to].push(tokenId);
}
```

Here's what this code does:

- `function mint(address to, uint256 tokenId) public {`: This function allows the contract owner to mint new tokens. It takes two arguments: the address to receive the tokens and the ID of the token to be minted.

- `_mint(to, tokenId);`: This is a function provided by the `ERC721` contract that mints the tokens and assigns them to the specified address.

- `totalSupply++;`: This increments the total supply of tokens.

- `owners[tokenId] = to;`: This updates the `owners` mapping to reflect the fact that the specified address now owns the token.

- `ownedTokens [to] .push(tokenId) ;`: This adds the token to the list of tokens owned by the specified address.

Now, let's look at the fourth section of code, which defines a new function called `transferFrom`:

```
    function transferFrom(address from, address to, uint256 tokenId)
public override {
        super.transferFrom(from, to, tokenId);
        parentToken.transferFromParent(from, to, tokenId);
        owners[tokenId] = to;
        removeTokenFromOwner(from, tokenId);
        addTokenToOwner(to, tokenId);
    }
```

Let's see what it does:

- `function transferFrom(address from, address to, uint256 tokenId) public override {`: This function allows users to transfer their tokens to another address. It takes three arguments: the address that currently owns the tokens, the address to transfer the tokens to, and the ID of the token to be transferred.
- `super.transferFrom(from, to, tokenId) ;`: This calls the `transferFrom` function from the parent ERC-721 contract to transfer the tokens.
- `parentToken.transferFromParent(from, to, tokenId) ;`: This calls the `transferFromParent` function from the parent ERC-998 contract to transfer the ownership of the token to the child contract.
- `owners [tokenId] = to;`: This updates the `owners` mapping to reflect the fact that the specified address now owns the token.
- `removeTokenFromOwner(from, tokenId) ;`: This removes the token from the list of tokens owned by the `from` address.
- `addTokenToOwner(to, tokenId) ;`: This adds the token to the list of tokens owned by the `to` address.

Now, let's look at the fifth section, which defines the functionality to add and remove an owner:

```
    function removeTokenFromOwner(address owner, uint256 tokenId)
private {
        uint256[] storage tokens = ownedTokens[owner];
        for (uint256 i = 0; i < tokens.length; i++) {
            if (tokens[i] == tokenId) {
                tokens[i] = tokens[tokens.length - 1];
                tokens.pop();
                break;
```

```
            }
        }
    }
    function addTokenToOwner(address owner, uint256 tokenId) private {
        ownedTokens[owner].push(tokenId);
    }
}
```

Let's take a closer look:

- `function removeTokenFromOwner(address owner, uint256 tokenId) private {`: This is a helper function that removes a token from `owner`
- `uint256[] storage tokens = ownedTokens[owner];`: This initializes a storage variable called `tokens` to the list of tokens owned by the specified address
- `for (uint256 i = 0; i < tokens.length; i++) {`: This loops through the list of tokens owned by the specified address
- `if (tokens[i] == tokenId) {`: This checks if the current token ID matches the ID of the token to be removed
- `tokens[i] = tokens[tokens.length - 1];`: This swaps the current token ID with the last token ID in the list
- `tokens.pop();`: This removes the last token ID from the list
- `break;`: This exits the loop once the token has been removed from the list

In this section, we covered the ERC-998 token standard, which introduced the concept of composable tokens with nested ownership structures. We learned that ERC-998 allows for the creation of tokens that can own and be owned by other tokens, enabling complex ownership relationships. This standard is particularly useful in gaming applications, collectibles, and digital assets that involve hierarchical ownership structures.

We examined an example of an ERC-998-based smart contract, where tokens can be transferred within a hierarchy and the ownership relationships are managed within the contract. We also discussed the benefits and use cases of ERC-998, including the ability to represent intricate in-game item ownership, tokenized real estate with nested ownership, and the creation of more dynamic and interactive collectibles.

Overall, ERC-998 expands the possibilities of NFTs by providing a standardized way to handle composable tokens and complex ownership structures. This opens exciting opportunities for developers and creators to build innovative applications and digital ecosystems that leverage nested ownership relationships.

Now, let's compare the standards that we've learned about in this chapter.

A quick comparison of ERC-721, ERC-1155, and ERC-998

Let's quickly compare the three token standards we've looked at – ERC-721, ERC-1155, and ERC-998:

Attribute	ERC-721	ERC-1155	ERC-998
Token type	Non-fungible	Fungible or non-fungible	Non-fungible
Token structure	Each token is unique	Multiple tokens can have the same ID	Tokens can be organized hierarchically
Token ownership	Each token has a single owner	Tokens can have multiple owners	Tokens can have multiple owners and be owned by other tokens
Token transfer	Tokens can be transferred one at a time	Multiple tokens can be transferred in a single transaction	Tokens can be transferred in groups and across contracts
Metadata	Token metadata is stored separately from the contract and accessed via a URI	Token metadata is stored in the contract and accessed by ID	Token metadata is stored separately from the contract and accessed via a URI
Gas efficiency	Requires more gas to transfer and manage individual tokens	More efficient for managing large numbers of tokens	Requires more gas to manage the hierarchical structure
Use cases	Crypto collectibles, gaming items, and unique assets	Gaming items, reward points, and multiple asset types	Tokens with complex ownership structures, in-game items, and collectibles

Table 11.1 – Comparison of different NFT standards

As you can see, each token standard has its strengths and weaknesses and is suited to different use cases. ERC-721 is ideal for representing unique assets such as crypto collectibles, while ERC-1155 is better suited for fungible tokens and NFTs that have multiple owners. ERC-998 is specifically designed for creating tokens with complex ownership structures, such as in-game items and collectibles that can contain other tokens. The choice of token standard depends on the specific requirements of the project or application.

In the next section, we will look at some of the other NFT types and standards that are popular in the industry.

Solbound tokens and why they are popular in the NFT industry

Solbound tokens are a new type of token that can be created on the Solana blockchain. These tokens are designed to be faster and more scalable than traditional Ethereum-based tokens as the Solana blockchain has much faster transaction times and lower transaction fees.

Solbound tokens can be used for a variety of purposes, including the following:

- Rewards and loyalty programs
- Gaming items and collectibles
- **Decentralized finance (DeFi)** applications
- Stablecoins

One example of a project that uses Solbound tokens is the Solanium project, which aims to create a decentralized fundraising platform on the Solana blockchain. Another example is the Phantom Wallet, which allows users to easily manage and trade Solbound tokens.

Unlike the Ethereum-based ERC standards we discussed earlier, Solbound tokens do not currently have a specific token standard or naming convention. However, Solana does provide a token program called SPL Token, which defines a standard set of functions that can be used to create custom token contracts on the Solana blockchain.

One key difference between Solbound tokens and Ethereum-based tokens is the programming language used to create them. Solana uses Rust, while Ethereum uses Solidity. This means that developers who want to create Solbound tokens will need to be familiar with Rust and the Solana development ecosystem, which might be a learning curve for some developers.

In terms of scalability and transaction speed, Solbound tokens offer significant advantages over Ethereum-based tokens. Solana has been designed to handle high transaction volumes and can process up to 65,000 transactions per second, compared to Ethereum's current limit of around 15 transactions per second. This makes Solbound tokens an excellent choice for applications that require fast transaction processing and low fees.

Next, we will learn about **rentable NFTs (rNFTs)**. These NFTs have taken tokenization to the next level, along with converting real work assets into digital assets.

Rentable NFTs

Rentable NFTs, also known as **rent-seeking NFTs** or **rNFTs**, are a type of non-fungible token that can be rented out to other users for a set period in exchange for payment. This means that the original owner of the NFT retains ownership and control of the asset but allows others to use it temporarily in exchange for a fee.

rNFTs are important for several reasons:

1. First, they can provide a new revenue stream for NFT owners and creators, allowing them to monetize their assets beyond just selling them outright. This can be especially beneficial for creators of assets that have a limited audience or are not in high demand, as renting them out can still provide a steady income.

2. Second, rNFTs can help increase the utility and functionality of NFTs. By allowing users to temporarily use an asset, it can enable new use cases and applications that were not possible before. For example, in gaming, rNFTs could allow players to use rare or powerful in-game items for a limited time without having to purchase them outright.

3. Finally, rNFTs can also help address issues of affordability and accessibility. For example, if a user cannot afford to purchase a high-value NFT outright, renting it for a shorter period may be a more feasible option. This can help democratize access to valuable and desirable assets, while still ensuring that the original owner is compensated for their creation.

rNFTs represent an exciting new development in the NFT ecosystem, with the potential to increase the utility and value of NFTs while also providing new revenue streams and accessibility options for creators and users alike.

The ECR-721X token standard

The ERC-721x standard is an extension of the ERC-721 standard that adds support for rentable tokens. It allows for the creation of NFTs that can be rented out to other users for a specified period.

The ability to rent out assets can be useful in a variety of scenarios:

*   **Sharing economy platforms**: Renting out physical assets such as cars or houses

*   **Gaming platforms**: Renting out in-game items or characters

*   **Digital art platforms**: Allowing users to rent out digital art pieces for a limited time

*   **Subscription services**: Providing access to content or services for a limited time

*   **Tokenized real estate**: Allowing investors to rent out portions of a real estate property for a specified period

One example of a smart contract that supports rentable assets is the *NiftyRentals* contract. This contract is built on top of the ERC-721x standard and allows users to rent out NFTs to other users for a specified period:

```
contract NiftyRentals is IERC721, IERC721Receiver {
    using SafeMath for uint256;
    // Mapping from token ID to owner
    mapping (uint256 => address) private _tokenOwner;
    // Mapping from token ID to approved address
```

```
    mapping (uint256 => address) private _tokenApprovals;
    // Mapping from owner to number of owned token
    mapping (address => uint256) private _ownedTokensCount;
    // Mapping from owner to operator approvals
    mapping (address => mapping (address => bool)) private _
operatorApprovals;
    // Token name
    string private _name;
    // Token symbol
    string private _symbol;
    // Base URI
    string private _baseURI;
    // Current rental rates for each token
    mapping (uint256 => uint256) private _rentalRates;
    // Time left on each rental
    mapping (uint256 => uint256) private _timeLeft;
    // Events
    event Rent(address indexed from, address indexed to, uint256
indexed tokenId, uint256 rentalRate, uint256 duration);
    event RentalExpired(address indexed from, uint256 indexed
tokenId);

    // Constructor
    constructor(string memory name, string memory symbol) public {
        _name = name;
        _symbol = symbol;
    }
    // ERC721 Interface Functions
    function balanceOf(address owner) external view returns (uint256)
{
        return _ownedTokensCount[owner];
    }
    function ownerOf(uint256 tokenId) external view returns (address)
{
        address owner = _tokenOwner[tokenId];
        require(owner != address(0), "Token does not exist");
        return owner;
    }
    function safeTransferFrom(address from, address to, uint256
tokenId, bytes calldata data) external {
        safeTransferFrom(from, to, tokenId);
        require(_checkOnERC721Received(from, to, tokenId, data),
"Transfer to non ERC721Receiver implementer");
    }
```

As per the specification, ERC-721x inherits all the mandatory functions from the ERC-721 standard, which include `balanceOf`, `ownerOf`, `approve`, `setApprovalForAll`, `getApproved`, `isApprovedForAll`, `transferFrom`, and `safeTransferFrom`.

In addition to these functions, ERC-721x adds the following new functions:

- `rent(uint256 _tokenId, uint256 _rentalPrice, uint256 _duration) external payable`: This function allows a token to be rented out for a specified period. It takes three arguments: the ID of the token to be rented, the rental price per unit time, and the duration of the rental period.

- `cancelRent(uint256 _tokenId) external`: This function cancels the rental of a token that was previously rented out.

- `getRentInfo(uint256 _tokenId) external view returns (uint256 rentalPrice, uint256 duration, uint256 deposit, uint256 startTime)`: This function returns information about the current rental status of a token.

- `batchTransferFrom(address _from, address _to, uint256[] calldata _tokenIds) external`: This function allows for the batch transfer of multiple tokens from one address to another.

- `batchSafeTransferFrom(address _from, address _to, uint256[] calldata _tokenIds, bytes calldata _data) external`: This function allows for the batch transfer of multiple tokens, with additional data that is sent along with each token transfer.

- `createGroup(uint256[] calldata _tokenIds) external`: This function creates a new group of tokens, with the specified token IDs.

- `removeGroup(uint256 _groupId) external`: This function removes a group of tokens, with the specified group ID.

- `getGroupSize(uint256 _groupId) external view returns (uint256)`: This function returns the number of tokens in a specified group.

- `getGroupToken(uint256 _groupId, uint256 _index) external view returns (uint256)`: This function returns the token ID at the specified index within a group.

- `setApprovalForAll(address _operator, bool _approved) external`: This function allows an owner to grant or revoke approval for a third-party operator to manage all their tokens.

- `isApprovedForAll(address _owner, address _operator) external view returns (bool)`: This function checks whether an operator has been granted approval to manage all the tokens of a specified owner.

- `supportsInterface(bytes4 interfaceId) external view returns (bool)`: This function checks whether a specified interface is supported by the contract.

ERC-721x is an optional extension of ERC-721, and not all NFTs are required to implement it. However, it can be useful in cases where rentable tokens, batch transfers, or token grouping are needed. For example, a game platform that allows players to rent out in-game items to each other could use ERC-721x to implement the rental functionality. Similarly, a platform that allows users to group their NFTs into portfolios could use ERC-721x to implement the grouping functionality.

Gas price and NFTs

When we discuss NFTs and standards and what platforms are suitable for launching your NFTs, the gas cost is a key factor that is sometimes also a showstopper.

Gas prices on the Ethereum network have been a major issue for the NFT ecosystem, especially during periods of high demand. **Gas** is the unit of measurement for the computational effort required to execute a transaction or contract on the Ethereum network. Gas prices are denominated in **ether** (**ETH**), and the higher the gas price, the more ETH it costs to execute a transaction or contract.

During periods of high demand, gas prices can rise significantly, causing delays in transaction processing and making it more expensive to buy, sell, or create NFTs. This has led to a phenomenon known as the *gas price war*, where users compete to outbid each other for the limited space available in each Ethereum block.

One example of the impact of gas prices on the NFT ecosystem can be seen in the sale of CryptoPunk #3100. This rare NFT sold for 1,600 ETH (approximately $3 million at the time) in March 2021, but the transaction cost over 200 ETH (approximately $380,000) in gas fees. This high gas cost was due to the number of bidders competing for the NFT and the complexity of the transaction.

Another example is the NFT drop for the popular artist Beeple on the Nifty Gateway platform in February 2021. The drop generated over $69 million in sales, but also resulted in significant congestion on the Ethereum network, with gas prices spiking to over 1,000 **Gwei** (a measure of gas price) at one point. This caused delays in transaction processing and made it more expensive for users to buy and sell NFTs on the platform.

Data from blockchain analytics firm Dune Analytics also shows a clear correlation between the popularity of NFT sales and the rise in gas prices. During peak periods of NFT activity, gas prices can reach hundreds or even thousands of Gwei, making it prohibitively expensive for some users to participate in the ecosystem.

To address the issue of high gas prices, various solutions have been proposed, including layer 2 scaling solutions, such as sidechains and state channels, which we will be covering in *Chapter 15*, and the move to alternative blockchain networks with lower fees, such as Binance Smart Chain and Polygon (formerly Matic). However, these solutions come with trade-offs and limitations, and the Ethereum network remains the dominant platform for NFTs and other blockchain-based assets.

Summary

In this chapter, we discussed several topics related to NFTs on the Ethereum network. First, we compared and contrasted several popular ERC standards for NFTs, including ERC-721, ERC-1155, ERC-998, and ERC-721x, outlining their key features, limitations, and potential use cases. We also discussed the emergence of new standards and technologies for rNFTs, which can provide a new revenue stream for creators and increase the functionality and accessibility of NFTs. Then, we explored a simple example of an ERC-721-based smart contract for creating and retrieving custom NFTs with specified names and metadata.

We also discussed the issue of gas prices on the Ethereum network, which can make it expensive and difficult to transact with NFTs during periods of high demand. We provided several examples of the impact of gas prices on NFT transactions and the NFT ecosystem as a whole. Our discussion highlighted the potential and challenges of NFTs on the Ethereum network, as well as the ongoing evolution of the NFT ecosystem through new standards and technologies.

In the next chapter, we'll create some cool NFTs and see how these ERC standards can be implemented.

12

Creating Your First Non-Fungible Token

In this chapter, you'll mint your first **non-fungible token** (**NFT**), create an ERC721 smart contract, deploy it, and then mint the NFT. You'll also use IPFS, a decentralized filesystem for building the next generation of the internet. You will also learn how to use Etherscan and one of the Ethereum explorers. This is a short chapter but a very important one as you will create your first NFT and experience a new digital economy out there.

In this chapter, we're going to cover the following main topics:

- Deploying your ERC-721 smart contract to Ethereum TestNet
- Minting your first NFTs
- Adding NFTs to your MetaMask wallet

Technical requirements

Before you begin ERC721 token creation, it is crucial to ensure that you have the necessary technical prerequisites in place. If you completed the hands-on work provided in *Chapter 8*, you have these set up already. However, I recommend running through the setup once more to ensure you have a valuable experience.

Here are the essential technical requirements:

- **Operating system** (**OS**): You can choose your preferred OS; macOS is used in the examples here, but they can be adapted to your OS of choice.
- **GitHub command-line interface** (**CLI**): Ensure you have the GitHub CLI installed and have access to GitHub. This is vital for version control and collaborative development.
- **Visual Studio Code** (**VS Code**): Install VS Code, a popular code editor that streamlines smart contract development.

- **Node.js**: Make sure Node.js is installed; it is a runtime environment necessary for running JavaScript-based applications. A better approach would be to use **Node Version Manager** (**NVM**).

- **Node Package Manager** (**npm**): npm comes bundled with Node.js and is used for managing packages and dependencies in your projects.

- **Hardhat**: Install Hardhat, a development environment for Ethereum that simplifies smart contract development and testing.

- **Web browser**: You will need a web browser of your choice. The examples here use Chrome but feel free to use your preferred browser.

- **Pinata account**: You will need a Pinata account (`https://www.pinata.cloud/`) to create the IPFS URI for the images we want to mint as NFTs. Please refer to `https://docs.pinata.cloud/docs/getting-started` for more information.

Once you have confirmed that these technical requirements have been set up and are running smoothly, you are ready to proceed with the next step – configuring the development environment.

Configuring and setting up the environment

In this section, we need to ensure that we have all the prerequisites in place and that they function so that we can execute the project.

> **Important note**
>
> Most of the installation instructions can be found in *Chapter 3*, *Chapter 8*, and *Chapter 10*; please refer to these chapters if you have not done the setup.

Once you have all the prerequisites set up, you can proceed to the next part, which is to Git clone the pre-coded project and build it successfully.

Here's a step-by-step guide on how to access and use the code repository:

1. Use the GitHub CLI, as shown here. The repository you need to clone is here. If you have already cloned this GitHub repository, you can ignore this step:

```
https://github.com/PacktPublishing/The-Essential-Guide-to-Web3
git clone https://github.com/PacktPublishing/
The-Essential-Guide-to-Web3
```

2. Once you have successfully cloned the project, open it in VS Code. Your workspace should resemble the configuration shown in *Figure 12.1*:

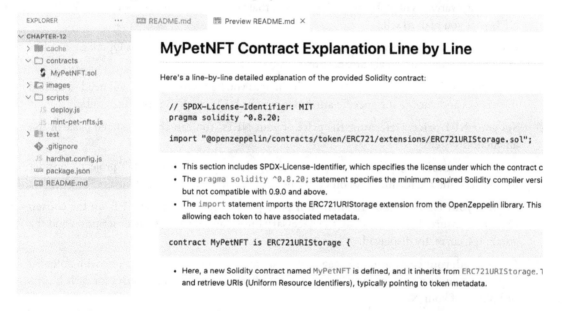

```
~     cd The-Essential-Guide-to-Web3/
~/The-Essential-Guide-to-Web3     main ±    cd Chapter-12
~/The-Essential-Guide-to-Web3/Chapter-12     main ±    code .
~/The-Essential-Guide-to-Web3/Chapter-12     main ±
```

Figure 12.1 – Git checkout and open project in VS Code

`code` . will open VS Code with the project folder; this should look as follows:

EXPLORER   ⋯   README.md   Preview README.md ×

∨ CHAPTER-12
  > cache
  ∨ contracts
      MyPetNFT.sol
  > images
  ∨ scripts
      deploy.js
      mint-pet-nfts.js
  > test
    .gitignore
    hardhat.config.js
    package.json
    README.md

MyPetNFT Contract Explanation Line by Line

Here's a line-by-line detailed explanation of the provided Solidity contract:

```
// SPDX-License-Identifier: MIT
pragma solidity ^0.8.20;

import "@openzeppelin/contracts/token/ERC721/extensions/ERC721URIStorage.sol";
```

- This section includes SPDX-License-Identifier, which specifies the license under which the contract c
- The `pragma solidity ^0.8.20;` statement specifies the minimum required Solidity compiler versi but not compatible with 0.9.0 and above.
- The `import` statement imports the ERC721URIStorage extension from the OpenZeppelin library. This allowing each token to have associated metadata.

```
contract MyPetNFT is ERC721URIStorage {
```

- Here, a new Solidity contract named `MyPetNFT` is defined, and it inherits from `ERC721URIStorage`. T and retrieve URIs (Uniform Resource Identifiers), typically pointing to token metadata.

Figure 12.2 – VS Code showing the project structure

Figure 12.2 shows the directory structure that is required for a Hardhat project. Here, you can find a line-by-line explanation of the smart contract code in the README . md file.

This section covered all the necessary prerequisites and ensured that they were in place and functional for the smooth execution of the project. You learned how to set up the required tools and software, including Node.js, Git, Hardhat, MetaMask, and a compatible web browser. You also learned how to clone the pre-coded project and successfully build and run it on your MacBook Pro.

Next, we'll deploy the ERC 721 contract into a testnet before we start minting some NFTs.

Launching an NFT project

Let's consider a use case where we want to launch an NFT project with a collection of 10,000 images with a theme of saving the planet and spreading awareness of global warming. Here are some of the main steps you may want to consider:

1. **Create your vision and strategy**: Define your mission statement, goals, and strategy for your NFT project. Consider what you want to achieve and what steps you need to take to get there.

2. **Create your artwork**: The artwork will be the core of your NFT project. Make sure that you create quality images that align with your vision, and the concept of saving the planet and spreading awareness of global warming. Ensure that you create an image for each of the 10,000 NFTs that you plan to sell.

3. **Choose the NFT platform**: Choose a platform to mint your NFTs, such as OpenSea, Rarible, or Nifty Gateway, and create an account.

4. **Mint your NFTs**: Mint your NFTs using the images you have created. You will need to upload the images and choose the specific attributes of your NFTs, such as rarity and traits.

5. **Set your NFT price**: Determine the price of your NFTs. You can choose a fixed price or use an auction system.

6. **Create your marketing plan**: Develop a marketing plan to promote your NFT project. Consider using social media, forums, and other online channels to reach potential buyers.

7. **Launch your NFT project**: Launch your NFT project by listing your NFTs on the chosen platform. Ensure that you have all the necessary information, such as the description and the attributes, correctly displayed.

8. **Engage with your community**: Engage with your community by communicating with potential buyers and answering their questions. Consider offering rewards and bonuses for early buyers or holders of your NFTs.

Remember, launching an NFT project requires careful planning, attention to detail, and continuous effort. By following these steps, you can create an impactful NFT project that aligns with your vision of saving the planet and raising awareness of global warming.

As you can see, there are several steps in launching an NFT. We will focus on smart contract creation and how to mint an NFT in this chapter. This will also set the foundation for all NFT-related projects that you may want to do next.

Next, we'll start writing the ERC-721 contract. We will reuse the Pet Store pets from *Chapter 8* and convert them into NFTs.

Deploying your ERC-721 smart contract to Ethereum TestNet

The Git project has already been unboxed for your convenience, which means it's been prepared for you to start compiling and testing smart contracts. Follow these steps to successfully compile and deploy the smart contract onto the Hardhat blockchain:

1. Launch VS Code on your computer. Navigate to the project folder that contains the unboxed Hardhat project. The following figure provides an example of how the project folder should look:

Figure 12.3 – VS Code with the Pet Store project open

2. Now that you are in the project folder within VS Code, you can proceed to compile and deploy the smart contracts to the Hardhat local blockchain. This process will involve using the Hardhat commands and interacting with the blockchain to simulate the deployment.

    The project folder in VS Code provides you with the environment to manage and interact with your smart contracts effectively. Remember to refer to the documentation or instructions specific to your project for accurate details on compilation and deployment procedures.

3. In your Terminal, run `npm install` to install project dependencies. This step ensures that the required packages and binaries are installed in the project root directory.

Figure 12.4 shows a sample of the expected output:

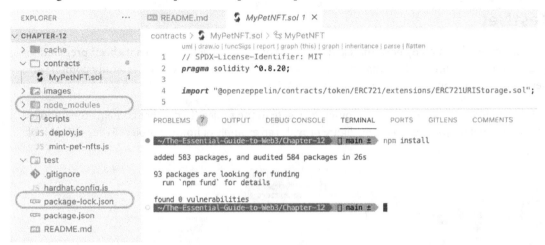

Figure 12.4 – Installing project dependencies

Now that the project dependencies and binaries have been installed in the project root directory, you are ready to move on to compiling the smart contracts.

4.   Next, compile your smart contract, `MyPetNFT.sol`, using the following command:

```
npx hardhat compile
```

This command will compile your smart contract and generate the necessary artifacts in the `artifacts/` folder:

Figure 12.5 – Compiling the Hardhat smart contract

Now that we have a compiled contract, the next step is to deploy this contract to the blockchain. We will use a live TestNet called **Sepolia** for this purpose.

5. Before deploying your contract to the Sepolia TestNet, you need to set up some configurations in the `hardhat-config.js` file:

    I. `INFURA_API_KEY`: Replace this variable with the URL for connecting to the Sepolia network via *Infura*. You can find this URL in your Infura account, which you set up earlier in *Chapter 7*.

    II. `YOUR_SEPOLIA_PRIVATE_KEY`: Replace this variable with your MetaMask wallet's private key for Sepolia. Remember, never share your private key in your code or configurations.

    Make sure you have only one `hardhat-config.js` file in your project directory to prevent conflicts:

```
JS hardhat.config.js > [@] <unknown> > 🔎 solidity
 1     require("@nomicfoundation/hardhat-toolbox");
 2
 3     // Go to https://infura.io, sign up, create a new API key
 4     // in its dashboard, and replace "KEY" with it
 5     const INFURA_API_KEY = "KEY";
 6
 7     // Replace this private key with your Sepolia account private key
 8     // To export your private key from Coinbase Wallet, go to
 9     // Settings > Developer Settings > Show private key
10     // To export your private key from Metamask, open Metamask and
11     // go to Account Details > Export Private Key
12     // Beware: NEVER put real Ether into testing accounts
13     const SEPOLIA_PRIVATE_KEY = "YOUR SEPOLIA PRIVATE KEY";
14
15     module.exports = {
16       solidity: "0.8.9",
17       networks: {
18         sepolia: {
19           url: `https://sepolia.infura.io/v3/${INFURA_API_KEY}`,
20           accounts: [SEPOLIA_PRIVATE_KEY]
21         }
22       },
23     solidity: {
24       version: "0.8.9".
```

Figure 12.6 – Infura key and wallet private key

6. Once you have made the required changes and have the variable shown in *Figure 12.6*, move on to deploy the smart contract to the **Ethereum Sepolia TestNet**.

7. Now, you can deploy the smart contract to the Ethereum Sepolia TestNet using the following command:

```
npx hardhat run scripts/deploy.js --network sepolia
```

This command initiates the deployment process. After a successful deployment, take note of the deployer address (your wallet address configured earlier) and the contract address that are generated upon completion. You will need this information for the next steps.

8. This will deploy the smart contract to the Sepolia TestNet. *Figure 12.7* shows a sample of the deployment output:

Figure 12.7 – Deployed smart contract to Sepolia TestNet

Please note the deployer address (this is your wallet address) that you configured in the previous step and the contract address that is created for you when the deployment is completed. We'll need this information for the Dapps in the next section.

9. Before moving on to Dapps in the next section, it's good practice to verify the contract's deployment on **Sepolia Testnet Explorer**. Open a new browser tab and navigate to `https://sepolia.etherscan.io/`:

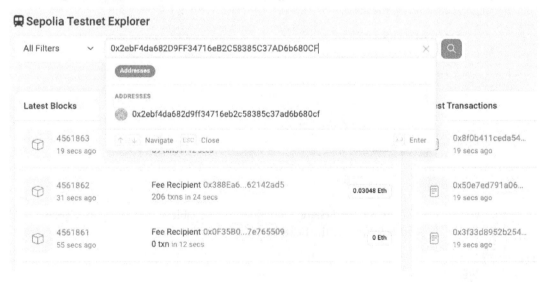

Figure 12.8 – Sepolia Etherscan page

Search for the contract address, as shown in *Figure 12.8*, and go to the smart contract details page.

10. Pay attention to the data highlighted in *Figure 12.9*. These attributes are very important and it is important to understand them:

Figure 12.9 – Smart contract details

11. In the **Overview** section, **ETH BALANCE** shows as **0**. This is because we haven't set any initial balance to the smart contract as this was not in our scope of things to do. In the **More Info** section, you will see the smart contract address and the transaction that created this contract. There is a table at the bottom that shows transaction details, including **Transaction Hash**, **Block**, and a few other details alongside **Txn Fee** (**transaction fee**). Right above here, there are a few tabs, including **Contract**:

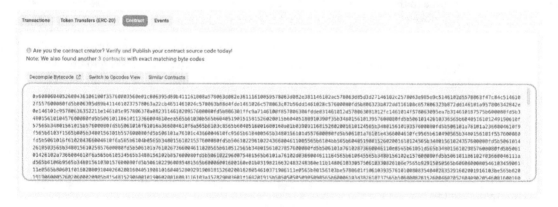

Figure 12.10 – Etherscan smart contract details

If you can't see the contract code and see something similar to what's shown in *Figure 12.10*, it means you haven't verified the contract. Verifying the contract is a separate step, not covered here. Refer to *Chapter 5*, the *Deploying and verifying smart contracts* section, for details.

12. Log in to MetaMask and select the Sepolia TestNet. Choose the corresponding account that's used for deploying the smart contract and ensure there is enough **SepoliaETH (ETH)** to cover gas fees, as shown in *Figure 12.11*:

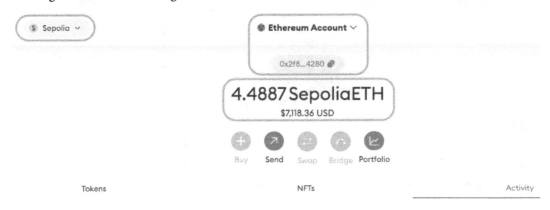

Figure 12.11 – MetaMask account details

With these steps completed, you're now ready to mint some NFTs.

Minting your NFTs

With that, we have come to the exciting part of this exercise, where our goal is to mint some cool pet NFTs and experience the process from end to end. Let's jump right into it.

The following steps could be automated and programmed for a better experience, but we are going to do this manually so that you can learn what exactly is happening here. We are going to upload the pet pictures in the images folder into Pinata and capture all the URIs that will be used in the `mint-pet-nfts.js` script later:

1. Log in to your Pinata account. Please make sure you have the necessary API keys, as mentioned in the *Technical requirements* section. The project folder contains an images folder with 24 images in it. These are pairs and they have thumbnails. First, let's load all the images into Pinata so that we can set the custom attributes. Use the **Upload** button or the drag-and-drop functionality to upload all the pet pictures:

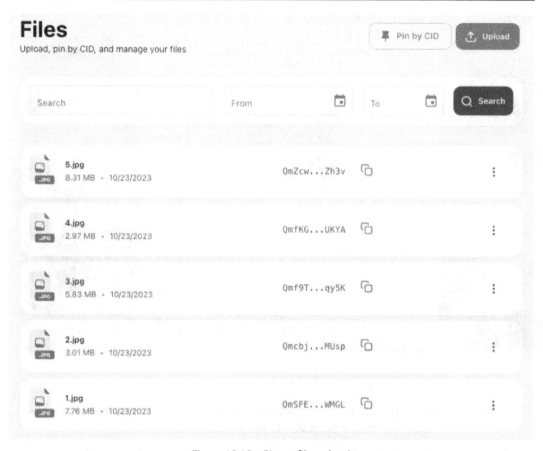

Figure 12.12 – Pinata file upload

Figure 12.12 shows a sample output of the uploads and how they will look in Pinata. Now, let's set up some attributes.

2. Next, click on the three dots, often referred to as the burger menu, where you'll find three options. Select **Content Preview** and proceed to upload the corresponding thumbnail, provide a title, and include a description:

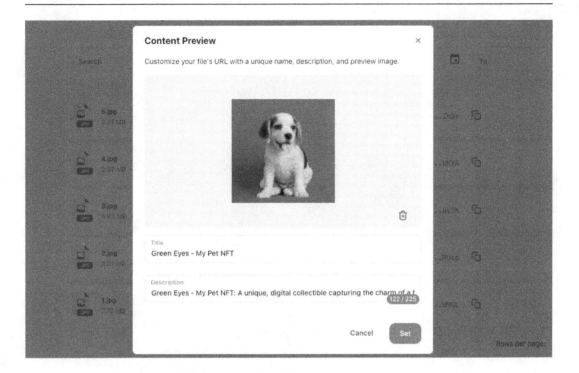

Figure 12.13 – Content Preview

Figure 12.13 shows a preview and the **Set** button, which you can use to save this setting. Make sure you get a **Content Preview Successfully Saved** message.

3. Copy the URI of the Pinata IPFS service (this should be similar to QmSFE...WMGL) for all the images that we uploaded in the previous step and keep it handy. This information is required to create the metadata.json file.

    Creating a metadata.json file for your NFTs is essential to provide essential information about the token, its attributes, and how it should be displayed. Here are the steps to create a metadata.json file for your NFT:

    I. **Define your metadata schema**: Determine what attributes and information you want to include in your NFT metadata. Common fields include name, description, image URL, attributes, and external links:

    II. **Structure your metadata**: Create a JSON object to structure your metadata. Here's a basic example:

```
{
    "name": "My Awesome NFT",
    "description": "A unique digital collectible",
    "image": "https://example.com/my-nft-image.jpg",
```

```
    "attributes": [
      {
        "trait_type": "Color",
        "value": "Blue"
      },
      {
        "trait_type": "Rarity",
        "value": "Common"
      }
    ],
    "external_url": "https://example.com/my-nft-details"
}
```

Customize the fields according to your NFT's details. You can add more attributes as needed:

- **Host your image:** Ensure that the `image` field contains a URL pointing to the image associated with your NFT. Host this image on a reliable server or an IPFS gateway.

- **Save as metadata.json:** Save the JSON object as a file named `metadata.json`. Make sure it follows the correct JSON format.

- **IPFS hosting (optional):** To ensure decentralization and immutability, you can host your `metadata.json` file on IPFS. There are IPFS services such as Pinata or Infura that can help you upload and pin your metadata file.

- **Link the metadata to your NFT:** When minting your NFT, include the URL in the hosted `metadata.json` file in the token's metadata field. This URL should be accessible and publicly available.

- **Verify the metadata:** Before finalizing the NFT minting process, ensure that the metadata is accessible and correctly formatted. You can test this by visiting the metadata URL in your web browser.

- **Store a copy:** Keep a backup copy of your `metadata.json` file, as well as the associated image, in case you need to make changes or updates in the future.

4. Once your `metadata.json` file is ready and linked to your NFT, anyone who owns your NFT can access this file to learn more about the token's attributes and details. This enhances the transparency and uniqueness of your NFT project.

5. You will see a set of `metadata.json` files under the `utils` folder that have been pre-created for you. Please use them as your `metadata.json` inputs:

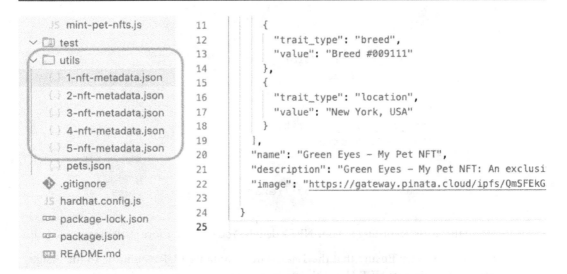

Figure 12.14 – metadata.json files for Pet NFT

As shown in *Figure 12.14*, make sure the `metadata.json` file exists and has the required attributes defined. The only attribute that needs to be changed in this file is `image`. You can customize this file with all the other name/key pair values as required.

6.   Upload all the `metadata.json` files to Pinata. *Figure 12.15* shows an example of this:

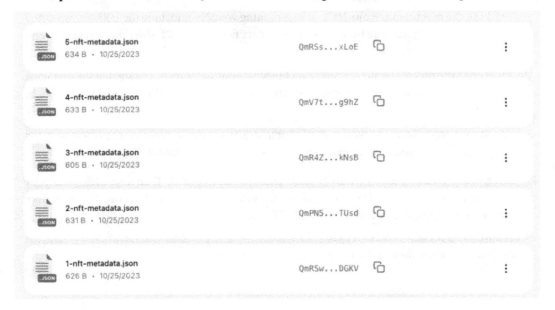

Figure 12.15 – metadata.json files in Pinata

7. Provide the following required values to the variable in `mint-pet-nfts.js`:

   - `MY_PET_TOKEN_ADDRESS`, which is the *smart contract address*

   - `API_KEY`, which is the *Infura API key*

   - `PRIVATE_KEY`, which is the *MetaMask private key*

   - `PINATA_IPFS_URI`, which is the *Pinata metadata JSON URI*

8. Now, let's mint our pet NFTs. Open a Terminal window and run the following command:

   ```
   npx hardhat run scripts/mint-pet-nfts.js --network sepolia
   ```

   Figure 12.16 shows the successful minting of an NFT:

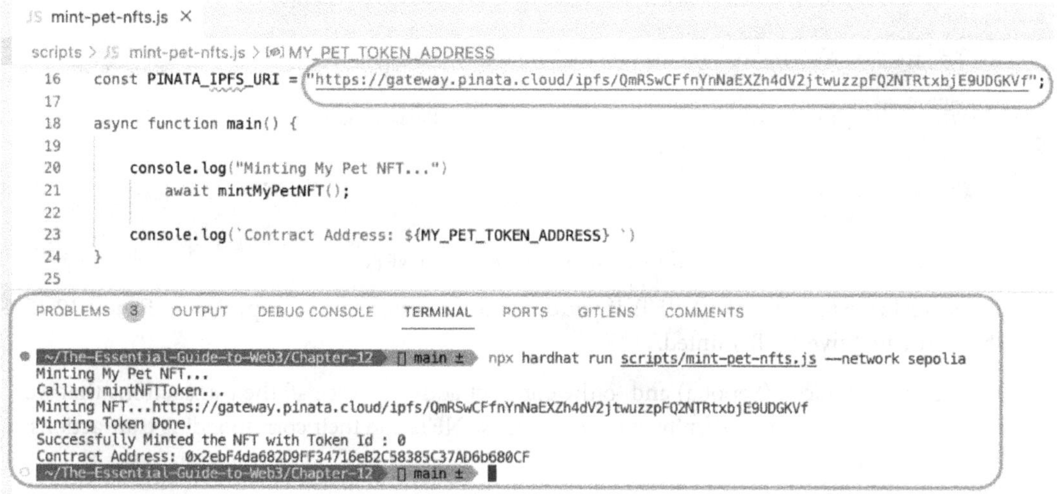

```
JS mint-pet-nfts.js ×

scripts > JS mint-pet-nfts.js > [∅] MY_PET_TOKEN_ADDRESS
  16      const PINATA_IPFS_URI = "https://gateway.pinata.cloud/ipfs/QmRSwCFfnYnNaEXZh4dV2jtwuzzpFQ2NTRtxbjE9UDGKVf";
  17
  18      async function main() {
  19
  20          console.log("Minting My Pet NFT...")
  21              await mintMyPetNFT();
  22
  23          console.log(`Contract Address: ${MY_PET_TOKEN_ADDRESS} `)
  24      }
  25

PROBLEMS 3    OUTPUT    DEBUG CONSOLE    TERMINAL    PORTS    GITLENS    COMMENTS

~/The-Essential-Guide-to-Web3/Chapter-12 [] main ±  npx hardhat run scripts/mint-pet-nfts.js --network sepolia
Minting My Pet NFT...
Calling mintNFTToken...
Minting NFT...https://gateway.pinata.cloud/ipfs/QmRSwCFfnYnNaEXZh4dV2jtwuzzpFQ2NTRtxbjE9UDGKVf
Minting Token Done.
Successfully Minted the NFT with Token Id : 0
Contract Address: 0x2ebF4da682D9FF34716eB2C58385C37AD6b680CF
~/The-Essential-Guide-to-Web3/Chapter-12 [] main ± █
```

Figure 12.16 – Minting your first NFT

This is your first NFT and you should be proud of it. This will remain in the blockchain so long as the blockchain lives.

9. Now, repeat the same steps but change the `PINATA_IPFS_URI` values one by one. Remember that `PINATA_IPFS_URI` is the `metadata.json` URI, not the image URI. This step should be automated for real-time projects:

```
~/The-Essential-Guide-to-Web3/Chapter-12  main ±  npx hardhat run scripts/mint-pet-nfts.js --network sepolia
Minting My Pet NFT...
Calling mintNFTToken...
Minting NFT...https://gateway.pinata.cloud/ipfs/QmRSwCFfnYnNaEXZh4dV2jtwuzzpFQ2NTRtxbjE9UDGKVf
Minting Token Done.
Successfully Minted the NFT with Token Id : 0
Contract Address: 0x2ebF4da682D9FF34716eB2C58385C37AD6b680CF
~/The-Essential-Guide-to-Web3/Chapter-12  main ±  npx hardhat run scripts/mint-pet-nfts.js --network sepolia
Minting My Pet NFT...
Calling mintNFTToken...
Minting NFT...https://gateway.pinata.cloud/ipfs/QmPN5BEyCmnM8HEddm674HdHjTYDyu4eznHUXrrF1TUsdy
Minting Token Done.
Successfully Minted the NFT with Token Id : 1
Contract Address: 0x2ebF4da682D9FF34716eB2C58385C37AD6b680CF
~/The-Essential-Guide-to-Web3/Chapter-12  main ±  npx hardhat run scripts/mint-pet-nfts.js --network sepolia
Minting My Pet NFT...
Calling mintNFTToken...
Minting NFT...https://gateway.pinata.cloud/ipfs/QmR4ZJ6PScuexZvB8fRYYZvc3JqnscgAZfViCeDE1kNsBp
Minting Token Done.
Successfully Minted the NFT with Token Id : 2
Contract Address: 0x2ebF4da682D9FF34716eB2C58385C37AD6b680CF
~/The-Essential-Guide-to-Web3/Chapter-12  main ±  npx hardhat run scripts/mint-pet-nfts.js --network sepolia
Minting My Pet NFT...
Calling mintNFTToken...
Minting NFT...https://gateway.pinata.cloud/ipfs/QmV7tDuGote7EGSZbnnUtY7vBB2gbSCqJngpaqSyog9hZz
Minting Token Done.
Successfully Minted the NFT with Token Id : 3
Contract Address: 0x2ebF4da682D9FF34716eB2C58385C37AD6b680CF
~/The-Essential-Guide-to-Web3/Chapter-12  main ±  npx hardhat run scripts/mint-pet-nfts.js --network sepolia
Minting My Pet NFT...
Calling mintNFTToken...
Minting NFT...https://gateway.pinata.cloud/ipfs/QmRSsUaBhmx2ZU16pVsK39xZcnaAB3WD9GMzmzq7jxLoER
Minting Token Done.
Successfully Minted the NFT with Token Id : 4
Contract Address: 0x2ebF4da682D9FF34716eB2C58385C37AD6b680CF
~/The-Essential-Guide-to-Web3/Chapter-12  main ±
```

Figure 12.17 – Minting your first NFTs

Please feel free to mint all 12 NFTs if you'd like to gain some more experience. *Figure 12.17* shows the first five NFTs minted.

10. Now, go to Etherscan (Sepolia) and to the contract address to see all the transactions that we created. Here, we can start learning more about these NFTs and their corresponding transactions:

Figure 12.18 – NFT mint transactions in Sepolia Etherscan

11. Here, you can see the transactions that were successfully executed and minted to your account address. *Figure 12.18* highlights the **More Info** section, which reveals a new attribute called **TOKEN TRACKER**. Upon clicking it, you will be taken to the **Token Tracker** page.

Figure 12.19 shows details about the selected NFT and its activities:

Figure 12.19 – MYPET NFT token details

With that, we have successfully minted a set of NFTs. Now, let's learn how to add these NFTs to our MetaMask wallet.

Adding your NFTs to your MetaMask wallet

Launch the MetaMask wallet on a web browser or desktop application. Ensure that the wallet is connected to the Ethereum Sepolia TestNet.

Follow these steps to add the NFTs you minted in the previous section to your MetaMask wallet:

1. In the MetaMask wallet, under the **NFTs** tab, select the **Import NFT** option:

Figure 12.20 – Importing NFTs into MetaMask

2. In the **Address** field, paste the contract address of the minted NFT smart contract:

Figure 12.21 – Adding an NFT contract and tokens to MetaMask

3. Enter the contract address and the token ID. Verify that these details match your NFT smart contract outputs from previous steps. Repeat this for all the tokens you minted:

0x2f8...4280

4.4659 SepoliaETH
$8,008.44 USD

Buy   **Send**   Swap   Bridge   **Portfolio**

Tokens   NFTs   Activity

MYPET (5)

Figure 12.22 – Minted NFTs displayed in MetaMask

Figure 12.22 shows the final and desired output for this exercise. Congratulations! You have successfully imported your NFT smart contract into your MetaMask wallet. You will now see your NFT collection listed within your wallet under the **Tokens** section.

You can now interact with your NFTs directly from your MetaMask wallet. This includes viewing detailed information about each NFT, transferring them to other addresses, or displaying them within supported NFT marketplaces.

You can also verify the minting of the NFTs with NFT marketplaces that support testnets, such as Sepolia. We will use **Opensea** to verify this. Use a new browser to open the *Opensea TestNet* website (https://testnets.opensea.io/) and search for the contract address of the NFT we created. *Figure 12.23* shows a sample of the listed NFTs in the Opensea marketplace:

Figure 12.23 – Minted NFTs displayed in the Opensea marketplace

You can now interact with your NFTs directly from your MetaMask wallet. This includes viewing detailed information about each NFT, transferring them to other addresses, or displaying them within supported NFT marketplaces.

Summary

This chapter painted a vivid picture of an NFT project aimed at saving the planet and raising awareness of global warming. You learned about the importance of strategic planning, high-quality artwork creation, and selecting the right NFT platform to bring your vision to life.

Before diving into the technical aspects, you were reminded of essential technical prerequisites such as OSs, the GitHub CLI, VS Code, Node.js, Hardhat, and web browsers. You also discovered the significance of Pinata accounts for creating IPFS URIs.

With the stage set, you delved into configuring and setting up a development environment, including cloning the pre-coded project and understanding its structure. After, you deployed your ERC-721 smart contract on the Ethereum Sepolia TestNet, securing vital details such as Infura API keys and private keys.

This chapter continued with an exhilarating exploration of minting NFTs, where you manually uploaded pet pictures to Pinata, configured attributes, and copied IPFS URIs. You gained hands-on experience by minting NFTs, eventually witnessing these unique tokens on the Sepolia TestNet and exploring their transaction details on Etherscan.

Finally, you learned how to add these minted NFTs to your MetaMask wallet, enhancing your grasp of the complete NFT creation and management process.

This chapter equipped you with the knowledge and practical skills needed to create, deploy, and interact with NFTs, an essential foundation for anyone venturing into the fascinating world of Web3 technology.

In the upcoming chapter, we delve into the fascinating world of oracles, uncovering their pivotal role in bridging the blockchain with real-world data and external information sources. Explore the dynamics and significance of oracles in our Web3 journey.

Part 6 – Web3 Advanced Topics

This is your gateway to exploring cutting-edge concepts and technologies that drive the decentralized web forward. It delves deep into advanced topics that are shaping the future of Web3 and blockchain ecosystems. The chapters cover a range of crucial subjects, beginning with an exploration of oracles, which enable smart contracts to interact with external data sources. You'll gain a comprehensive understanding of their role in bringing real-world data into the blockchain. The chapters explore **layer 2 (L2)** networks and rollups, providing insights into scaling solutions that enhance the efficiency and scalability of blockchain networks. You'll discover how these technologies address congestion and high gas fees on the Ethereum network. The journey continues into the realm of zero-knowledge proofs, a fascinating field of cryptography that enables data privacy and authentication without revealing sensitive information. You'll learn about their applications in blockchain and privacy-focused projects. Finally, dive into **Decentralized Autonomous Organizations (DAOs)**, where you'll explore the principles of decentralized governance and how DAOs empower community-driven decision-making.

This section has the following chapters:

- *Chapter 13, Understanding Oracles*
- *Chapter 14, Zero-Knowledge Proofs and Zero-Knowledge EVMs*
- *Chapter 15, L2 Networks and Rollups*
- *Chapter 16, Decentralized Autonomous Organizations – Overview*

Understanding Oracles

We have come to the last few chapters in this book, where we will get into some of the advanced topics that are essential to work in the Web3 ecosystem. We covered some of these advanced topics at a high level in earlier chapters. In this chapter, we'll understand what an oracle is.

Oracles open the door for the decentralized Web3 world to connect with traditional data sources, older systems, and complex calculations. In this chapter, you will learn about Oracles, types of blockchain Oracles, the Oracle problem, and how to become an Oracle if you are a data provider or a node operator. You will also learn about quick start guides through which you can run an Oracle node in 20 minutes.

In this chapter, we're going to cover the following main topics:

- Understanding oracles
- Understanding the Oracle problem in Web3
- Understanding Chainlink as an Oracle
- Running a Chainlink node

Technical requirements

The following are the prerequisites for running the exercise in this chapter:

- An operating system you are comfortable using. We will be using macOS.
- VSCode or any other editor you are comfortable using.
- Docker and Docker Compose. We will be using Docker Desktop for macOS.
- A browser you are comfortable with. We will be using Chrome.
- An Infura account with a valid WebSocket URI.

Please make sure that you've met these technical requirements before you attempt to run the example in this chapter.

Understanding oracles

Before we understand what an Oracle is, try to answer some of the questions presented here. Mark down your answers as *Yes* or *No*. Once you've completed this chapter, revisit your answers; everything will be clearer to you:

- Is an oracle a corporation?
- Is an oracle a database?
- Is an oracle a program?
- Is an oracle a source of information?
- Is Oracle a data provider?
- Is an oracle a node?
- Is an oracle an API?
- Is an oracle mandatory?

> **Oracle definition**
>
> A blockchain oracle is a third-party service that retrieves and verifies data from external sources and delivers it to a blockchain-based smart contract. Smart contracts are self-executing computer programs that run on a blockchain, but they are limited in that they can only access data that is stored on the blockchain. Oracles provide a way for smart contracts to access data from external data sources and execute it based on real-world conditions.

Oracles are programs that can retrieve external data and trigger events on the blockchain when a smart contract needs information that is not present in the blockchain or from an external data source. They are used to connect the decentralized world of blockchain with the centralized world of traditional data sources, such as web APIs, databases, and IoT devices. The following figure illustrates a simple centralized oracle that provides weather-related information to a smart contract:

Figure 13.1 – Oracle providing weather data to a smart contract

Oracles act as a bridge between the blockchain and the off-chain world, providing a way for smart contracts to access external information, such as the current price of a stock or the weather forecast. An oracle can be either a centralized or a decentralized solution, and each has its advantages and disadvantages.

A **centralized oracle** is controlled by a single entity, which handles retrieving and supplying data to smart contracts. This can provide a fast and reliable service, but it also has the potential to lead to problems such as data tampering, data censorship, and a single point of failure. The following figure shows an example of a centralized oracle supplying external data to the Ethereum blockchain (smart contracts):

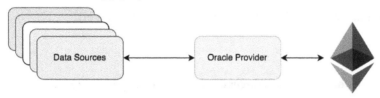

Figure 13.2 – Centralized Oracle as a data provider to Ethereum

A **decentralized oracle**, on the other hand, is a network of independent oracle providers that work together to provide data to smart contracts. This can provide a more secure and transparent service as the data is provided by multiple sources and can be cross-referenced. Later in this chapter, we will discuss more on the need for the decentralization of oracles.

It is important to consider the use case and the requirements when choosing between a centralized or a decentralized Oracle solution. For example, if the data provided by the oracle is critical to the functioning of a dApp, it may be more appropriate to use a decentralized oracle network to ensure the integrity and accuracy of the data.

In any case, it is important to choose the Oracle solution carefully, based on the use case, the data it provides, as well as the reputation and reliability of the Oracle. Additionally, it is important to have a transparent and decentralized oracle network, where the data providers are incentivized to provide correct data, and the community can assess the reputation of the oracles to ensure the integrity of the data.

An oracle can also be a smart contract that can retrieve external data and trigger events on the blockchain. Oracles act as a bridge between the decentralized world of blockchain and the centralized world of traditional data sources, such as web APIs, databases, and IoT devices.

Blockchain oracles provide a way for smart contracts to access external information, such as the current price of a stock or the outcome of a sporting event, and use this information to trigger specific actions or make decisions. Oracles are used in a variety of dApps, such as prediction markets, insurance, and stablecoins, as they enable smart contracts to access external information and interact with the real world.

An oracle is typically implemented as a smart contract on the blockchain that can be called by other smart contracts. It may also include off-chain components, such as an oracle node, that retrieves data from external sources and gives it to the oracle smart contract.

It is important to note that oracles should be chosen carefully as the quality of the data they provide can have a significant impact on the functionality and security of the smart contract. Additionally, oracles can be a center point of failure as they can be compromised or manipulated, so it is important to have multiple oracles to cross-reference data.

Now, let's look at some of the types of Oracles we have and how they work.

Types of oracles

There are several types of oracles. Let's discuss some of the most popular ones:

- **Software oracles** are programs that retrieve data from external sources and send it to the blockchain
- **Hardware oracles** are physical devices that are connected to the blockchain and can retrieve data from the physical world, such as sensor data from IoT devices
- **Inline oracles** are smart contracts that are designed to retrieve data from external sources and process it within the smart contract itself
- **Reputation oracles** are oracles that rely on the reputation of the data source to ensure data integrity, instead of a trusted third party

Oracles are a key part of many dApps, such as prediction markets, insurance, and stablecoins, as they enable smart contracts to access external information and interact with the real world.

Next, we'll learn why we need Oracles in the first place.

Why do we need Oracles?

Smart contracts, by design, are self-executing and run solely on the information that is stored on the blockchain. However, many use cases for smart contracts require access to external information, such as the current price of a stock or the weather forecast. Oracles enable smart contracts to fetch data from external sources. Here are some examples of why we need oracles:

- **Decentralized finance (DeFi) applications**: Many DeFi applications, such as lending and borrowing platforms, require access to external data, such as the current price of an asset, to function properly.
- **Predictions markets**: Oracles can be used to provide the outcome of events to prediction market (`https://www.investopedia.com/terms/p/prediction-market.asp`) smart contracts, enabling them to settle bets and pay out winnings.
- **Supply chain management**: Oracles can be used to provide information about the location and status of goods as they move through the supply chain, allowing smart contracts to automatically execute actions based on the data.

- **IoT integration**: Oracles can be used to retrieve data from IoT devices and trigger actions on the blockchain, enabling smart contracts to interact with the physical world. Automatic order placements based on inventory usage and level in a warehouse is a good example of this.

- **Gaming and non-fungible tokens** (**NFTs**): Oracles can be used to provide game state and item data to smart contracts that manage the ownership and trading of in-game items and NFTs.

Even though Oracles solve many real problems, they fundamentally have one core issue known as *the oracle problem*. Let's discuss this problem in detail.

Understanding the oracle problem in Web3

In Web3, *the oracle problem* refers to the challenge of ensuring the integrity and accuracy of data provided by oracles to smart contracts on the blockchain. The problem arises because smart contracts rely on external data to trigger actions and make decisions, but that data may be untrusted, unreliable, or manipulated. *Figure 13.3* shows that blockchains or smart contracts do not have a direct way to take or look up external data sources such as weather data. This is also because of the core operating principles of a blockchain, which means it is non-deterministic. Another problem with blockchains is that they have limited integrations with enterprise systems, market data, and data based on events. Therefore, you need an oracle so that a smart contract can really be smart!

Figure 13.3 shows a view of a single point of failure for the data sources. Imagine that all your data comes from one place, such as a single giant computer. If that computer has a problem or stops working, everything relying on it breaks too. This is a common issue when using centralized data sources for smart contracts, and it's a big risk because if that source fails, it affects the whole system:

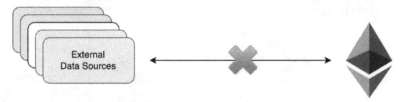

Figure 13.3 – Single point of failure with the data sources

Several potential issues can arise with oracles in Web3, including the following:

- **Data tampering**: Oracles may supply manipulated data to smart contracts, leading to incorrect decisions and actions being taken

- **Data censorship**: Oracles may be controlled by a central authority and can choose to not supply certain data to certain smart contracts, leading to biased decisions

- **Single point of failure**: If an oracle is compromised or goes offline, the smart contract may not be able to access the necessary data and may not function correctly

- **Scalability**: If many smart contracts rely on the same oracle, it can become a bottleneck, and its reliability may become a concern

To mitigate these issues, several solutions have been proposed, such as using multiple oracles, providing incentives for oracles to supply correct data, and using decentralized oracle networks that are less susceptible to censorship.

Furthermore, having a transparent, decentralized oracle network, where the data providers are incentivized to provide correct data and the community can assess the reputation of the oracles, can help solve *the oracle problem* in Web3. So, what is the solution here? We'll learn how decentralized oracles can solve *the oracle problem* in the next section.

Solving the oracle problem with decentralized oracles

A **decentralized oracle network** is a network of independent oracle providers that work together to supply data to smart contracts. These oracle providers can be individuals, companies, or other organizations, and they supply data to the network in exchange for incentives or rewards:

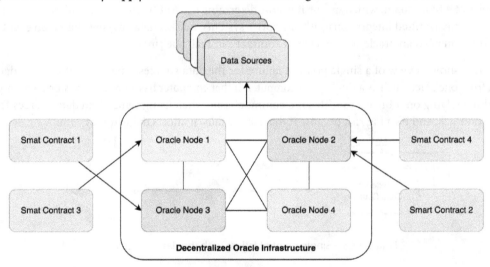

Figure 13.4 – Decentralized oracle network

Decentralized oracle networks aim to overcome the limitations of centralized oracles by providing a more secure, transparent, and reliable way of accessing external data. They provide the following benefits:

- **Decentralization**: By having a network of multiple oracle providers, a decentralized oracle network is less susceptible to censorship, data tampering, and manipulation

- **Security**: By cross-referencing data provided by multiple oracles, a decentralized oracle network can increase the accuracy and integrity of the data provided

- **Transparency**: Decentralized oracle networks can provide a transparent process to verify the authenticity of the data provided, helping build trust in the network

- **Scalability**: With a decentralized network, the data that's been requested can be distributed among multiple oracles, reducing the risk of overloading a single oracle

- **Flexibility**: Decentralized oracle networks can adapt to different data sources and supply different types of data, making them suitable for a wide range of use cases

Several decentralized oracle networks are available in the market, such as Chainlink, Band Protocol, Tellor, and Oraclize. Each of these networks has its unique features and capabilities, and it is important to choose the one that best suits your use case. Let's look at some of the popular oracles we have:

- **Chainlink** is a decentralized oracle network that allows smart contracts to securely access off-chain data. It uses a network of independent oracle providers to supply data to smart contracts, allowing for greater security and scalability.

- **Band Protocol** is a decentralized oracle platform that allows dApps to query off-chain data in a secure and decentralized way. It uses a network of validators to curate and support the data feeds, supplying a transparent and decentralized oracle solution.

- **Tellor** is a decentralized oracle platform that allows dApps to access off-chain data in a secure and decentralized way. It uses a network of miners to provide data to smart contracts and incentivizes them to supply correct data by paying them for the data provided.

- **Oraclize** is an oracle service that supplies a wide range of data to smart contracts, from web APIs to IoT data. It uses a combination of trusted and decentralized sources to supply data to smart contracts and provides a transparent process to verify the authenticity of the data.

- **Provable** is an oracle service that provides smart contracts with access to off-chain data. It uses a combination of trusted and decentralized sources to provide data to smart contracts and provides a transparent process to verify the authenticity of the data.

These are a few examples of popular oracles in the Web3 ecosystem, though there are many more oracles available, and new ones are being created as the ecosystem is being developed further. It is important to choose an oracle carefully based on the use case and the data it provides, as well as its reputation and reliability. Since Chainlink is widely used and known in the Web3 community, we will learn more about it next.

Exploring Chainlink as an Oracle

Chainlink (`https://chain.link/`) is a decentralized oracle network that expands the capabilities of smart contracts by providing secure access to off-chain data and computation. It is a large and growing network with hundreds of node operators and thousands of oracle services supporting more than dozens of blockchains and helping billions of secured DeFi funds to be settled.

Some of the popular oracle services provided by Chainlink are as follows:

- Crypto pairs
- FX exchange rates
- Keepers network
- Verifiable randomness
- Equity data
- Weather data with historical information
- Carbon measurements
- Carbon offsets

Chainlink offers the most time-tested oracle infrastructure for helping **centralized finance systems** securely access the rapidly growing blockchain economy. It delivers data to smart contracts from premium sources, ensuring critical contract outputs are based on the highest quality inputs. It is architected with layers of decentralization and is composed of multiple security-reviewed nodes, providing strong resistance to Sybil attacks. Chainlink secures billions of dollars for in-production applications across multiple blockchain networks. It also provides a universal abstraction layer for connecting to all leading public and private blockchain environments, enabling cross-network connectivity. It allows users to independently watch and verify the performance of its oracle networks and the quality of individual node operators. *Figure 13.5* shows an example of how Chainlink provides weather-related information to smart contracts as an Oracle in a decentralized architecture:

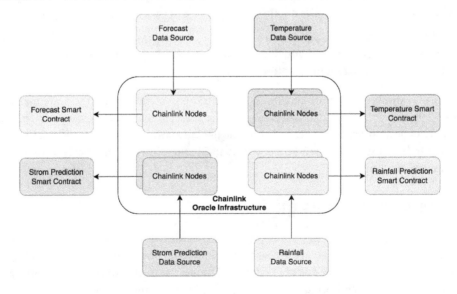

Figure 13.5 – Chainlink decentralized oracle network

LINK is the token of the Chainlink decentralized oracle network. It is used to incentivize and compensate node operators who provide data and ensure the security of the network. The token is used to pay node operators for their services in the network and serves as a means of exchanging value between users of the network. The token is also used to govern the network, allowing holders to vote on proposals to upgrade and improve the network.

LINK uses. ERC-677 ERC-677 is an Ethereum token standard that extends the capabilities of the ERC-20 token standard. It provides more functionality to the standard, such as the ability to transfer tokens with a specified data payload and the ability to interact with smart contracts directly from a token transfer. This allows for more flexible and efficient transactions and can enable new use cases for tokenized assets on the Ethereum blockchain.

Chainlink offers various categories of oracles for EVM chains. Chainlink provides high-quality **data feeds** (`https://docs.chain.link/data-feeds/`) such as pricing feeds, proof of reserve feeds, and NFT pricing feeds for dApps in NFTs, DeFi, gaming, and the Metaverse. The quickest way to use and connect external data in your smart contracts is to use the data feed from Chainlink.

Through a reliable and decentralized automation platform that makes use of the same external network of node operators that secures billions of dollars worth of value, **Chainlink Automation** (`https://docs.chain.link/chainlink-automation/overview`) enables conditional execution of your smart contract functions. By using Chainlink Automation, you can market your product more quickly and avoid the risks, setup costs, and ongoing maintenance associated with a centralized automation stack. Read the entire documentation to become familiar with the features of Chainlink Automation to make the most of the infrastructure. You can use Chainlink Automation to execute smart contract functions based on predefined conditions without building and supporting a centralized stack. Developers can deploy applications more quickly thanks to Chainlink Automation's high dependability and decentralization, as well as its support from an expert team.

The Chainlink documentation defines "A provably fair and verifiable **random number generator (RNG)** called **Chainlink Verifiable Random Function (Chainlink VRF)**, which enables smart contracts to access random values without sacrificing security or usability. Chainlink VRF creates one or more random values and a cryptographic proof of how those values arrived at, for each request." (`https://docs.chain.link/vrf/v2/introduction/`) Before being used by any consuming applications, the proof is published and confirmed on the blockchain. Through this procedure, it is ensured that no single party, including oracle operators, miners, users, or smart contract developers, can tamper with or manipulate the results.

There are two ways to request randomness in Chainlink VRF v2:

- **Subscription**: Set up a subscription account and use LINK tokens to fund it. The subscription account can then have multiple consuming contracts connected to it by users. Following the fulfillment of the randomness requests made by the consuming contracts, the transaction costs are determined, and the subscription balance is adjusted as necessary. Using this technique, you can fund requests for several consumer contracts using a single subscription.

- **Direct funding**: When you use smart contracts that need random data, you have to use a cryptocurrency called LINK to pay for it. You need to put enough LINK tokens directly into your smart contract to cover the cost of getting random information.

Your contracts can access any outside data source through a decentralized oracle network by connecting to any external API (`https://docs.chain.link/any-api/introduction/`) with Chainlink. We are aware that building smart contracts is more difficult when they must be compatible with off-chain data. To allow developers to concentrate more on the functionality of smart contracts rather than what fuels them, Chainlink has developed a framework with a minimum set of requirements and unrestricted flexibility. Smart contracts can push and pull data thanks to Chainlink's decentralized oracle network, enabling communication between on-chain and off-chain applications.

Now, let's do some hands-on work and set up a simple Chainlink node.

Running a Chainlink node

There are several ways to run a Chainlink node. In this section, we will look at two ways to become an operator.

Running nodes are always complex and resource-oriented tasks. The architecture of an oracle can vary depending on the specific implementation and use case, but an oracle can be broken down into several key components:

- **Data source**: The data source is where the oracle retrieves the external data that it will provide to the smart contract. This can include web APIs, databases, IoT devices, and more.

- **Data integration**: This part handles integrating the data from the data source into the oracle. This can include parsing the data, formatting it, and making it suitable for the smart contract to consume.

- **Data validation**: This part handles confirming the data provided by the data source. This can include checking the integrity and authenticity of the data and ensuring that it is fit for purpose.

- **Data submission**: This part handles sending the data to the smart contract. This can include encoding the data, signing it, and broadcasting it to the blockchain.

- **Reputation and incentives**: Many oracles include a system to incentivize the oracles to provide correct data and to have a reputation system to assess the oracle's reliability.

- **Decentralized network**: This part allows for a decentralized network of oracles where multiple oracles can provide the same data and cross-reference it.

- **Smart contract**: The smart contract is the part that receives and processes the data provided by the oracle.

It is important to note that the architecture of an oracle can vary depending on the specific implementation and use case. Some oracles are centralized, while others are decentralized; some are built as standalone solutions, while others as a part of a larger network. Additionally, the oracles may have more components, depending on the use case and the requirements.

Next, we will start with an easy method to run a full node locally on your laptop or desktop.

Running a Chainlink node locally

Running a Chainlink node locally involves setting up and configuring the necessary software and infrastructure to participate in the Chainlink network. Let's look at the steps involved in setting up a Chainlink node:

1. Set up a database to store the required data from a Chainlink node. We will use Docker for PostgreSQL.

2. Set up an Ethereum node provider for the Goerli testnet. We will use Infura.

3. Set up a Chainlink node using Docker.

4. Link the Chainlink node and PostgreSQL database.

5. Check the logs with the Docker container.

6. Check the Infura dashboard to see the usage for the newly set-up node.

Open a new Terminal window and execute the following commands one by one:

```
$ docker run --name cl-postgres -e POSTGRES_PASSWORD=mychainlinknodedb
-p 5432:5432 -d postgres
```

The preceding command will set up a new PostgreSQL database using the standard Docker image for PostgreSQL. The password is passed as a parameter. Here, we are using a simple password; please follow the password best practices if you are setting things up in a production environment.

```
$ docker ps -a -f name=cl-postgres
```

The preceding command will show whether the PostgreSQL database is up and running. The following figure shows a sample output:

```
docker run --name cl-postgres -e POSTGRES_PASSWORD=mychainlinknodedb -p 5432:5432 -d postgres
81520e98273219c1b9a2a826ed4e22fc9866d91df9a6d3f85c8435ca3d472e36
docker ps -a -f name=cl-postgres
CONTAINER ID   IMAGE      COMMAND            CREATED         STATUS        PORTS                    NAMES
81520e982732   postgres   "docker-entrypoint.s…"  10 seconds ago  Up 8 seconds  0.0.0.0:5432->5432/tcp   cl-postgres
```

Figure 13.6 – PostgreSQL using Docker

Once you see and confirm the postgresql is up and running with the docker go to the next step and start creating a directory using the following command.

```
$ mkdir ~/.chainlink-goerli
```

The preceding command will create a working director for everything we need to run a Chainlink node. This directory or folder will host a couple of property files so that we can pass in values to the node when it boots up.

Next, edit the `.env` file and add the environment variable as shown below. These environment variables are essential for the Chainlink node to work correctly.

```
echo "LOG_LEVEL=debug
ETH_CHAIN_ID=5
CHAINLINK_TLS_PORT=0
SECURE_COOKIES=false
ALLOW_ORIGINS=*
ETH_URL=
DATABASE_URL=postgresql://postgres:mychainlinknodedb@host.docker.
internal:5432/postgres?sslmode=disable" > ~/.chainlink-goerli/.env
```

The preceding code shows some instructions for setting up the environment file, `.env`. The last two properties are the most important ones – ETH_URL and DATABASE_URL. ETH_URL is a WebSocket URI from the Infura account we have been using all along. Make sure YOUR_PROJECT_ID is replaced with your Infura YOUR_PROJECT_ID. DATABASE_URL has all the required parameters set; just use it as-is, as shown in this example. The `cat` command will show you the values you have set up:

```
~/.chainlink-goerli  cat .env
LOG_LEVEL=debug
ETH_CHAIN_ID=5
CHAINLINK_TLS_PORT=0
SECURE_COOKIES=false
ALLOW_ORIGINS=*
ETH_URL=wss://goerli.infura.io/ws/v3/7b0c11b3a96646738019e01f55a07f0e
DATABASE_URL=postgresql://postgres:mysecretpassword@host.docker.internal:5432/postgres?sslmode=disable
~/.chainlink-goerli
```

Figure 13.7 – Chainlink .env file

Now, set up the Chainlink node by running the following command.

```
$ cd ~/.chainlink-goerli && docker run --name chainlink  -v
~/.chainlink-goerli:/chainlink -it --env-file=.env -p 6688:6688
--add-host=host.docker.internal:host-gateway smartcontract/
chainlink:1.11.0 local n
```

You should see the following output in your command/console window:

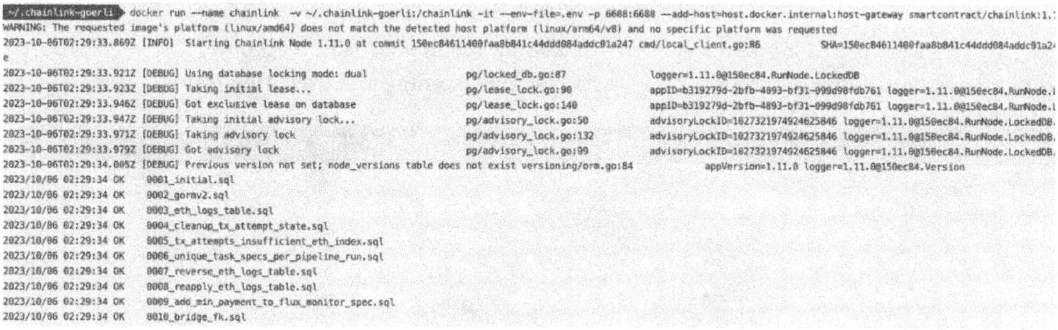

Figure 13.8 – Chainlink local node starting up

When prompts appear for the following, please use the values mentioned:

- **New key store password**: 1234567890123456. The key store password is 16 digits in length.

- **Enter API Email**: user@example.com. You can use any email.

- **Enter API Password**: password12345678. The password is eight digits or more in length.

The following figure shows the output you should see in your command or console window:

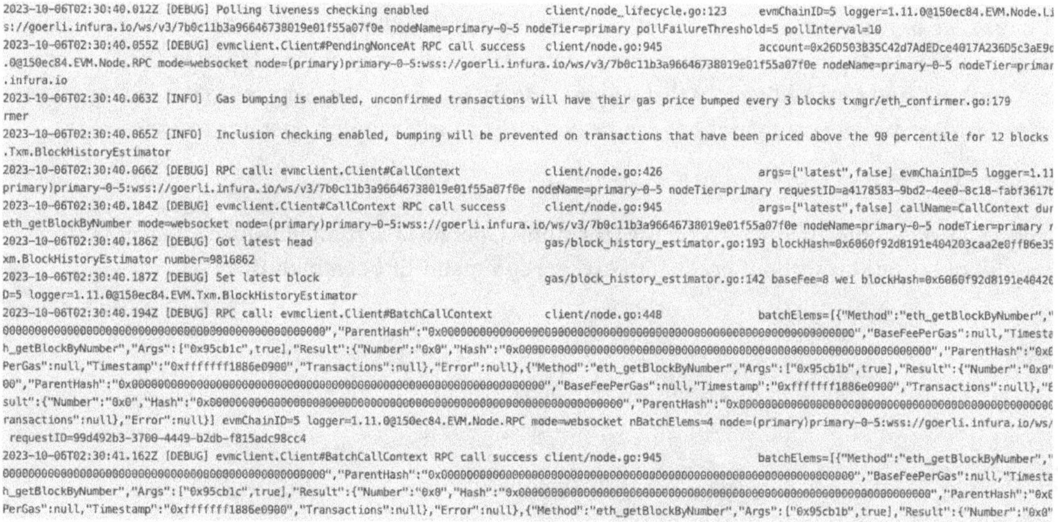

Figure 13.9 – Chainlink local node run state

You should see the node up and running and doing some transactions using the Infura connection. Now, navigate to the Infura dashboard to see some of the API calls the Chainlink node is executing.

Figure 13.10 shows the dashboard stats that you should see in your Infura account. These graphs in Infura's dashboard confirms that the node is successfully running and executing transactions.

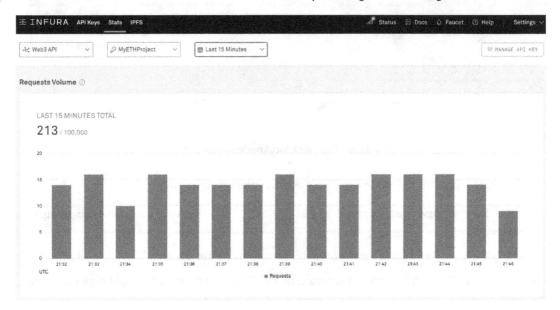

Figure 13.10 – Infura dashboard

With that, we have a configured and working Chainlink node. All you need to do now to become a data provider is to deploy an Operator smart contract, whitelist your node address in the Operator smart contract, and start adding jobs that will provide data from the data sources to the calling smart contracts. Most of these configurations can be done using the Chainlink operator console.

Go to `http://localhost:6688/signin`.

Figure 13.11 shows the login screen for the Chainlink Operator UI, through which you can perform a handful of operations without needing to execute command-line commands:

Figure 13.11 – Chainlink Operator UI

Chainlink Operator is a software tool that helps manage the deployment and maintenance of Chainlink nodes on the Ethereum blockchain. Chainlink Operator simplifies the deployment and management of Chainlink nodes, making it easier for developers, system administrators, and DevOps engineers to run and support a reliable and secure Chainlink network.

Chainlink nodes are an essential part of the Chainlink network as they handle securely retrieving data from off-chain data sources and delivering it to smart contracts on the blockchain. By using Chainlink Operator, users can automate the deployment, scaling, and maintenance of Chainlink nodes, reducing the complexity and effort needed to run a Chainlink network.

Chainlink Operator provides a simple and intuitive interface for deploying and managing Chainlink nodes, making it easier for users to run and maintain a secure and reliable network. This helps reduce the risk of downtime and ensures that smart contracts can access the data they need in a timely and secure manner.

If you are interested in setting up a Chainlink node at a production scale, there is an easy method to run a full node with AWS Quick Starts.

AWS Quick Starts is a collection of automated reference deployments that use AWS CloudFormation templates to launch, configure, and run key workloads on the AWS cloud. The Quick Starts guides provide step-by-step instructions for deploying and configuring popular software solutions on AWS, such as databases, big data analytics, security, and more.

These guides can be useful for customers who are new to AWS or for experienced customers who are looking for a quick and effortless way to deploy and configure common solutions on AWS.

Figure 13.12 shows a sample architecture for running the Chainlink node on AWS with high availability, auto scaling, and some of the advanced DevOps tools from AWS:

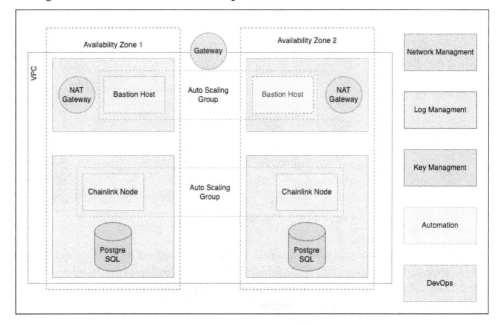

Figure 13.12 – AWS Chainlink node

To use AWS Chainlink Node, navigate to `https://aws.amazon.com/solutions/partners/chainlink-node/` and follow all the instructions here. This may incur costs on the AWS cloud platform, so use it at your discretion.

Comparing oracles with blockchains

Before we conclude this chapter, let's briefly look at the similarities, differences, and synergies between an oracle and a blockchain.

Blockchains and oracles are both important technologies in the decentralized ecosystem, but they have distinct characteristics and functions.

First, let's talk about the similarities:

- Both oracles and blockchain are based on decentralized principles and work in a trustless environment. Both technologies can be used to ensure the integrity and authenticity of data.

- **Decentralized Nature**: Both blockchains and oracles operate within decentralized ecosystems. Blockchains are decentralized ledgers where data is distributed across a network of nodes, and oracles often use decentralized data sources or multiple oracles to provide information to smart contracts.

- **Security**: Both blockchain networks and reputable oracle services prioritize security. Blockchains use cryptographic algorithms to secure data and transactions, while oracles implement various security measures to ensure the integrity of data they provide to smart contracts.

- **Trust**: In both cases, users and developers often rely on trust in the technology and the network. Blockchain users trust in the consensus mechanism and immutability of the ledger, while oracle users trust that the oracle provides accurate, tamper-resistant data.

- **Data Validation**: Both blockchains and oracles may use cryptographic techniques to validate data. Blockchains use cryptographic hashes and signatures to ensure data integrity, and some oracles employ cryptographic proofs to verify data authenticity.

There are a few differences as well. A blockchain is a decentralized and distributed ledger technology that records transactions and enables smart contracts. An oracle, on the other hand, is a mechanism for providing external data to smart contracts:

- Blockchains are designed to be self-sufficient and run independently, while oracles depend on external data sources to provide data to smart contracts.

Oracles and blockchains can work together to provide a complete solution for dApps:

- Oracles enable smart contracts to access external data and interact with the real world, while blockchains provide a secure and transparent way to record and execute these interactions.

- Oracles can help blockchains overcome their limitation of being unable to access external data, thus providing a way for smart contracts to access data from external data sources.

Decentralized oracle networks can help ensure the integrity and authenticity of the data provided to smart contracts by cross-referencing data provided by multiple oracles.

Summary

In this chapter, we explored the concept of blockchain oracles and their role in bridging the gap between blockchain-based smart contracts and external data sources. We discovered that while smart contracts are powerful in their ability to execute predefined conditions, they are limited in their access to real-world data.

In our exploration of blockchain oracles, we defined them as vital third-party services that responsibly source and validate external data for smart contracts. Acting as trustworthy intermediaries, oracles safeguard data integrity within smart contracts. We emphasized their pivotal role in expanding blockchain capabilities by connecting contracts to real-world information, enabling applications such as supply chain management, DeFi, and prediction markets. We also distinguished between software, hardware, and consensus-based oracles, each tailored to specific use cases. Additionally, we stressed the importance of secure data transmission and verification to maintain smart contract integrity and thwart potential manipulation or false information. In conclusion, blockchain oracles play a pivotal role in unlocking the potential of smart contracts by providing access to real-world data and enabling automation in blockchain-based applications. With oracles acting as trusted intermediaries, smart contracts can execute based on real-time external information, revolutionizing industries and expanding the possibilities of decentralized systems.

In the next chapter, we will be learning about one of the most advanced and niche technology Zero Knowledge Proofs and how they are playing an important role in ZK based Ethereum Virtual Machines.

14
Zero-Knowledge Proofs and Zero-Knowledge EVMs

In this chapter, we'll take a beginner-friendly dive into some advanced topics – **Zero-Knowledge Proofs** (**ZKPs**) and **Zero-Knowledge EVMs** (**ZKEVMs**). We'll introduce you to these concepts, explore where they can be useful, and understand their vital role in the future of Ethereum technology. Here's what we'll focus on:

- Understanding ZKPs
- Understanding ZKEVMs

This chapter will set the stage for your journey into these intriguing concepts.

A classic example of a ZKP is the "Ali Baba's cave" analogy. In this scenario, the prover wants to convince the verifier that they know the secret password to open a door inside a cave without revealing the password itself. They do this by entering the cave through the door while the verifier is not looking, and then exiting the cave through another entrance. The verifier can be convinced that the prover knows the password, since they were able to navigate the cave, but they do not learn the password itself.

Exploring ZKPs and their integration with the Ethereum Virtual Machine

ZKPs are cryptographic techniques that enable one party to prove the validity of a statement without revealing any information beyond the statement's truth. They play a crucial role in enhancing privacy and security in various applications, including blockchain technology.

ZKPs allow users to prove the correctness of their actions, such as transactions or smart contract executions, without disclosing the underlying data or details. This ensures privacy and confidentiality, which is particularly valuable in public blockchains where transaction data is visible to all participants.

In the world of blockchain and smart contracts, there's a new technology called zkEVM that's being added to Ethereum's "brain," known as the **Ethereum Virtual Machine** (**EVM**). The EVM acts like the engine that powers smart contracts on Ethereum, making things work in **decentralized apps** (**dApps**). However, there's a challenge - the EVM doesn't know how to handle secrets, but this issue is being solved with zkEVM.

The zkEVM is designed to overcome this limitation of not being able to handle secrets by introducing something called **Zero-Knowledge Proofs** (**ZKPs**) into the EVM. This means that users can create and interact with smart contracts while keeping their input, output, and state changes private. In a zkEVM, users can prove that their smart contract executions are correct without revealing the actual data underneath, ensuring privacy and confidentiality. In simple terms, zkEVM makes it possible for Ethereum to handle private and confidential transactions and operations.

Integrating ZKPs into the EVM offers several potential benefits and use cases, including privacy-preserving smart contracts, which can process confidential data and open up new possibilities for various industries, such as **decentralized finance** (**DeFi**), supply chain management, and healthcare. Furthermore, ZKPs can help with blockchain scalability by enabling off-chain computations with verifiable results, reducing on-chain computation and storage costs.

ZkEVM is an ongoing area of research and development, with various projects and researchers exploring different approaches to implement ZKP systems into Ethereum or create privacy-preserving smart contract platforms. Each of these approaches may have different properties, trade-offs, and degrees of compatibility with the existing EVM.

ZKPs play a critical role in enhancing privacy, security, and scalability in the blockchain ecosystem, enabling a wide range of applications that require confidentiality and data protection. The idea of zkEVM is like adding a superpower to the EVM. It lets Ethereum do things with super privacy, such as secret smart contracts and calculations. This is a big move toward making Ethereum more private and secure.

Now that we have a basic idea of what ZKPs and zkEVMs are, let's look at ZKPs in detail.

Understanding ZKPs

ZKPs are like a magic trick in cryptography. They let one person prove to another that they know something or that something is true, without actually revealing what that thing is or any extra details about it. It's a way to share secrets without giving away the whole story. This concept is essential in preserving privacy in various cryptographic applications, as it enables secure authentication and verification without disclosing sensitive information.

A ZKP has three main properties:

- **Completeness**: If the statement is true and both the prover and verifier follow the protocol, the verifier will be convinced that the statement is true.

- **Soundness**: If the statement is false, a dishonest prover cannot convince the verifier that the statement is true, except with negligible probability.

- **Zero-knowledge**: If the statement is true, the verifier learns nothing beyond the fact that the statement is true. In other words, the verifier cannot extract any additional information about the prover's secret or the statement itself.

You can find more details about ZKPs and their aforementioned properties in this research paper: `https://arxiv.org/pdf/2307.00521.pdf`.

ZKPs in cryptography

ZKPs are widely used in cryptography, especially in secure communication, authentication, and privacy-enhancing technologies such as cryptocurrencies (e.g., *Zcash*) and secure multiparty computation.

Cryptography used in ZKPs often relies on various cryptographic primitives and protocols to achieve the desired properties of completeness, soundness, and zero knowledge. Some of the common cryptographic techniques used in ZKPs include the following:

- **Commitment schemes**: These are used to "commit" to a specific value while keeping it hidden. Later, the committed value can be "revealed" without the possibility of altering it. This is useful in ZKP protocols to ensure that the prover does not change their secret information during the proof process.

- **Interactive proofs**: These are protocols where the prover and verifier exchange a series of messages, with each message depending on the previous ones. The verifier's acceptance or rejection is based on the final message. Many ZKP protocols are interactive, although they can often be transformed into non-interactive proofs, using techniques such as the Fiat-Shamir heuristic (`https://en.wikipedia.org/wiki/Fiat%E2%80%93Shamir_heuristic`).

- **Homomorphic encryption**: This is a form of encryption that allows specific operations to be performed on encrypted data without decrypting it first. It can be used in ZKPs to enable the prover to perform computations on encrypted data, without revealing the underlying plaintext.

- **Zero-Knowledge Succinct Non-Interactive Argument of Knowledge (zk-SNARKs)**: This is a specific type of ZKP that is non-interactive, requires a small number of cryptographic operations, and has short proofs. zk-SNARKs are used in cryptocurrencies such as Zcash for private transactions. We will learn more about these later in the chapter.

There are several cryptography libraries and frameworks available that support ZKP implementation. These include the following:

- `libsnark` **(C++)**: A library for zk-SNARKs that provides a collection of algorithms to construct non-interactive ZKPs. It is widely used in blockchain projects, including Zcash:

  - GitHub: `https://github.com/scipr-lab/libsnark`

- `Zokrates` (**Rust**): A toolbox for zk-SNARKs on Ethereum that allows developers to create and verify ZKPs on the Ethereum blockchain. It includes a high-level **domain-specific language (DSL)** for writing ZKP circuits:

    - GitHub: `https://github.com/Zokrates/ZoKrates`

- `Bellman` (**Rust**): A library for building zk-SNARKs, using a domain-specific language based on Rust. It was developed by the **Electric Coin Company** (**ECC**) for use in Zcash and other projects:

    - GitHub: `https://github.com/zkcrypto/bellman`

- `Bulletproofs` (**Rust**): A library for implementing Bulletproofs, which are short non-interactive ZKPs without a trusted setup. Bulletproofs are used in projects such as *Monero* to enable confidential transactions:

    - GitHub: `https://github.com/dalek-cryptography/bulletproofs`

- `zk-STARKs` (**C++**): A library for building zk-STARKs, which are a more scalable and transparent alternative to zk-SNARKs. They do not require a trusted setup and are considered post-quantum secure:

    - GitHub: `https://github.com/starkware-libs/stark`

These libraries and frameworks provide the necessary tools and abstractions for developers to create and work with ZKPs in various applications, including cryptocurrencies, privacy-preserving smart contracts, and secure multiparty computation.

ZKPs in the blockchain ecosystem

ZKPs have become an essential component in the blockchain ecosystem, providing enhanced privacy and security features. They enable a party to prove the validity of a statement without revealing any additional information beyond the statement's truth. ZKPs have a wide range of applications in blockchain technology, including privacy-focused transactions, secure identity management, off-chain computations, and Layer 2 scaling solutions. Here are a few examples of ZKP usage in blockchain:

- **Zcash**: Zcash is a privacy-focused cryptocurrency that uses zk-SNARKs to enable confidential transactions. Users can choose to shield the transaction details (sender, recipient, and amount) while still proving the transaction's validity on the blockchain, without revealing any sensitive information.

- **Monero**: Monero is another privacy-focused cryptocurrency that uses bulletproofs, a type of ZKP, to enable confidential transactions. Bulletproofs allow Monero users to hide the transaction amount, providing a more efficient range-proof mechanism compared to its predecessor, *RingCT*.

- **Ethereum**: Ethereum has been exploring the integration of ZKPs for various purposes, such as privacy-preserving smart contracts and Layer 2 scaling solutions such as `zkSync`, which uses `zk-Rollups` to bundle multiple transactions into a single proof, improving transaction throughput and reducing gas fees.

- **The AZTEC protocol**: The AZTEC protocol is a privacy solution built on top of the Ethereum blockchain that uses ZKPs to enable confidential transactions and privacy-preserving smart contracts. Users can transact and interact with smart contracts while keeping their transaction details private.

- **Scroll**: Scroll is a unique project that combines privacy-preserving smart contracts with the existing EVM, making it one of the few solutions available that can offer this kind of functionality.

These are some of the popular blockchains that use ZKP today, and there are many more that are not listed here. ZKP will become a core technology requirement for blockchain soon.

Next, we will learn some of the basic and common use cases where ZKP can be applied.

Use cases

There are many use cases where ZKP can come in remarkably effective. The following is a list of some of the popular and upcoming use cases of ZKPs in blockchain technology:

- **Privacy-preserving transactions**: ZKPs allow users to transact privately on a public blockchain while still proving the validity of their transactions, as seen in cryptocurrencies such as Zcash and Monero.

- **Secure identity management**: ZKPs can be used for secure identity verification without revealing sensitive personal information. Users can prove they possess certain credentials or meet specific requirements without disclosing the underlying data.

- **Layer 2 scaling solutions**: ZKPs are used in scaling solutions such as `zk-Rollups` to improve transaction throughput and reduce fees on blockchains such as Ethereum.

- **Confidential smart contracts**: ZKPs enable the creation of privacy-preserving smart contracts, allowing users to interact with a contract while keeping their inputs and outputs private. This has applications in DeFi, supply chain management, and various other sectors.

- **Secure multi-party computation**: ZKPs can be used to enable secure multi-party computation, where multiple parties can jointly compute a function over their inputs while keeping them private. This can be useful in voting systems, auctions, or any scenario where privacy is crucial.

ZKPs play a crucial role in enhancing privacy, security, and scalability in the blockchain ecosystem, enabling a wide range of applications that require confidentiality and data protection.

We will look at ZK-SNARK and ZK-STARK at a very high level in the next section.

Introducing ZK-SNARK and ZK-STARK

It's time to introduce ZK-SNARK and ZK-STARK, two cutting-edge cryptographic technologies that bring advanced privacy and security to the world of blockchain and beyond. **ZK-SNARK** stands for **Zero-Knowledge Succinct Non-Interactive Argument of Knowledge**, while **ZK-STARK** stands for **Zero-Knowledge Scalable Transparent Arguments of Knowledge**. These mouthful acronyms represent powerful tools that allow one party to prove they know something, without revealing what that knowledge is. This has far-reaching applications, from enhancing privacy in cryptocurrency transactions to ensuring the integrity of data in various industries. zk-SNARK and zk-STARK are at the forefront of innovations that are reshaping how we handle sensitive information in the digital age. Let us do some more digging into these two topics next.

zk-SNARKs

zk-SNARKs are a type of ZKP. These proofs are "succinct" and "non-interactive," meaning they can be quickly verified and do not require back-and-forth communication between the prover and verifier. In the context of zk-SNARKs, an "argument of knowledge" is a computational assertion that the prover knows a certain piece of information without revealing it.

zk-SNARKs are used extensively in blockchain technologies, particularly in Layer 2 scaling solutions such as zk-Rollups. These bundle multiple transactions into a single proof that can be verified on-chain, significantly improving the throughput of a network and reducing gas costs. The use of zk-SNARKs in this context allows for the scalability of blockchains without sacrificing security.

zk-STARKs

zk-STARKs are an alternative to zk-SNARKs that removes the need for a trusted setup (a common criticism of zk-SNARKs), but they are currently more computationally intensive and produce larger proofs.

Zcash, a privacy-focused cryptocurrency, is one of the most well-known examples of zk-SNARKs in use. Zcash uses zk-SNARKs to allow users to transact privately, proving transaction validity without revealing additional information.

Some of the pros of zk-SNARKs include the following:

- **Efficiency**: zk-SNARKs proofs are small and fast to verify, making them practical for blockchain applications
- **Privacy**: zk-SNARKs provide strong privacy guarantees, allowing users to prove knowledge or correctness without revealing any additional information

Some cons include the following:

- **Trusted setup**: zk-SNARKs require a one-time trusted setup. If the setup is compromised, it could lead to the creation of false proofs.
- **Complexity**: zk-SNARKs are complex to understand and implement correctly, requiring expertise in advanced cryptography.

zk-SNARKs are a powerful cryptographic tool that can enhance privacy and scalability in blockchain applications. They are used in Layer 2 scaling solutions such as zkRollups and privacy-focused cryptocurrencies such as Zcash. However, they come with trade-offs, including the need for a trusted setup and their complexity. Alternatives such as zk-STARKs are being developed to address some of these limitations.

Creating a fully functional smart contract with integrated ZKPs requires a complex setup and a deep understanding of both the smart contract language (such as Solidity for Ethereum) and the underlying ZKP technology (such as zk-SNARKs). However, I can provide a high-level outline of a smart contract example for an age verification system that uses ZKPs.

In this example, we assume that we have a pre-compiled zk-SNARK circuit that checks whether a user's age is above a certain threshold (e.g., 18 years), without revealing the user's actual age. The user generates a proof, using their age as the input, and submits it to the smart contract.

Here is a high-level outline of the age verification smart contract:

```solidity
pragma solidity ^0.8.0;

contract AgeVerification {
    // Address of the zk-SNARK verifier contract
    address public verifierAddress;

    // Mapping to store whether a user has been verified
    mapping(address => bool) public isVerified;

    // Constructor that sets the verifier contract's address
    constructor(address _verifierAddress) {
        verifierAddress = _verifierAddress;
    }

    // Function for users to submit their ZKP of age
    function submitProof(
        // Proof elements (depends on the specific ZKP scheme)
        uint256[2] memory a,
        uint256[2][2] memory b,
        uint256[2] memory c,
        uint256[] memory input
    ) public {
        // Instantiate the verifier contract
        Verifier verifier = Verifier(verifierAddress);

        // Verify the submitted ZKP
        bool isValid = verifier.verifyProof(a, b, c, input);
```

```
        // If the proof is valid, set the user as verified
        if (isValid) {
            isVerified[msg.sender] = true;
        }
    }
}

// Example of a zk-SNARK verifier contract interface
// The actual implementation depends on the specific ZKP scheme used
abstract contract Verifier {
    function verifyProof(
        uint256[2] memory a,
        uint256[2][2] memory b,
        uint256[2] memory c,
        uint256[] memory input
    ) public virtual returns (bool);
}
```

In this example, the AgeVerification smart contract allows users to submit their ZKP of age to the submitProof function. The contract interacts with a separate zk-SNARK verifier contract, which is responsible for verifying the submitted proof. If the proof is valid, the user's address is marked as verified in the isVerified mapping.

Please note that this example is a high-level outline and does not include the actual implementation of the zk-SNARK verifier contract, which depends on the specific ZKP scheme and tools used (e.g., *ZoKrates*, *Circom*, etc.). Additionally, creating and verifying ZKPs involves complex cryptographic operations, requiring careful implementation to ensure security and privacy.

Understanding the zkEVM

zkEVM is an implementation of the EVM that leverages ZKPs to enable privacy-preserving smart contracts and computations on the Ethereum blockchain.

The EVM is the runtime environment for smart contracts on the Ethereum network. It is a Turing-complete virtual machine that processes and executes smart contract code, making it possible to build and deploy dApps on Ethereum. However, one of the limitations of the current EVM is the lack of native support for privacy-preserving computations and transactions.

The zkEVM aims to address this limitation by integrating ZKPs into the EVM, allowing users to create and interact with smart contracts while keeping their input, output, and state changes private. In a zkEVM, users can prove the correctness of their smart contract executions without revealing the underlying data, thus ensuring privacy and confidentiality.

Integrating ZKPs into the EVM has several potential benefits and use cases:

- **Privacy-preserving smart contracts**: zkEVM enables the creation of smart contracts that can process confidential data, opening new possibilities for privacy-focused applications in various industries, such as DeFi, supply chain management, and healthcare.

- **Scalability**: Using ZKPs can also help with blockchain scalability. For example, zk-Rollups is a Layer 2 scaling solution that leverages ZKPs to bundle multiple transactions into a single proof, improving transaction throughput and reducing gas fees.

- **Off-chain computations**: zkEVM can enable off-chain computations with verifiable results, allowing users to perform complex operations off-chain and submit only proof of correctness to the blockchain, reducing on-chain computation and storage costs.

Soon, zkEVM is set to become a central part of Ethereum, making it even more powerful. However, while we wait for that to happen, roll-up providers are building a special lane next to the highway. This lane will connect smoothly to the highway when it is ready, allowing a vast number of transactions to flow quickly and cheaply. This process will also keep everything private and confidential, thanks to zkEVM technology. While zkEVM is a promising concept, it is essential to note that implementing a fully functional zero-knowledge EVM is an ongoing area of research and development. Several projects in the blockchain ecosystem are working on zkEVM implementations or exploring the integration of ZKPs into the EVM, with the goal of enabling privacy-preserving smart contracts and computations on the Ethereum network.

Summary

In this chapter, we delved into the world of ZKPs and their wide-ranging applications in cryptography, blockchain technology, and smart contracts. Here are the key takeaways.

We discussed the fundamental concept of ZKPs, which allows one party to prove a statement's validity without revealing any additional information, enhancing privacy and security.

We explored how ZKPs are integral to privacy-focused cryptocurrencies such as Zcash and Monero, as well as Layer 2 scaling solutions such as zkSync, which leverage zk-Rollups to enhance transaction throughput and reduce gas fees on Ethereum.

Then, we introduced the concept of the zkEVM, highlighting how ZKPs can enable privacy-preserving smart contracts and computations, revolutionizing blockchain technology.

Although various zkEVM types exist, there is not a widely accepted classification system yet. Nevertheless, numerous projects and researchers are actively working on implementing ZKPs in Ethereum and creating platforms for privacy-preserving smart contracts.

We reviewed a practical example – an age verification smart contract, employing ZKPs to allow users to prove their age without disclosing it. This illustrated how ZKPs enable privacy-centric smart contracts, opening new doors for applications in industries such as DeFi, supply chain management, and healthcare, where data confidentiality is paramount.

In the next chapter, we will take a deep dive into the Layer 2 networks and look at a couple of them using zkEVM-based rollups.

15

L2 Networks and Rollups

In this chapter, we will look into various topics related to scaling solutions in the blockchain ecosystem. We will start with the concept of Layer 2 networks, which provide scalability by proceeding with transactions off-chain while maintaining the security and privacy of the blockchain. We will also explore different types of Layer 2 networks, including optimistic rollup, ZK rollup, and side chains at a very high level.

This is again an advanced topic and we will be covering only an introduction to L2 and rollups.

In this chapter, we're going to cover the following main topics:

- Understanding L2 networks
- Understanding how Polygon works (Matic)
- Understanding rollups

Understanding Layer 2 networks

You may be familiar with the term *Autobahn*. The Autobahn is a network of federal highways in Germany that is known for its reputation for high speeds and efficient transportation. It is an essential part of Germany's transportation infrastructure, connecting various cities and regions across the country. But how does one get onto an Autobahn from home, office, or anywhere? You need to get into a service lane or a secondary road and follow signs to get onto the Autobahn highway. L2s are your service roads to L1, the Autobahn.

The following figure illustrates a comparison of the L1 and L2 networks with the Autobahn.

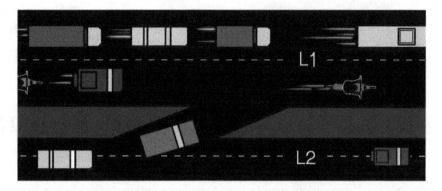

Figure 15.1 – Autobahn L1 and L2 example

Although it's not shown in the figure, the Autobahn also connects back to the service roads, which is also especially important. This ensures smooth entry and exit onto and off the Autobahn and the service roads. Now, let us see how this is related to blockchain and the nuances around it.

A blockchain L2 network is a type of blockchain network that operates at *Layer 2* of the blockchain stack, built on top of a *Layer 1* blockchain network.

In a traditional blockchain network, all transactions and smart contract executions are recorded on the *Layer 1* blockchain, which is a decentralized and distributed ledger that is maintained by a network of nodes.

A blockchain L2 network, on the other hand, is an additional layer that sits on top of the *Layer 1* blockchain. It aims to improve the scalability, privacy, and/or security of the underlying blockchain by moving some of the transactions and/or smart contract executions off-chain.

There are several reasons why a Layer 2 blockchain network may be needed:

- **Scalability**: The main benefit of a Layer 2 blockchain network is scalability. By moving some of the transactions and smart contract executions off-chain, a Layer 2 network can handle a much larger number of transactions than the *Layer 1* blockchain, making it more suitable for decentralized applications with high throughput requirements.

- **Lower fees**: Transactions on a Layer 2 network are cheaper than on Layer 1, as they do not need to be recorded in the global ledger, thus reducing the cost of maintaining the network.

- **Speed**: Transactions on Layer 2 networks are faster than on Layer 1, as they do not need to be validated by the entire network. They are only validated by parties involved in the transaction.

- **Privacy**: Layer 2 networks can provide more privacy than Layer 1, by keeping the transaction details off-chain and away from the public.

- **Security**: Layer 2 networks can provide more security than Layer 1, by allowing more complex smart contract execution and by being less susceptible to censorship.

Different L2 networks focus on different priorities when it comes to the scope and goal of what they want to achieve. But speed, privacy, and security are the top priorities.

Layer 2 networks have a wide range of potential use cases. Let us look into some of the common examples:

- **Decentralized Finance (DeFi)**: Layer 2 networks can be used to improve the scalability and speed of DeFi applications, such as lending, borrowing, and trading platforms

- **Micropayments**: Layer 2 networks can be used to handle a large number of small transactions, such as micropayments, without congesting the main blockchain network

- **Gaming**: Online gaming transactions and smart contract executions, including in-game purchases, trading of digital assets, and game state updates, can be handled by a sizable number of Layer 2 networks

- **Supply chain management**: Applications for supply chain management, such as tracking the movement of goods and ensuring product authenticity, can be made faster and more scalable by utilizing Layer 2 networks

- **Identity management**: Identity management applications, such as those that create and manage digital identities for people and organizations, can be made faster and more scalable by utilizing Layer 2 networks

- **Data management**: Layer 2 networks can be used to improve the scalability and speed of data management applications, such as storing and sharing enormous amounts of data securely and privately

- **Privacy**: By keeping the specifics off-chain and hidden from the public, Layer 2 networks can be used to enhance the privacy of transactions and the execution of smart contracts

The use cases mentioned are only the most obvious and most popular ones. In fact, most of the use cases for an L1 network can be done with L2 networks.

Now let us look at some of the popular Layer 2 network types.

Types of Layer 2 networks

There are many types of Layer 2 networks. Every type has some specific pain points it solves. Some are remarkably successful and some are not. Some address speed while others could address security and privacy. Let us see where it all started and how we came to the most recent L2 trend called **Rollups**.

Some of the widely known L2 network types are as follows:

- **State channels**, where transactions and smart contract executions occur off-chain between a small number of participants and are only recorded on the *Layer 1* blockchain as opening and closing transactions

- **Plasma**, which allows the creation of child chains that execute smart contracts, record transactions off-chain, and periodically submit the results to the *Layer 1* blockchain

- **Sidechains**, which are independent blockchain networks that are pegged to the main blockchain

Now let us start with state channels and learn a little more about these types before jumping into the exciting world of rollups in the next section.

State channels

State channels are a type of Layer 2 blockchain network that allows for the execution of transactions and smart contracts off-chain between a small number of participants. The state of the channel is recorded on the *Layer 1* blockchain as opening and closing transactions, but the details of the transactions and smart contract executions within the channel are not recorded on the blockchain.

State channels work by creating a direct communication channel between the participants, allowing them to transact and execute smart contracts without the need for every transaction to be recorded on the blockchain. This can increase the scalability of the blockchain and lower transaction costs as they do not need to be validated by the whole network, only by the parties involved in the transaction.

An example of a state channel use case is a game of poker between two players. Both players would open a state channel, deposit some funds, and then play the game, updating the balance of the channel with each hand. Once the game is finished, the final balance of the channel will be recorded on the blockchain, and the funds will be released to the winning player.

State channels can be used for a variety of different use cases, not only for games, but also for micropayments, digital asset trading, and more.

Plasma

Plasma is a type of Layer 2 blockchain network that allows for the creation of child chains that execute transactions and smart contract executions off-chain. The child chains are connected to the *Layer 1* blockchain, typically Ethereum, and periodically submit the results of the off-chain transactions to the main blockchain, allowing them to be verified and recorded on the global ledger.

The main goal of Plasma is to increase network scalability by offloading a significant portion of transactions and smart contract execution from the primary blockchain. To do this, one must establish child chains that oversee processing particular kinds of transactions, such as gaming or micropayments.

In Plasma, child chains are created by any user and are connected to the main blockchain using a smart contract. These child chains can handle a large number of transactions and smart contract executions, and when the user wants to exit the child chain, the final state of the chain is submitted to the main blockchain.

Plasma chains can also be used for security, by providing a mechanism for users to exit the child chain and move their funds back to the main blockchain in case of a security issue.

Side chains

Side chains are independent blockchain networks that are pegged or connected to a main blockchain, typically known as the parent chain. The main idea behind side chains is to allow for the transfer of assets or value between different blockchain networks, enabling interoperability and scalability.

Side chains can be used to handle specific types of transactions or use cases, such as micropayments, digital asset trading, or gaming, without congesting the main blockchain network. They can also be used to test new features and technologies before they are implemented on the main blockchain.

For assets to be transferred between the parent chain and side chain, a mechanism known as a two-way peg is used. This mechanism allows users to lock their assets on the parent chain and receive an equivalent amount of assets on the side chain, and vice versa.

Side chains can also be used to increase security, as they can be designed to have different consensus mechanisms and security levels, depending on the use case.

There are several popular Layer 2 networks in public blockchains, some of which are as follows:

- **Lightning Network** is a state channel network that is built on top of the Bitcoin blockchain. It is designed to handle micropayments and to increase the scalability of the Bitcoin network.

- **Raiden Network** is another state channel network that is built on top of the Ethereum blockchain. It aims to handle many small transactions and to increase the scalability of the Ethereum network.

- **Truebit** is a Layer 2 scaling solution that is built on top of the Ethereum blockchain. It aims to improve the scalability of smart contract execution by offloading computationally expensive tasks to off-chain workers.

- **Optimistic Rollup** is a Layer 2 scaling solution that utilizes a smart contract on the Ethereum blockchain to record the results of off-chain transactions and smart contract executions.

- **ZK Rollup** is a scaling solution that utilizes zero-knowledge proofs to verify the validity of off-chain transactions and smart contract executions. It is built on top of Ethereum blockchain.

- **Polygon Matic Network** is a Layer 2 scaling solution for Ethereum that utilizes a network of sidechains to handle many transactions and to increase the scalability of the Ethereum network.

Next, we will dive into a couple of these Layer 2 solutions, learn how they operate, and discuss some of the pros and cons, some technical architectures, and their fundamental operating principles.

We're going to focus on one special network called Polygon. It's a great example of how a side road on the blockchain can be incredibly successful. Polygon has also given us some important ideas for making the main blockchain (Layer 1) and the super-fast networks (Layer 2) work together better.

Polygon (Matic)

The core of Polygon's vision is Ethereum, the platform on which numerous Dapps are hosted. Users now find it simple to interact with new financial products, purchase artwork, play games, and even join virtual worlds thanks to these decentralized apps. The amount of activity on Ethereum, however, clogs the network and drives up transaction costs.

By offering a sidechain solution, Polygon aims to tackle some of the issues that the Ethereum network is currently facing, such as high transaction costs and a lack of community governance. *One Layer 2 solution built on Ethereum is called Polygon.* This sidechain was built to help Ethereum increase efficiency, security, size, and usefulness rather than to be an *Ethereum killer*.

Understanding how Polygon works

Polygon uses a decentralized network of **Proof-of-Stake** (**PoS**) validators as well as sidechains for off-chain computation to meet scalability requirements.

By utilizing the current developer community and ecosystem, Polygon aims to address scalability and usability issues without sacrificing decentralization. By giving Dapps and user functionalities greater scalability and better user experiences, it seeks to enhance existing platforms.

For public blockchains, it is a scaling solution. The existing Ethereum tooling is supported by Polygon PoS, along with quicker and less expensive transactions.

Figure 16.2 shows the basic architecture behind Polygon Matic.

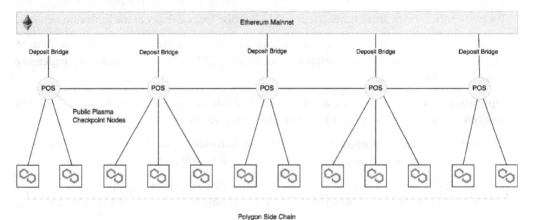

Figure 15.2 – Polygon architecture

This is a simplified version of the Polygon architecture and the figure is shown to get a high-level view. Each component that is shown in the diagram has many moving parts.

On Polygon sidechains, transactions are quick, inexpensive, and secure, and finality is made possible on Polygon and Ethereum, the first compatible Layer 1 base chain. On the internal testnet, a single sidechain was able to reach up to 10,000 **Transactions Per Second (TPS)**; additional chains will be added for horizontal scaling. It also provides a smooth user interface, developer abstraction from the mainchain to the Polygon chain, native mobile apps, and an SDK with **WalletConnect** support. Stakeholders in the PoS system include polygon chain operators and it has really grown rapidly in the last couple of years.

For any blockchain, the heart of the network is the consensus layer, also called the validator layer. Next, we will learn about Polygon validators.

Validators

The **Heimdall** validator and Bor block producer nodes (`https://wiki.polygon.technology/docs/home/architecture/heimdall-chain/`) are run by network participants known as validators, who also lock up MATIC tokens within the system and participate in the network by running these nodes. To contribute to the network's security and receive compensation for their efforts, validators stake their MATIC tokens as collateral.

At each checkpoint, rewards are given to all stakeholders in proportion to their stake, with the proposer receiving an additional bonus. In the contract that is referred to when claiming rewards, the user reward balance is updated.

If the validator node engages in malicious behavior, such as double-signing, which also affects the linked delegators at that checkpoint, the stakes could be drastically lowered.

On the Polygon network, validators are chosen through an on-chain auction that takes place periodically. Participating as block producers and verifiers are these chosen validators. Updates are made to the parent chain (the Ethereum mainnet) following participant validation of a checkpoint, which releases rewards for validators based on their network stake.

To protect the network, Polygon uses a number of validators. The responsibilities of validators include managing a full node, generating blocks, validating consensus, taking part in it, and committing checkpoints on the Ethereum mainnet. One must stake their MATIC tokens with Ethereum mainnet-based staking management contracts to become a validator.

To choose the validators for the current set with their updated stake ratio, Heimdall reads the events released by the staking contracts. Bor also uses this method when generating blocks.

Delegation is also noted in the staking contracts, and any changes to the validator power, node signer address, or unbinding requests take effect when the next checkpoint is committed.

Now let us dive into delegators – a little contrast in behavior when compared with validators – in the next section.

Delegators

Delegators are token owners who are unable or unwilling to manage a validator node themselves. They play a crucial part in the system because they oversee selecting validators, and securing the network instead of ceding control of their stake to validator nodes. They execute their delegation transaction on the Ethereum mainnet staking contract.

The following commit on the Ethereum mainnet bonds the MATIC tokens to that checkpoint. Additionally, delegators have the choice to withdraw from the system at any time. Like validators, delegators must wait until the unbonding period (the unbonding period is a specific duration during which your cryptocurrency holdings are "locked up" and cannot be used for transactions or withdrawn), which lasts for about nine days, is over before they can withdraw their stake.

Delegators stake their tokens by giving them to validators, and in return, they receive a portion of the rewards. In addition to sharing risks, delegators also share rewards with their validators. Each validator's delegators run the risk of having their stakes reduced in proportion to their delegated stake if they behave badly.

The portion of rewards going to validators is determined by a commission percentage. Delegators can view each validator's commission rate to understand how their rewards are distributed as well as the relative rate of return on their stake.

This should give you a good understanding of why we need side chains and how they keep the traffic flow into the L1 from L2 and keep the Autobahn moving.

Next, we will look at rollups, next-generation L2 networks.

Understandings rollups

The main idea behind rollups is to move many transactions and smart contract executions off-chain, while still maintaining their security and trustlessness. They do this by using a smart contract on the Ethereum blockchain to record the results of off-chain transactions and smart contract executions.

In a rollup, multiple transactions are grouped or batched together and then *rolled up* into a single transaction on the Ethereum blockchain. This reduces the number of transactions that need to be recorded on the blockchain, increasing the scalability of the network.

Figure 16.3 shows a high-level overview of how a rollup technology works with Layer 1 and Layer 2 networks working in parallel and L2 posting transaction blocks into Layer 1 and L1, posting receipts back to L2.

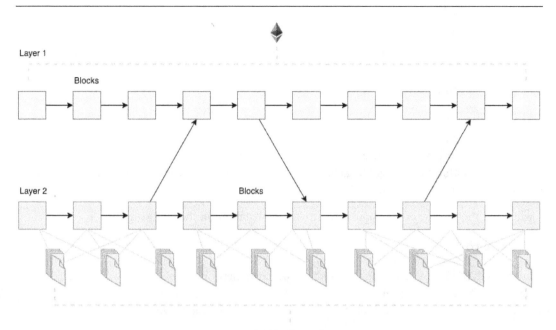

Figure 15.3 – Rollups

The rollup smart contract is responsible for verifying that the off-chain transactions and smart contract executions are valid and that the final state of the rollup is correct. It does this by using a data availability mechanism, which allows users to prove the existence of the off-chain data if necessary.

There are a handful rollups already on the market now. Even rollups have some subtypes already and we have even started hearing about Layer 3, Layer 4, and Layer 5 solutions. We will take a look at rollup types now.

Types of blockchain rollups

Rollups are a type of Layer 2 scaling solution for blockchain networks that aim to increase the transaction processing capacity of the network by aggregating multiple transactions into a single, larger transaction. There are several different types of rollups, including the following:

- **Optimistic Rollup (ORU)**: This type of rollup uses a smart contract to allow multiple transactions to be processed off-chain and then aggregated into a single transaction, which is then submitted to the main chain. The transactions are valid, or *optimistic*, until proven otherwise.

- **ZK-rollup**: This type of rollup uses **zero-knowledge proofs** (**ZKPs**) to ensure the privacy and security of the transactions being processed off-chain. ZKPs allow for the verification of a computation without revealing any information about the inputs or the computation itself.

- **Validation Rollup**: This type of rollup combines the benefits of both ORUs and ZK-rollups, offering both scalability and security. The transactions are processed off-chain and aggregated into a single transaction, which is then submitted to the main chain for validation.

- **Hybrid Rollup**: This type of rollup combines elements of other rollup solutions to offer a customized solution that is tailored to the specific requirements of the blockchain network.

Each type of rollup has its own advantages and disadvantages, and the choice of rollup will depend on the specific requirements of the blockchain network. In general, rollups offer a more efficient and cost-effective solution for scaling blockchain networks, as they reduce the number of transactions that must be processed on-chain.

We will learn about some of the popular rollup implementations in the following section.

Optimistic rollups

Optimistic rollup is a Layer 2 scaling solution for blockchain networks, designed to increase scalability by processing many transactions off-chain while maintaining the security and trustlessness of the main blockchain. Here is a high-level overview of how optimistic rollup works:

- **Off-Chain Execution**: In optimistic rollup, most of the transaction processing and smart contract execution occurs off-chain. Transactions are grouped into batches and executed on the rollup chain, which is a sidechain connected to the main blockchain.

- **Optimistic Execution**: During the off-chain execution, the transactions are assumed to be valid without immediate verification. This optimistic approach allows for fast and low-cost processing, as it avoids the need for immediate on-chain validation.

- **Fraud-Proof Mechanism**: While transactions are considered valid optimistically, any malicious or invalid behavior is detected through a fraud-proof mechanism. Anyone can challenge the validity of a transaction by submitting proof of invalidity to the main blockchain.

- **Verification Period**: After a batch of transactions is processed off-chain, a verification period begins on the main blockchain. During this period, any participant can submit a fraud-proof to challenge the correctness of the off-chain execution.

- **Dispute Resolution**: If a fraud-proof is submitted, a dispute resolution process is initiated. The rollup chain and the main blockchain evaluate the proof and determine the validity of the challenged transaction. If the proof is valid, the transaction is reverted, and appropriate penalties may be imposed. If the proof is invalid, the challenger may face penalties.

- **On-Chain Commitment**: Once the verification period concludes, a summary or commitment of the off-chain transactions is posted to the main blockchain. This summary acts as a compressed representation of the off-chain execution, serving as proof of the correct state of the rollup chain.

- **Finality and Security**: As the summaries are periodically posted on the main blockchain, the finality and security of the transactions are anchored to the main blockchain's consensus mechanism, ensuring the integrity of the entire system.

Optimistic rollup allows for a significant increase in scalability by minimizing on-chain operations while leveraging the security and decentralization of the main blockchain. It strikes a balance between scalability and security, providing a promising solution for handling a larger volume of transactions on blockchain networks.

Optimistic rollups use a data availability mechanism, which allows users to prove the existence of the off-chain data if necessary.

There are a few examples of optimistic rollup projects that have been developed for the Ethereum blockchain:

- **Optimism** is a Layer 2 scaling solution that uses optimistic rollup to increase the scalability of the Ethereum network. It allows for the execution of transactions and smart contract executions off-chain, while still maintaining their security and trustlessness. It is being developed as a full-featured L2 platform that allows for the creation of dApps that can handle substantial amounts of transactions and high-speed smart contract execution.

- **Arbitrum** is an optimistic rollup scaling solution that aims to increase the scalability and privacy of the Ethereum network. It uses a combination of smart contracts and off-chain computation to allow for the execution of complex smart contracts and the handling of many transactions.

- **Skale** is an optimistic rollup scaling solution that aims to increase the scalability of the Ethereum network. It uses a network of sidechains to handle many transactions and to increase the speed of smart contract execution.

The following figure shows a representation of the optimistic rollup implementation.

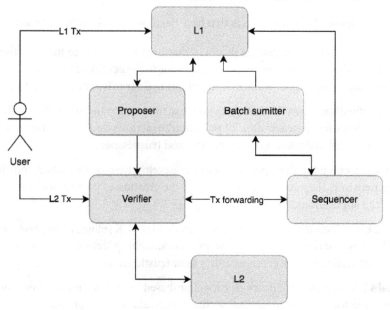

Figure 15.4 – Optimistic rollup architecture

Optimism and Arbitrum were the most popular rollups in the L2 space before the ZK-based rollups.

These are just a few examples of the many optimistic rollup projects that have been developed for the Ethereum blockchain. In the next section, you will learn about ZK rollups and how they are different from optimistic rollups.

ZK rollups

A **ZK rollup**, also known as zero-knowledge rollup, is a type of Layer 2 scaling solution for blockchain networks, specifically for Ethereum. It uses ZKPs to verify the validity of off-chain transactions and smart contract executions and to ensure their privacy.

Like other rollup solutions, a ZK rollup aims to increase the scalability of the Ethereum network by moving many transactions and smart contract executions off-chain, while still maintaining their security and trust-lessness. They do this by using a smart contract on the Ethereum blockchain to record the results of off-chain transactions and smart contract executions, but instead of storing all the data on-chain, they only store small, private proof of the data.

The main difference between a ZK rollup and other rollups is their use of ZKPs, which allow privacy-preserving transactions. This means that the details of the off-chain transactions and smart contract executions are not recorded on the blockchain and are only visible to the parties involved in the transaction.

ZK rollups also use a validity-proof mechanism that ensures the safety of assets on the rollup, even if the operator of the smart rollup contract is malicious.

There are a few examples of ZK rollup projects that have been developed for the Ethereum blockchain:

- **Loopring**, a decentralized exchange protocol that uses ZK rollups to increase the scalability and security of the Ethereum network. It allows for the execution of transactions and smart contract executions off-chain, while still maintaining their privacy and trust-lessness.

- **Aztec** is a protocol that uses ZK rollups to increase the privacy and scalability of the Ethereum network. It allows for the execution of private transactions and smart contract executions off-chain, while still maintaining their security and trustlessness.

- **StarkWare** is a company that specializes in the development of ZK-rollup solutions for the Ethereum network. They provide a platform for the creation of private, scalable, and trustless decentralized applications.

- **ZkSync** is a Layer 2 scaling solution for Ethereum that uses ZK rollups to increase scalability and security. It allows for the execution of fast, private, and cheap transactions and smart contract executions off-chain, while still maintaining their trustlessness.

- **Matter Labs** is a company that develops ZK-rollup-based Layer 2 scaling solutions for Ethereum. They offer a platform to create fast and secure decentralized applications.

- **Scroll** enables the direct verification of an Ethereum block using concise proof. The fundamental concept involves ensuring the accuracy and reliability of each opcode within the EVM execution trace. This approach facilitates the smooth migration of L1 smart contracts to the Scroll platform. Notably, instead of relying on novel ZK-friendly primitives, we took a reverse approach. By focusing on supporting native EVM with customized optimizations, we gained a substantial advantage. This advantage lies in our compatibility with all current Ethereum infrastructures without necessitating any modifications.

- **Linea** is a zkEVM-based Layer 2 solution for Ethereum that replicates the Ethereum environment in the form of a rollup. With Linea, developers can build and deploy smart contracts just as they would on the Ethereum mainnet. It offers the flexibility to use familiar tools and frameworks, providing a seamless development experience. Users benefit from the same level of security and familiarity as Ethereum, but with reduced transaction costs, making Linea an attractive choice for more cost-effective transactions.

You can find more information about these projects from `https://l2beat.com/`, which is an analytics and research website for Ethereum scaling L2 solutions.

The following figure shows a representation of the Scroll rollup implementation.

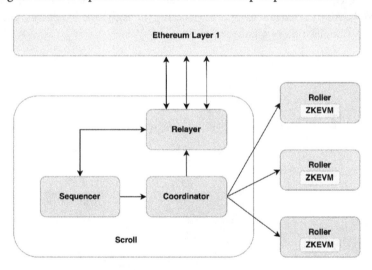

Figure 15.5 – Scroll architecture

The Scroll architecture diagram lays out the overview of how it operates with different homegrown components and concepts and which components interact with Layer 1. Again these are complex topics for future reading, but you should be ready to start rollup yourselves now to get into the exciting world of web3 and blockchains with L1 and L2.

In the next chapter, we'll be learning about **Decentralized Autonomous Organizations**, also known as **DAOs**.

Summary

In this chapter, we took a deep dive into the fascinating world of blockchain scaling solutions. We started by unraveling the concept of Layer 2 networks, which are like superhighways for blockchain transactions, allowing them to speed up while preserving security and trust. We examined various types of Layer 2 networks, such as optimistic rollup, ZK rollup, and side chains, each with its own superpower.

As we explored these networks, we discovered their wide-ranging applications, from transforming DeFi to revolutionizing gaming, supply chain management, identity verification, and data handling. Layer 2 networks proved their worth by offering scalability, lightning-fast transactions, and enhanced privacy for these diverse use cases.

We also delved into the magic of rollups, where optimistic rollups brought off-chain execution with a trusty fraud-proof system, while ZK rollups worked their wonders with privacy and security through ZKPs.

Speaking of which, we unveiled the secret world of ZKPs, both interactive and non-interactive. They're like digital detectives, verifying things without revealing confidential details.

To wrap up, we dissected Scroll, a project making Ethereum even more efficient by verifying its blocks using succinct proofs. All these advancements are clearing the path for a blockchain future that's not only bigger and faster but also more secure and private.

16
Decentralized Autonomous Organizations – Overview

This is the concluding chapter of this book and is where we will learn about **decentralized autonomous organizations** (**DAOs**), digital organizations that operate autonomously through smart contracts on a blockchain network. This is only an introductory chapter to DAOs, so we will only touch upon some of the very basics. We will learn about DAOs, how they function, and what impact they may have in the future.

DAOs represent a new paradigm in organizational structure, where digital entities operate autonomously via smart contracts on a blockchain network.

While scratching the surface of DAOs, we'll offer a glimpse into their fundamental concepts and functionalities. While we'll cover only the basics, you'll gain valuable insights into how DAOs work and the potential they hold for shaping our future.

As we explore this topic, consider it not as an endpoint but as a beginning – an invitation to dive deeper into the limitless possibilities of DAOs and the broader realm of blockchain technology. The future promises exciting developments, and your understanding of DAOs is a stepping stone toward realizing their transformative potential.

In this chapter, we're going to cover the following main topics:

- Understanding DAOs
- Popular DAOs
- The future of DAOs

Understanding DAOs

A DAO is a digital entity that operates autonomously, governed by a set of rules encoded on a blockchain. It eliminates the need for centralized control, allowing decision-making and operations to be transparent and community-driven. DAOs enable participants to engage in a wide range of activities, such as voting, proposal submission, and funding allocation, all through smart contracts. With their decentralized nature, DAOs provide a framework for collective decision-making, promoting transparency, inclusivity, and trust. By leveraging blockchain technology, DAOs have the potential to revolutionize governance structures across industries, fostering innovation, collaboration, and community empowerment.

There are countless DAOs in the world now; all popular cities have a DAO named after them.

Let's consider a real-life scenario where a DAO could be applicable for a a community group: a neighborhood or community association.

In a traditional neighborhood association, decisions about community projects, funds, and rules are typically made by a small group of individuals, such as a board of directors or committee members. This can sometimes lead to power imbalances and limited input from the broader community.

Now, imagine transforming this neighborhood association into a DAO. Here is how it could work:

- **Decision-making**: Instead of a small group making decisions, the DAO allows every member of the community to have a say. Each member would have a voting right proportional to their stake or contribution within the community.

- **Proposals**: Any member can propose a project or initiative they believe would benefit the community. For example, a proposal could suggest building a community garden, organizing events, or allocating funds for local improvements.

- **Voting**: Community members can vote on these proposals using a decentralized platform associated with the DAO. This could be a user-friendly website or mobile application that allows members to cast their votes securely.

- **Funding**: The DAO can have a treasury funded through membership fees, donations, or other sources. Community members can contribute to this treasury, and funds can be allocated based on the outcome of the voting process. This ensures that community resources are managed transparently and democratically.

- **Execution and accountability**: Once a proposal has been approved, the DAO can automatically disburse funds to the responsible individuals or teams. Progress and updates on the projects can be shared with the community, ensuring accountability and transparency.

By implementing a DAO in a neighborhood association, every member gets a voice and a vote in decision-making processes. It fosters a sense of community ownership and empowerment. It also provides a transparent and efficient way to allocate funds and resources for community projects.

Of course, implementing a DAO for a neighborhood association would require technical infrastructure, education, and participation from community members. However, this example highlights how a DAO can bring decentralized governance, collective decision-making, and transparency to a real-life scenario, empowering individuals to shape and improve their community.

One example of a DAO is *The DAO* (`https://en.wikipedia.org/wiki/The_DAO`), which was created in 2016 as a decentralized venture capital fund. It was built on the Ethereum blockchain and was designed to allow members to propose and vote on investments in various projects. The DAO raised over $150 million in its **initial coin offering** (**ICO**) and became one of the largest crowdfunding campaigns in history at the time. However, due to a vulnerability in its code, an attacker was able to drain a substantial portion of its funds. This led to a hard fork of the Ethereum blockchain to restore the stolen funds, and The DAO was subsequently dissolved. Despite its failure, the project served as an important early example of the potential for DAOs to disrupt traditional venture capital.

Another example is *MakerDAO* (`https://docs.makerdao.com/`), which is a decentralized autonomous organization built on the Ethereum blockchain. Its goal is to create a stable cryptocurrency by pegging its value to that of the US dollar. It achieves this by using a system of **collateralized debt positions** (**CDPs**) in which users can lock up collateral in exchange for a loan of the stablecoin DAI, which can then be used for transactions or trading. The value of DAI is maintained by the system automatically adjusting the interest rates on CDPs to ensure that the demand for DAI remains in line with the supply.

These are just two examples, but many different types of DAOs have been created for various purposes. They are being used for a wide range of applications, from **decentralized finance** (**DeFi**) and prediction markets to gaming and social media.

DAOs can offer several advantages over traditional centralized organizations. Some of the main reasons why people might choose to use a DAO are as follows:

- **Decentralization**: Because DAOs are not controlled by a single central authority, they can be more resistant to censorship and manipulation. This can make them have a more democratic and transparent way of making decisions.

- **Automation**: Smart contracts can be used to automate many of the functions of an organization, such as **voting** and **asset management**. This can make DAOs more efficient and reduce the need for intermediaries.

- **Transparency**: DAOs can be built on a blockchain, which provides an immutable record of all transactions. This can make it easy for anyone to see how the organization is being run and how funds are being used.

- **Flexibility**: DAOs can be customized to suit the specific needs of a particular organization or project. They can also be easily updated or modified as needed.

- **Incentivization**: DAOs can be used to align the incentives of all its participants by providing rewards based on the value they contribute.

- **Open source**: DAOs are based on open source technology, which means that anyone can access and contribute to the development of the platform.

Overall, DAOs can enable new ways for communities to organize, collaborate, and govern themselves effectively.

DAOs can be used for a wide variety of purposes, depending on the specific needs of the organization or project. Let's look at some potential use cases:

- **DeFi**: DAOs can be used to create decentralized lending, borrowing, and trading platforms. This can make it possible to access financial services without the need for a traditional intermediary.

- **Community management**: DAOs can be used to manage and govern online communities, such as social media platforms or forums. This can enable users to make decisions about the direction and management of the platform collectively.

- **Governance**: DAOs can be used to govern the decision-making process of a company, organization, or project. This can make it possible for stakeholders to vote on proposals and have a say in how the organization is run.

- **Crowdfunding**: DAOs can be used to raise funds for a project or venture. This can be done through an ICO or by allowing members to make contributions in exchange for a stake in the organization.

- **Supply chain management**: DAOs can be used to track and manage the flow of goods and services within a supply chain. Smart contracts can be used to automate the process of tracking inventory, managing payments, and ensuring compliance with regulations.

- **Gaming**: DAOs can be used to create decentralized gaming platforms. This can enable developers to create and monetize games without the need for a centralized platform.

- **Social impact**: DAOs can be used to align incentives and coordinate actions of people and organizations toward common goals, such as environmental sustainability, poverty reduction, or global health.

These are just a few examples, but the potential uses for DAOs are still being explored and new use cases are continuously emerging. DAOs can be customized and tailored to suit the specific needs of a particular organization or project, making them a versatile tool for various sectors and industries.

Popular DAOs

There are so many popular DAOs that highlight the diversity of applications and opportunities that arise from decentralized governance and community-driven decision-making in the blockchain space. As mentioned earlier, we have many DAOs in popular cities around the world.

Here is a list of popular DAOs, with details about their founding date, location, purpose, and their current level of success:

- **The DAO**: Founded in April 2016, in Zug, Switzerland. It aimed to operate as a decentralized venture capital fund, allowing members to vote on investment proposals. However, due to a security vulnerability, it suffered a major hack and funds were eventually recovered through a hard fork. The DAO was dissolved, but it served as an influential precursor to other DAO projects.

- **MakerDAO**: Founded in December 2017, in Santa Cruz, California, USA. MakerDAO is one of the pioneering DeFi DAOs. It operates on the Ethereum blockchain and its primary purpose is to provide a decentralized stablecoin called DAI, collateralized by other cryptocurrencies. MakerDAO has been successful, with DAI becoming one of the most widely used stablecoins in the DeFi ecosystem.

- **Aragon**: Founded in February 2017, in Zug, Switzerland. Aragon aims to enable the creation and management of decentralized organizations. It provides tools and frameworks for creating DAOs, including features for governance, voting, and dispute resolution. Aragon has gained popularity and has been utilized by various projects and organizations to establish their decentralized entities.

- **MolochDAO**: Founded in February 2019, in Boulder, Colorado, USA. MolochDAO focuses on supporting funding for Ethereum-based projects and initiatives. It aims to provide a way for Ethereum community members to pool their resources and collectively fund projects that align with their goals. MolochDAO has seen success in funding various Ethereum ecosystem projects and has inspired the creation of similar DAOs.

- **dxDAO**: Founded in May 2019, in various global locations. dxDAO is a decentralized autonomous organization focused on **decentralized exchange** (**DEX**) governance. It aims to provide a community-led governance model for the operation and decision-making of decentralized exchanges. dxDAO has been active in governing the DutchX and Mesa protocols, among other initiatives.

- **Curve Finance DAO**: Founded in January 2020, in various global locations. Curve Finance is a decentralized exchange optimized for stablecoin trading. Its DAO, which has community governance, plays a role in making decisions about fee distribution, protocol parameters, and partnerships. Curve Finance has gained significant traction and liquidity in the DeFi space.

- **Yearn.finance**: Founded in February 2020, in various global locations. Yearn.finance is a decentralized ecosystem of yield-optimizing protocols and products. Its governance DAO, governed by YFI token holders, determines strategies, fee structures, and ecosystem development. Yearn.finance has experienced substantial growth and innovation in the DeFi landscape.

- **Compound Governance**: Founded in May 2020, in San Francisco, California, USA. Compound is a leading decentralized lending protocol. Its governance DAO allows token holders to vote on proposals related to protocol parameters and upgrades. Compound has gained prominence in the DeFi space, with its lending platform attracting significant usage and adoption.

- **SushiSwap**: Founded in August 2020, in various global locations. SushiSwap is a decentralized exchange protocol and an **automated market maker** (**AMM**) platform. Its governance DAO plays a crucial role in determining the protocol's direction, managing liquidity incentives, and introducing new features. SushiSwap emerged as a popular alternative to Uniswap and has continued to innovate in the DeFi ecosystem.

- **DAOstack**: Founded in March 2018, in Tel Aviv, Israel. DAOstack provides a framework and tools for the creation and management of decentralized organizations. Its platform enables the development of custom DAOs with customizable governance mechanisms. DAOstack has facilitated the creation of various communities.

- **Aavegotchi**: Aavegotchi, founded in 2020, is a blockchain-based collectibles game and DAO. It combines DeFi lending protocols with NFT-based virtual pets called "Gotchis." Aavegotchi's DAO governs decisions related to game development, community initiatives, and tokenomics.

- **Gitcoin**: Gitcoin, established in 2017, is a decentralized platform that connects developers with open source projects and provides funding through its DAO. It allows developers to contribute to projects, earn rewards, and receive grants for their work, all decided upon by the community.

- **RaidGuild**: Raid Guild, formed in 2020, is a decentralized collective of freelancers specializing in blockchain development. It operates as a DAO, allowing members to collaborate on projects, negotiate work, and collectively make decisions about the guild's operations and partnerships.

- **DAOhaus**: DAOhaus, founded in 2020, provides a platform for creating and managing DAOs. It offers modular and customizable tools for community governance, voting, and treasury management. DAOhaus empowers communities to create DAOs and tailor them to their specific needs.

- **MetaCartel**: MetaCartel, established in 2019, is a venture DAO that supports early-stage blockchain projects and start-ups. It provides funding, mentorship, and resources to selected projects through its community-driven decision-making process. MetaCartel aims to foster innovation in the Ethereum ecosystem.

- **WhaleShark**: WhaleShark, launched in 2019, is a social money experiment that enables individuals to create personal tokens. It operates as a DAO and allows token holders to participate in governance decisions. WhaleShark explores the concept of social currencies and tokenized communities.

- **Decentraland**: Decentraland, created in 2017, is a virtual reality platform built on the Ethereum blockchain. It allows users to buy, sell, and trade virtual land and create decentralized applications within the virtual world. Decentraland's DAO manages decisions related to governance, land development, and user-driven experiences.

- **The MetaFactory**: The MetaFactory, formed in 2019, is a DAO-driven marketplace for limited edition and community-designed fashion and merchandise. It allows creators and designers to collaborate, mint NFTs, and participate in the production and distribution of physical goods. The MetaFactory's DAO governs decision-making and incentives for the community.

These diverse DAOs span various industries, including gaming, open source development, venture funding, virtual reality, art, fashion, and more, highlighting the broad applications and possibilities of decentralized autonomous organizations.

Before we wrap up, let's investigate the state of DAOs, how we should prepare for the future, and how DAOs impact us.

The future of DAOs

Let's start with the current state of DAOs. DAOs have gained significant traction and momentum in the blockchain and DeFi space. They have evolved from conceptual experiments to practical implementations with real-world applications. Here is the state of DAOs as of now:

- **Growing number of DAOs**: The number of DAOs has been steadily increasing, spanning various industries and sectors. From DeFi protocols to art collectives and community governance, DAOs are being established to tackle diverse use cases.

- **DeFi dominance**: Many prominent DAOs operate in the DeFi sector, driving innovation and transforming traditional financial systems. These DAOs enable lending, borrowing, DEXs, liquidity provision, and more, creating a vibrant and rapidly evolving DeFi ecosystem.

- **Governance experimentation**: DAOs continue to experiment with governance models to enhance transparency, inclusivity, and decision-making processes. Various voting mechanisms, tokenomics, and incentive structures are being explored to ensure effective governance within DAO communities.

- **Adoption and funding**: DAOs have attracted substantial attention and funding. They have garnered support from venture capitalists, individual investors, and the broader crypto community, leading to increased adoption and growth.

- **Regulatory challenges**: DAOs operate in a regulatory gray area in many jurisdictions as they often do not fit within traditional legal frameworks. Regulatory clarity and compliance measures are ongoing challenges that need to be addressed for broader adoption and mainstream acceptance.

- **Security and scalability improvements**: Security vulnerabilities and scalability limitations have been significant concerns for DAOs. However, ongoing research and development efforts aim to enhance smart contract security and scalability solutions, making DAOs more robust and efficient.

- **Community collaboration and knowledge sharing**: The DAO ecosystem is characterized by vibrant and active communities. Participants collaborate, share knowledge, propose ideas, and engage in discussions, fostering a sense of collective ownership and shared decision-making.

- **Experimentation and innovation**: DAOs are at the forefront of blockchain experimentation and innovation. New concepts, protocols, and **decentralized applications** (**DApps**) are continually being developed within the DAO ecosystem, pushing the boundaries of what is possible with decentralized governance.

It is important to note that the state of DAOs is dynamic and ever-evolving. As the blockchain ecosystem continues to mature and new challenges and opportunities emerge, DAOs are expected to evolve and play a significant role in shaping the future of decentralized governance, economic systems, and community collaboration.

Let's delve deeper into the future impact of DAOs, key takeaways, and how to prepare for their rise with more examples and details:

- **Democratization of decision-making**: DAOs empower individuals by providing direct involvement in decision-making processes. They enable the common man to participate in voting, propose ideas, and shape the direction of projects or organizations. This fosters a more inclusive and transparent governance model:

  - *Example 1*: **DAOstack's** platform enables users to create and participate in decentralized organizations, giving individuals the power to propose and vote on proposals that shape the organization's direction

  - *Example 2*: **Polkadot's** governance system allows token holders to vote on network upgrades and parameter changes, ensuring that decisions are made collectively and democratically

- **New economic models**: DAOs introduce new economic opportunities through tokenomics and incentive structures. They allow individuals to participate, contribute, and earn rewards directly within the DAO ecosystem, fostering a collaborative economy:

  - *Example 1*: **MolochDAO** enables Ethereum community members to pool funds and collectively support projects through funding proposals, incentivizing collaboration, and innovation

  - *Example 2*: Decentralized prediction market platforms such as Augur incentivize participants to provide accurate predictions by rewarding them with native tokens, aligning their incentives with the success of the platform

- **Collaborative ownership**: DAOs facilitate shared ownership and management of assets, intellectual property, and digital goods. Through fractional ownership and transparent governance, individuals can participate in the value creation of shared resources:

  - *Example 1*: **Aragon's DAO** framework allows communities to create decentralized organizations and collectively manage assets such as real estate, digital art, or intellectual property rights

- *Example 2*: The **Artist DAO**, a collective of artists, leverages NFTs and DAO governance to enable shared ownership and control over digital artworks, creating a collaborative art ecosystem

- **Disintermediation and trustlessness**: DAOs eliminate intermediaries and increase efficiency by leveraging blockchain technology. Smart contracts ensure transparency, automate processes, and reduce reliance on centralized authorities.

  - *Example 1*: **Uniswap**, a decentralized exchange protocol operating as a DAO, enables users to trade tokens directly from their wallets, removing the need for intermediaries

  - *Example 2*: DAO-based lending platforms such as **MakerDAO** and **Aave** allow individuals to borrow and lend assets directly, eliminating traditional intermediaries such as banks and enabling decentralized and permissionless financial services

- **Challenges and considerations**: While DAOs offer significant potential, challenges remain. These include governance scalability, decision-making processes, security vulnerabilities, and regulatory frameworks. Overcoming these challenges will be critical for the long-term success of DAOs.

So, how do we prepare for the future with DAOs?

There could be several factors and reasons why we should be prepared to accept this new culture. The reason I call it "culture" here is because it is something that we, as citizens, are not used to in our lifetimes so far, so it is more a cultural change than anything else. It includes the following:

- **Education and awareness**: Stay updated on blockchain technology, decentralized governance, and the evolving landscape of DAOs. Engage with online communities, attend conferences, and explore educational resources to deepen your knowledge.

- **Active participation**: Join DAO communities aligned with your interests, contribute ideas, vote on proposals, and actively engage in the decision-making process. This participation fosters collective decision-making and strengthens the DAO ecosystem.

- **Risk management**: Understand the risks associated with DAO participation, including security vulnerabilities and potential financial risks. Conduct due diligence before engaging with DAOs or investing in DAO tokens.

- **Regulatory landscape**: Stay informed about regulatory developments around DAOs in your jurisdiction. Advocate for clear and favorable regulations that support innovation while ensuring user protection.

The success of DAOs depends on technological advancements, community adoption, regulatory frameworks, and the ability to address challenges. Continuous development, improved governance models, and community-driven innovations will shape the success and impact of DAOs in the future. We'll look at some of these factors next.

Will DAOs be successful?

The success of DAOs can be evaluated based on several factors, including adoption, functionality, governance efficiency, community engagement, and impact on industries. Here is a detailed elaboration on the potential success of DAOs:

- **Adoption and growth**: The success of DAOs can be measured by the level of adoption and the growth of their respective communities. As more individuals and organizations embrace DAOs and actively participate in their governance and activities, this indicates a growing acceptance and recognition of their potential.

- **Functionality and innovation**: Successful DAOs often demonstrate functional and innovative features that address real-world challenges. This includes efficient decision-making mechanisms, smart contract automation, decentralized finance solutions, collaborative ownership structures, and other innovative applications:

  - *Example*: **MakerDAO's** success can be attributed to its creation of DAI, a widely used decentralized stablecoin, and its **collateralized debt positions** (**CDPs**) model, which has enabled efficient lending and borrowing within the decentralized finance ecosystem.

- **Governance efficiency**: A successful DAO implements governance processes that are efficient, transparent, and inclusive. The ability to propose and vote on proposals, manage funds, and allocate resources in a decentralized and consensus-driven manner is crucial for a DAO's success:

  - *Example*: Aragon's governance framework provides tools and mechanisms for decentralized organizations to manage decision-making, voting, and dispute resolution efficiently, making it easier for communities to govern themselves effectively.

- **Community engagement and participation**: A thriving community is a key indicator of a successful DAO. Engaged community members who actively contribute, vote on proposals, provide feedback, and drive initiatives forward demonstrate the strength and potential of the DAO:

  - *Example*: MetaCartel's success lies in its active community of developers, entrepreneurs, and investors who collaborate, mentor, and fund early-stage blockchain projects. Their participation and support contribute to the overall success of the DAO.

- **Impact on industries and society**: The success of a DAO can be measured by its impact on industries, markets, and society at large. A DAO that introduces disruptive solutions, democratizes access, fosters innovation, and brings positive change to traditional systems can be considered successful:

  - *Example*: DAOs such as **Gitcoin** and **MolochDAO** have made significant impacts on the open source and Ethereum communities by funding projects and promoting collaboration, resulting in the development of innovative technologies and advancements in the decentralized ecosystem.

- **Sustainability and longevity**: A successful DAO exhibits sustainability and longevity by adapting to changing circumstances, fostering resilience, and maintaining the trust and support of its community over time:

  - *Example*: The success of **DAOstack** is evident in its continued growth and evolution as it provides a platform for the creation and management of DAOs, contributing to the sustainability and long-term viability of the DAO ecosystem.

It is important to note that the success of DAOs is not guaranteed, and challenges such as security vulnerabilities, scalability limitations, regulatory uncertainties, and governance complexities must be addressed. However, as DAOs continue to evolve, innovate, and overcome these challenges, they have the potential to reshape industries, governance models, and community collaboration in a decentralized and inclusive manner.

Summary

In this chapter, we explored the concept of DAOs and their potential impact on industries, governance, and community collaboration. We began by introducing DAOs, highlighting their decentralized nature, community-driven decision-making, and transparency.

We discussed the various functions and purposes of DAOs, including their role in DeFi, governance, crowdfunding, community management, and supply chain management. We examined real-life examples of popular DAOs such as MakerDAO, Aragon, and MetaCartel, highlighting their founding dates, functions, and current levels of success.

The future of DAOs was a focal point in this chapter. We explored the potential democratization of decision-making, new economic models, collaborative ownership, and the disintermediation and trustlessness that DAOs offer. Through diverse examples, such as neighborhood associations transformed into DAOs, we demonstrated how DAOs can impact everyday people, providing a voice in decision-making, economic opportunities, and shared ownership.

This chapter emphasized the challenges and considerations surrounding DAOs, including regulatory uncertainties, security vulnerabilities, and scalability limitations. However, we emphasized that ongoing efforts to address these challenges are crucial for the success and wider adoption of DAOs.

To prepare for the future and embrace DAOs, we discussed the importance of education and awareness, active participation, risk management, and staying informed about regulatory developments. By engaging with DAO communities and advocating for favorable regulations, individuals can contribute to the growth and success of DAOs.

We concluded this chapter by highlighting the dynamic state of DAOs, their growing adoption, and the need for continuous innovation, improved governance models, and community collaboration. DAOs hold the potential to reshape industries, governance structures, and economic systems, but their success will depend on addressing challenges and evolving with the changing landscape.

Through this chapter, you gained insights into the transformative potential of DAOs. You learned about the democratization of decision-making, the power of collaborative ownership, and the disruptive impact of DAOs on various industries. Understanding the key takeaways and preparing for the future will empower individuals to navigate the DAO ecosystem, contribute to governance processes, and embrace the decentralized future that DAOs offer.

As we conclude this journey through the fascinating world of Web3, blockchain, and decentralized technologies, remember that your learning does not stop here. The world of Web3 is ever-evolving, and your newfound knowledge is your passport to its exciting future. Keep exploring, innovating, and pushing the boundaries of what is possible. Whether you are building decentralized applications, investing in cryptocurrencies, or simply curious about the technology shaping our digital landscape, you are now equipped with the tools and understanding to navigate this dynamic space. Thank you for joining us on this transformative journey, and here is to a future powered by Web3!

Index

Packtpub.com

Subscribe to our online digital library for full access to over 7,000 books and videos, as well as industry leading tools to help you plan your personal development and advance your career. For more information, please visit our website.

Why subscribe?

- Spend less time learning and more time coding with practical eBooks and Videos from over 4,000 industry professionals

- Improve your learning with Skill Plans built especially for you

- Get a free eBook or video every month

- Fully searchable for easy access to vital information

- Copy and paste, print, and bookmark content

Did you know that Packt offers eBook versions of every book published, with PDF and ePub files available? You can upgrade to the eBook version at packtpub.com and as a print book customer, you are entitled to a discount on the eBook copy. Get in touch with us at customercare@packtpub.com for more details.

At www.packtpub.com, you can also read a collection of free technical articles, sign up for a range of free newsletters, and receive exclusive discounts and offers on Packt books and eBooks.

Other Books You May Enjoy

If you enjoyed this book, you may be interested in these other books by Packt:

Blockchain with Hyperledger Fabric - Second Edition

Nitin Gaur, Anthony O'Dowd, Petr Novotny, Luc Desrosiers, Venkatraman Ramakrishna, Salman A. Baset

ISBN: 978-1-83921-875-0

- Discover why blockchain is a technology and business game changer

- Set up blockchain networks using Hyperledger Fabric version 2

- Understand how to create decentralized applications

- Learn how to integrate blockchains with existing systems

- Write smart contracts and services quickly with Hyperledger Fabric and Visual Studio Code

- Design transaction models and smart contracts with Java, JavaScript, TypeScript, and Golang

- Deploy REST gateways to access smart contracts and understand how wallets maintain user identities for access control

- Maintain, monitor, and govern your blockchain solutions

Mastering Blockchain - Fourth Edition

Imran Bashir

ISBN: 978-1-80324-106-7

- Grasp the mechanisms behind Bitcoin, Ethereum, and other cryptocurrencies
- Understand cryptography and its usage in blockchain
- Become familiar with the theoretical foundations of smart contracts and blockchain consensus
- Develop DApps using Solidity, Remix, Truffle, and Ganache
- Solve issues relating to privacy, identity, scalability, and security in enterprise blockchains
- Dive into the architecture of Ethereum 2.0
- Delve into emerging trends like DeFi, NFTs, and Metaverse
- Explore various applications, research topics, and future directions of blockchain

Packt is searching for authors like you

If you're interested in becoming an author for Packt, please visit `authors.packtpub.com` and apply today. We have worked with thousands of developers and tech professionals, just like you, to help them share their insight with the global tech community. You can make a general application, apply for a specific hot topic that we are recruiting an author for, or submit your own idea.

Share Your Thoughts

Now you've finished *The Essential Guide to Web3*, we'd love to hear your thoughts! Scan the QR code below to go straight to the Amazon review page for this book and share your feedback or leave a review on the site that you purchased it from.

`https://packt.link/r/1-801-81347-7`

Your review is important to us and the tech community and will help us make sure we're delivering excellent quality content.

Download a free PDF copy of this book

Thanks for purchasing this book!

Do you like to read on the go but are unable to carry your print books everywhere? Is your eBook purchase not compatible with the device of your choice?

Don't worry, now with every Packt book you get a DRM-free PDF version of that book at no cost.

Read anywhere, any place, on any device. Search, copy, and paste code from your favorite technical books directly into your application.

The perks don't stop there, you can get exclusive access to discounts, newsletters, and great free content in your inbox daily

Follow these simple steps to get the benefits:

1. Scan the QR code or visit the link below

https://packt.link/free-ebook/9781801813471

2. Submit your proof of purchase
3. That's it! We'll send your free PDF and other benefits to your email directly

www.ingramcontent.com/pod-product-compliance
Lightning Source LLC
Chambersburg PA
CBHW080615060326
40690CB00021B/4700